THE LAST WORKSHOP

I was immediately drawn in. The treatment of addiction, bonding, avoidance, intimacy and risk all come together as the therapists and the clients each bring their best to a one-week workshop. The big question each reader will have to ask themselves is who changes more and is enriched more in a therapy session—the therapist or the client. I truly enjoyed going on this journey.

> —SHARON WEGSCHEIDER-CRUSE Therapist, Founder of
> Onsite Workshops, Co-founder of The National Association
> for Children of Alcoholics, Author of the bestseller *Hope and*
> *Health for the Alcoholic Family*

As I continued reading and got to know the participants and their stories, I was no longer a spectator, I became one of them. Their struggles and their breakthroughs became my struggles and my breakthroughs. More importantly, I felt the fundamental lesson woven into the fabric of *The Last Workshop*: nothing is more powerful than telling the truth to yourself and to others while holding each as an equal worthy of respect. Hearts open and minds are stretched to embrace realities larger than one's own.

For those who are familiar with Esalen, this book is like coming home. Those who have never been there may hear a call. Leaders and therapists will be inspired by the examples of skill, honesty, and humility. I know I will read it again.

> —ISABELLA CONTI Psychologist, Executive Coach,
> Entrepreneur, Co-author of *From Power to Partnership:*
> *Creating the Future of Love, Work, and Community*

The book captured the diversity, depth and vulnerability of the characters and drew me into their stories, their struggles and the emergence of the people they were capable of being. The relationships between and among the people were developed with great care and grace. It would have been so easy to take leaps and miss out on the subtlety of how relationships were encouraged and cultivated, especially those between unlikely characters. I was drawn into the miracle of the amazing group work that can happen when it is facilitated well and members open themselves to the unexpected.

The book held my attention from start to finish. A worthy undertaking very skillfully done. Thank you for the gift of this story!

—CHRIS STUART Communications Consultant

The style makes me feel like I'm right in the story as it unfolds.

—CATHY ROBINSON-WALKER President of The Leadership Studio, Leadership expert, Executive Coach, Author of *Leading with Mastery and Heart: The Coaching Companion for Thriving Nurse Leaders*

Engaging, insightful, brave and vulnerable ... The writing was so mesmerizing, I felt I was a participant in the room, processing in real time with the rest of the group. A profound and revealing representation of an Esalen experience.

—JJ JEFFRIES Workshop Leader, Esalen staff

It was an absolute thrill ... I devoured it. The details of three people working together, facilitating a group together were wonderful. The trust, the non-verbal communication, the doubts, the synergies were really wonderfully expressed and rendered.

—ISABEL PRYSTAWIK Founder Motionally, Former Esalen Resident

I can't put it down. It takes me right back to Esalen. I can picture every location, image and experience.

—KATE INGERSOLL Former Esalen Resident, Author of *Open Road: a life worth waiting for*

I just spent a wonderful evening with the three of you at Esalen. I'm thoroughly enjoying the book. It's quite emotional for me to read it.

—LYNNE VON TRAPP

GUESTHOUSE PUBLICATIONS
Sausalito

978-1-7331978-1-6 (paperback)
978-1-7331978-2-3 (ebook)

Cover design by Laura Duffy
Book design by Karen Minster

Guesthouse Publications
Sausalito, California

guesthousepublications@gmail.com

QUOTED MATERIAL: Chapter 2, from Thomas F. Crum's *The Magic of Conflict: Turning a Life of Work into a Work of Art* (Touchstone, 1987), by permission of the author; Chapter 3, from Oriah Mountain Dreamer's *The Invitation* (HarperONE, 1999), by permission of the author; Chapter 4, a translation by Coleman Banks from *The Essential Rumi* (HarperCollins, 1995), by permission of the author; Chapter 5, the poem "Faith" from Patrick Overton's *The Leaning Tree* (Bethany Press, 1975), by permission of the author; Chapter 6, a translation by Wade Baskin from Jean-Paul Sartre's *Essays in Aesthetics* (Philosophical Library, 1963), by permission of the publisher; Chapter 7, from Alan Cohen's *Dare to Be Yourself* (Random House, 1991), by permission of the author; Chapter 12, from *Letters to a Young Poet* by Rainer Maria Rilke, translated by Stephen Mitchell (Penguin Random House LLC, 1984), by permission of the publisher.

This book is dedicated to

our dear friend Armando Quiros,

who urged us on at every turn,

always curious about our content and process.

Brilliant, loving man … we miss you.

CONTENTS

WORKSHOP PARTICIPANTS

CARMEN: Emotionally young, parents fought, mother belittled her, wants to stop being scared

DIANE: Low self-esteem, expresses feelings, wants to feel better in her relationships

TODD: Aspiring musician, blames failures on others, came to Esalen to hang out

FRANK: Lawyer in career crisis, looking for a future

TEX: Works with horses, suffered childhood physical abuse, wants to save his marriage

MAX: Retired teacher afraid of aging, likes to talk

RONALD: Therapist, wants a relationship

ALISON: Married with children, recovering alcoholic, unhappy with self and family

1

Friday

THE FLIGHT ATTENDANT THREW BACK THE DOOR OF the small jet and Santa Barbara's morning light poured in. Rae could smell the sea as a cool marine breeze mixed with the stale cabin air. Taking a deep breath and letting it out slowly, Rae felt a tightness in her stomach, like an indigestible lump. Her anxiety was back, as if it had been waiting patiently at the airport, watching for her return. All the excitement of her successful trip drained away. Alan would be waiting for her at the other end of a short cab ride home.

Following the line of passengers down the gantry steps onto the tarmac, she listened to the first message on her cell phone. It was Alan, and he sounded irritated. "You didn't call me this morning. I'm waiting. Call me back right away."

The next message was also from Alan. "This is my second call today. Why haven't you called me?" By the third message, his voice had a familiar whine. "You know I have a doctor's appointment today. I'm anxious. Where are you?"

The lump in Rae's stomach hardened.

Rae rolled her suitcase across the blacktop and through the airport to the lineup of cabs on the street. The trunk of the closest cab bounced open and a turbaned cabbie got out of the driver's side. As he reached for her bag, she smiled at him, pressing her palms together and bowing slightly.

"*Sat Shri Akaal.*"

He hesitated. A bemused smile spread across his face, and he ducked his head and said, "*Satsriakaal,*" dropping her suitcase in the trunk. Rae climbed into the back seat. "One-thirty-two Beach Road, please."

As the cab headed toward the on-ramp to Highway 101 South, she squinted in the bright sunlight, searching a distant eucalyptus grove for herons' nests. Finding none, she resumed listening to her messages: two from clients, followed by a congratulatory call from an organizer of the New York psychology conference.

"Rae, hi. It's Jack Shaw from the APA. Congratulations! Your keynote got rave reviews and the bookstore sold out of your new book. I want you to consider heading up a panel on childhood trauma at the Las Vegas conference. I'll be in touch. You're the top."

Rae smiled, remembering how nervous she had been about the trip east. She hadn't taken the main stage since her dressage performance in middle school. But strangely, after all her anxiety the night before the presentation, she'd risen from a deep, dreamless sleep feeling calm and completely composed. She had known, as if from a source outside herself, she would perform with clarity and confidence.

Her reverie broke with a disquieting thought and a wave of foreboding. *Another conference. Alan isn't going to like it.*

She saw a sign for the Las Positas exit fly by overhead. She was almost home. Rae closed her eyes and counted thirty slow, deep breaths. Her eyes opened just as the cab came to a stop in front of her Spanish-style home, its tiled roof poking out from the midst of a luxuriant semitropical garden. She paid the fare and collected her bag.

Before she had crossed the sidewalk, the front door of the house flew open and Alan popped out like a jack-in-the-box. He was freshly shaven, his thinning hair combed straight back partially covering his balding pate. He stopped abruptly at the edge of the landing and stood at the top of the steps in his slippers, heavy gray sweats and an open-neck Hawaiian shirt.

Rae collapsed the handle of her suitcase and looked up at her husband expectantly. *Please welcome me,* she thought. The sun was behind him and Rae couldn't read his expression. "Hello, sweetheart," she said.

Alan made no move to help her with her bag. "I can't believe you didn't call me," he said. "You know how important today is to me. I don't ask for much, but I do expect you to show concern when you leave me alone.

"This is a very difficult time for me," he added petulantly.

The warmth drained from Rae's face. "Sorry, sweetheart." She hoisted her suitcase up the steps and walked past him, dropping her bag inside the front door and heading into the large, open kitchen.

Alan followed her. "You have no idea how upset I am, how sick with worry I've been. My health is fragile, and I need all my strength to fight this thing. My cancer coach says the strain between us is hindering my immune system."

Rae straightened her shoulders.

"Alan, I've had a long flight. I need you to go into the other room while I settle in and make lunch. I'm not having this conversation with you right now."

Alan's face reddened. He paused, as if restraining himself, then shook his head disapprovingly. "You're so selfish!"

He turned on his heel and stormed off.

Rae was shaken. *Am I?*

Somewhere in her heart, Rae knew that she really cared for him. They had laughed and loved and done great work together. Rae pictured driving up the California coast with Alan years ago on their way to teach their first workshop. Their attraction had been so exciting and compelling when she was a single mom and he was unhappily married.

Now their life together was mostly shared conflicts, and she didn't know what to do about it. Rae felt her panic rising. *I know he doesn't want to be this way. Would it hurt me to call him more often when I'm away?*

No answers came. She thought of her clients' relationship struggles and the wreckage left in the wake of their various childhood traumas. *I see my clients' issues and choices so clearly, why I can't see my own?*

She was right back in the confusion she had felt fourteen years ago, telling her teenage children that she and their father were splitting up. She had refused to continue putting up with his emotional absence, but somehow that hadn't seemed reason enough when she saw the hurt in their eyes.

Is there something wrong with me?

She didn't know the answer and she didn't know if she could face another breakup. Closing her eyes, Rae inhaled deeply and exhaled slowly. *Let go and let God,* she thought.

After several breaths she consciously turned her thoughts to the upcoming workshop with David and Gil. There would be time next week to think about her marriage.

DAVID'S SECOND FLOOR OFFICE went from bright to dim, to bright again, as a flotilla of billowing clouds sailed over Bloomington's rolling hills. He watched them chasing their shadows across the wooded campus of Indiana University even as he listened intently to his client's story.

It was the last psychotherapy session of the day. The young man looked every bit the grad student he was, slouched on the overstuffed sofa in a T-shirt, faded jeans and bare feet halfway sticking out of a pair of beat-up loafers. He paused after reciting a laundry list of shortcomings of his current girlfriend and said, "I don't know why I always lose interest."

This was just the latest in a string of girlfriends, and David was losing patience. He gave his client a wry look and said, "It's easier to love an idea than to live in reality."

The grad student waited for further explanation. When none came, he asked, "That's it?"

David said, "If you want a real person in your life, you have to become more curious about reality. Who are you? Who is she? What are you like together? To do that, you need to let go of your fantasies."

"What do you mean, fantasies?" he asked, furrowing his brow.

"Good." David's eyes widened slightly behind his wire-rim glasses. "Asking questions is the first step." David leaned forward, resting his elbows on his knees. "Why don't you start by telling me how you felt about her before the two of you had sex?"

"That's easy. I had to have her. She was new and strange and exciting. She drove me crazy. Everything she did seemed sexy to me. When we weren't together, I worried about whether she was really into me."

"How long did that last?"

"The whole first week, until I slept with her."

"And then?"

"The sex was great, and I felt more relaxed around her."

"But that wore off?"

"Well, yeah..."

"You began to suspect she wasn't exactly the person you thought she was."

"Yeah..."

"And you were right. She didn't exist beyond the chemical cascade in your limbic system. If you want a relationship, you're going to have to take a completely different approach."

"I have no idea what you're talking about."

"No, you don't." David paused to let him take that in and glanced at the clock. The fifty-minute hour was up. "One definition of insanity is doing the same thing over and over again, and expecting a different result."

The student laughed nervously. "Okay, so what do I do?"

"For a start, I'd suggest you forgo sex for the first three months of your next relationship."

The young man looked stunned. He shook his head. "I wouldn't know where to begin."

"Good. That's a great place to start." David's face softened. "I'll see you next week."

His client grabbed his coat and left, shutting the door behind him. David stood over his desk and jotted a note in the file. He bounced on his toes as he wrote, his calves already anticipating his after-work doubles match, and his mood rising with the thought of the coming week at his favorite West Coast retreat center teaching with Rae and Gil.

He turned off the lights, locked the office door behind him and walked down the hall to the wide staircase down to the lobby. The old wooden steps were broad and, feeling particularly chipper, he started taking them two at time. After three small leaps, he felt slightly off balance and returned to taking them one at time. Still, he was pleased with himself. He thought of his childhood home on North-lawn Street in Detroit. As a teenager he routinely took the whole staircase in three grand leaps, launching from landing to landing.

Smiling to himself as he left the building, David stopped at the curb to look left, right and left again, making sure there were no cars coming as he stepped into the street. What he didn't see was the empty Coke bottle right in front of him. He felt a sharp pain as his foot slipped off it and rolled under him. Taking two hopping steps he recovered his balance but limped the rest of the way to the other side of the street.

Safely on the far sidewalk, he stood still, keeping the weight off his right foot and waiting for the pain to subside. It didn't, and his thoughts took a dark turn. He would have to miss tonight's game. His tennis days could be over. Without tennis his stamina and strength would drain away, his heart and lungs succumb to sedentary disorders and finally, his brain would shrink from a lack of oxygenated blood. He was doomed to repeat his father's horrifying descent into dementia.

He recognized the familiar catastrophic thinking and smiled. He rotated his right foot slowly and was comforted when he found his ankle had a full range of motion. The sharp pain had subsided. He took a tentative step. The pain didn't spike, so he tried walking slowly. His ankle tolerated it well enough and he continued on his way to the Russell Road Racquet Club. The old tennis pro would know what to do. It would make him a few minutes late but his pals would be waiting for him at the net.

"GAME, SET, MATCH," David called out after his momentum carried him to the winning volley, slicing the ball away from the desperate reach of his opponent. David gave his partner, George, a high five and walked off the court favoring his thickly-taped right ankle.

Back in the locker room, he stripped down and cautiously shuffled into the showers, where two octogenarians were soaping down. David registered their thin legs and hanging guts, and wondered how many more years it would be before he looked like that.

He showered quickly, toweled off and looked himself over in the mirror, straightening his shoulders, sticking out his chest and sucking in his stomach. His bone structure was starting to show through his retreating muscle, and his belly was definitely softer and more rounded than he remembered.

He shook off the gloom. His reflection in the mirror couldn't take away from the thrill of beating two guys who were thirty years younger. *They may have been stronger and faster, but they were no match for a couple of grizzled veterans.*

David dressed, picked up his tennis bag and headed out of the locker room. He was looking forward to the weekly Shabbat dinner with his wife Joann and their adult sons.

The evening air was brisk against his skin. Joann was parked out front in her well-preserved 1994 Prelude. She had her ear buds in and was talking on her phone as David opened the door. He threw his bag in the back and slipped into the passenger seat. She smiled and accepted a kiss on the cheek.

While he sat there waiting for her to finish, David took a long look at her. She was slim and still had the lines of a younger woman's body under her slacks and blouse. Her soft, mid-length hair remained a natural brown, and at 66, the lines around her eyes and loose skin under her throat appeared as a gentle settling. They both were showing signs of aging, but he still felt the longing and desire he'd felt for the young single mother he had married thirty-one years ago. He felt his eyes watering and he blinked to clear them. Then his ankle started to throb and he bent over to rub it.

Joann ended her call and turned to see what he was doing.

"What's wrong, honey?"

"I twisted my ankle. It seemed to get better, but towards the end of my match, it started hurting again."

"You played on it?"

"Like I said, I was feeling better."

"You know you're leaving for the workshop on Sunday and there are no doctors there. You should have gone right over to see Sam at the clinic." She briskly slipped the car into gear and eased into traffic.

David tucked his chin in toward his chest, and let his expression go blank. "I hear that you're concerned about my trip."

"Don't use that therapist trick on me; you have responsibilities. We have a lot to do this weekend, and the last thing we need is for you to be laid up with a sprained ankle."

"But..."

"No ifs, ands, or buts. Call Sam right now and ask him if he can see you before dinner."

David started to feel his neck and shoulders tightening like curing concrete. He looked at Joann, but before he could speak, she glanced at him and smiled that disarming smile of hers. "Now don't get your hackles up. I'm just concerned about you."

David laughed. He loved Joann's light touch. She was so tough, but she could turn soft and funny in an instant. He looked at her and beamed.

She glanced at him again. "What? What?"

"I'm just appreciating you."

"Well, yeah. What's not to appreciate?"

They both laughed.

Saturday

THE TIP OF THE RISING SUN POURED ITS PALE LIGHT over Rae as she sat in the lotus position, wrapped in a shawl against the chill sea air. She felt the slight sensation of warmth on her cheeks and noticed the red translucence of her closed eyelids. Opening her eyes, Rae saw the tiny molten eruption of sunrise on the distant ridgeline.

Tears came to her eyes as she experienced the sun's warming rays as deeply personal and intentional. Joy welled up within her, yet she had no idea why. *Was her practice deepening? Was her pain opening her to the Source?*

Rae had a lot to do before leaving for the workshop. She had a half day of clients and a couples counseling session with Alan. She sighed and thought, *Another marriage counselor for Alan to reject.*

Taking a deep, slow breath, she stood and bowed. She knew how to get through this. Put one foot in front of the other and do what she had learned to do with her first husband's drinking. Take it one day at a time.

GIL SAT IN CAFFE PUCCINI and listlessly stirred the white froth atop his cappuccino. Streaks of mocha brown appeared in the wake of the stainless steel spoon, but he had no interest in the pattern and stared vacantly out the large plate glass window. Morning traffic streamed by, headlights muted by a wet blanket of fog that lay on the city like a sedative, damping sounds, holding back the dawn and leaving everyone alone with their thoughts. He wasn't focusing. Even the sweet, yeasty smell of the fresh baked brioche sitting on a plate in front of him didn't break through his torpor.

He was functioning out of habit, and brooding on the futility of last night's pursuits while waiting for the coffee to work its magic. He comforted himself. At least he'd gone home at midnight knowing well enough that everyone else would stay on until closing. Since he'd stopped drinking, he was better at knowing when to call it quits. Best of all, he no longer had to deal with hangovers, just this occasional dull emptiness the morning after.

Why did he tag along with his old friends to the clubs south of Market every weekend? Was it loyalty, or did he really think he was going to meet the love of his life among the animated altered states of club diving? He hadn't had anything like a date in months, and his current sex life had been reduced to an occasional erotic dream.

By the time he'd pulled his second cup toward him, he was interested enough in the world to open his current issue of *Science*. Skimming down the table of contents, he felt an echo of the excitement and curiosity he'd had as a graduate student in ecology, something he missed during his tenure as a lab rat at Genentech. Now he rarely read anything that was relevant to his former job. He preferred the long view of evolution and the broad scope of ecology to the intricate biochemistry at its foundation. He still read for pleasure the original observations and theories of the eighteenth- and nineteenth-century naturalists, who wrestled with the meaning of giant bones that couldn't be explained by the known fauna of the day. He loved the way others' careful observations helped him understand what he saw as he roamed over the countryside on his many walks. Science was a language, a vocabulary built on the accumulation of observations and experiments over the centuries. And even though he hadn't worked in his field since grad school, Gil was still fluent.

It had been six months since he resigned. Biotech had been booming and the work was well-paid but the sterile labs and corporate attitudes never sat well with him. Now he had the money he'd saved up and more time to explore his interests, which at the moment mostly revolved around recovery from his former drinking habits.

He thought about the daily round of Alcoholics Anonymous meetings during his last year at Genentech. Gil smiled ironically at what a slippery slope recovery had been: the other 12-step meetings that quickly followed as his sobriety revealed the stuck places in his personal habits and relationships. One thing led to another and before he knew it, he was taking weekend courses in psychology and attending workshops with Rae and David at Esalen. There he discovered his gift, the ability to navigate the jarring twists and turns of others' personal processes. Rae and David encouraged him, took him on as an assistant, and asked him to teach with them. He could use more of that kind of affirmation.

Gil looked up to see Grant walking towards him holding a cup and saucer in one hand and his portfolio in the other, with the weekend *Wall Street Journal* tucked under his arm. He took in the puffy eyes and the two bits of reddened tissue stuck to Grant's freshly shaven face. Gil smiled in recognition, the left corner of his mouth edging upwards.

"Look what the cat dragged in."

"Easy for a loser to say." Grant scowled. "If you'd stuck around and had anything like the night I did, you'd be in bed for a week."

Gil took it in and decided not to volley back. "Lucky at cards, unlucky in love," he shrugged.

Grant laid his portfolio on the window bench and sat down, placing his cup and saucer on the round linoleum tabletop in front of him. "You're not having much luck with either these days, are you?"

Gil winced. "You're right about that." Then he smiled and added, "But at least when I woke up, I didn't have a swollen brain throbbing in a skull two sizes too small."

"That will be handled directly." Grant forced a grin, took a long pull from under the foam of his latte and breathed out a satisfied, "Ah!"

Gil wrinkled his nose at the aroma of alcohol. "You're back on the Vov?"

"Just hair of the dog."

"Yeah, I just hope you don't have clients this morning."

"Saturday, no clients," Grant beamed. "The partners and I are flying east this morning to be fawned over by the Boston Society of Architects."

Seeing Grant's gloat coming on, Gil settled back in his chair, resigned to another tale of success in Grant's quest for fame and fortune. It was the least he could do for an old friend, but he took little joy in it. By comparison his own career seemed like aimless wandering. Grant went on at length about how yet another award would hang on the wall behind his desk.

Gil looked at his watch. "Shit."

He rose, slinging his messenger bag over his head and leaning in, congratulated Grant and gave him a squeeze on the shoulder.

"I've got an eight o'clock class. Have a good trip."

IT WAS ALMOST MIDNIGHT, the end of a long day. Rae ruminated about Alan and their couple's therapy session. He had accused her of being cold and distant, while Rae made no effort to defend herself. The therapist's efforts to focus Alan on his own feelings and his cancer had momentarily raised Rae's hopes. But Alan twisted that into an opportunity to complain about how Rae had fallen short of meeting his needs.

She went into the bathroom to brush her teeth. Looking at herself in the mirror, Rae noted the dark circles under her eyes. She looked tired and old. She washed her face and put on a layer of moisturizing cream, then smiled ironically and thought, *As if this is going to help.*

She walked into the bedroom, climbed into bed, turned away from Alan and nestled her head into the soft down pillow. *By this time tomorrow, I'll be at a world renowned persoal growth center, laughing with David and Gil, deep into the business of running a group.*

Smiling, she fell asleep.

2

Sunday

G IL DOWNSHIFTED HIS FADED RED ISUZU TROOPER and turned right at the old wooden Esalen sign. Keeping his foot on the brake, he rolled down the steep driveway on the ocean side of Highway 1. In fifty yards, he came to a complete stop beside a small windowed guard shack. A young man with shoulder-length blond hair and a red beard stepped out and walked over to the passenger side of the car.

Leaning over and peering in he asked, "What workshop are you in?"

"Life Beyond Your Limitations."

Holding a clipboard with one hand, he flipped through the attached sheets until he found the page he wanted.

"Your name?"

"Gil Broadbent."

Gil was disappointed. No matter how often he'd been here, a different person checked him in each time, and he had to reintroduce himself. He thought wistfully of Sam's Grill, where in his drinking days not only did the maître d' know his name but the bartender served his usual without asking. He had a sudden urge to tell the guy with the clipboard, *I take my Gibsons straight up, very dry, very cold with two onions.*

"I don't see you listed. Are you sure you signed up for this workshop?"

"Well, actually, I'm leading the workshop." He felt a flicker of doubt. Maybe Rae and David hadn't added him to the leaders' list.

But before Gil's thoughts went any further, crinkles appeared around the young man's eyes and his white teeth flashed.

"Ha, here you are." The young man looked up. "You should've told me you're a leader, I never would have guessed."

He handed Gil a key. "You have a sleeping bag space in Fritz. Do you need a map?"

"No, thanks." *Never would have guessed?*

Gil released the parking brake and rolled down the hill, turning left around the oval of grass and parking by the low stone wall in front of the lodge. He was hoping to find Rae and David inside or out back, but no one was there. So he decided to wait. He lay down on the bench on the ocean side of the deck, just twenty feet from the cliff's edge. He stuffed his fleece jacket under his head and looking up at the sky through the long branches of the Monterey Cypress he listened to the rhythmic roll and crash of the Pacific on the rocks a hundred feet below. Slowly his thoughts drifted off.

RAE AND DAVID sat gazing out at the ocean as they floated in a shallow hot springs pool lined with rounded river rock.

The other tubs of the bathhouse deck were empty at the moment and the rest of the retreat center, just fifty yards up a steep dirt road, seemed miles away. The last of the weekend crowd had left already and those arriving for the week were still checking in and getting settled in their rooms.

They'd had a long talk about the upcoming workshop on the drive up from Santa Barbara and now were relaxing, taking in the vast blue water stretching to the horizon. After several minutes of silence, David turned around, carefully placed his wire-rimmed glasses on the stone lip of the tub and submerged himself in the warm water. Half a minute later, he came up sputtering and blinking.

Rae was shocked how different he looked without his glasses. His eyes were big and bulged slightly like those of a deep water fish brought up too quickly from the depths. She noted how vulnerable he looked.

"You have a birthday coming up, don't you?" Rae asked.

David wiped the excess water from his face with one hand while reaching for his glasses with the other.

He broke into a rueful grin, "It's not here … yet."

"How old will you be?"

"You know, it's funny, but I have to stop and think. Isn't that one of those questions the paramedics ask you after an accident to make sure your brain is working?"

"No, they ask you your name, what day it is and how many fingers they're holding up."

"In that case, I'd pass," David smiled. "I'll be 68 next Thursday."

"Have you ever thought about retiring?" Rae noticed him wince and immediately regretted asking the question. She knew that aging was a sore subject for him.

David leaned back against the seaward edge of the tub and spread his arms, holding his legs out straight on the surface of the water and then allowing them to slowly sink.

"Sixty-eight's not *that* old. Besides, I love what I do, and I still think I'm getting better at it; so why stop?" David smiled for a moment; his brow furrowed. "Not to mention the mortgages on our house in Bloomington and our condo in Florida. And Joann is still working. So the answer is no, I'm not really thinking about retiring."

"Haven't you ever wanted to do something different? What about all the things you always dreamed of but haven't gotten around to doing?"

"Well, I wanted to get married, have a family and be good at what I do. I wanted to help people. And I've done all those."

Rae didn't know whether or not to challenge his denial. No one was that content. Certainly she wasn't. She thought of the Nathaniel Hawthorne quotation she latched onto in high school: *"The world owes all its onward impulses to men ill at ease."*

As if further explanation might be necessary, David said, "I started late at being a husband and father." He paused. "Being a father came naturally, but being a husband didn't. I've worked hard at it for years. Now my kids have families of their own, and my life is full and rich. Joann and I feel very grateful for our life together but we still have to work on our relationship."

Wish I felt that way about Alan and me, thought Rae.

"My practice is like that, too," David added. "I worked hard to develop it. There was a lot to learn, and I made mistakes along the way. But now every time I meet with a client,

I feel like I'm harvesting the richness of a lifetime's worth of experience."

"You never cease to surprise me," Rae replied. She looked at David for a moment, then turned to a man who was just arriving at the pool. "Do you happen to have the time?"

The man looked at his wristwatch. "Quarter to four."

"Thanks." Rae stood up and turned toward David. "Let's head up the hill."

"Okay." David slid back down to a prone position, then rolled over. Grabbing the edge of the tub to balance himself, he stood up.

They wrapped themselves in towels. As Rae followed him up the steps, she noticed he was favoring his right leg.

GIL OPENED HIS EYES and saw Rae and David beaming down at him. The warmth of their countenances filled his chest and spread through his body. A thought flitted across his mind: *What would it have been like to have parents like these?* He grabbed David's extended hand and pulled himself up, engulfing David in an enthusiastic embrace.

David laughed. "Whoa, lover boy!"

Gil felt a surge of energy he hadn't felt since his college football days. He squeezed all the harder and bending backward lifted David off the ground. David moaned dramatically. Worried that he might have hurt him, Gil quickly set him down. He was relieved to see David smiling and turned to Rae. This time he took it slowly, looking in her eyes before folding her gently into his arms. Holding her, he let out a long slow breath and allowed his body to soften into the embrace. He held her several seconds longer than was natural for him, concentrating on maintaining a relaxed posture. He was sure she expected it as if hugging were a spiritual practice. He whispered softly in her ear, "It's good to see you."

Rae eased the hug and Gil stepped back. She smiled up at him. "It's good to see you too."

David interjected, "I hate to break up this love fest, but we have a workshop to plan."

Gil shot David a look and then said, "Okay, let's get it done quickly so I can get a swim in before dinner."

A FEW MINUTES before six, Rae stood behind David in the line of guests waiting to be served dinner. She felt invigorated after a brisk walk around the property. The wooden tables in front of them held two large, covered trays of main dishes and several smaller platters of fresh vegetables. A slender rope stretched across the approach to the food, indicating that they weren't ready to serve yet. A hum of conversation surrounded her as the guests lined up for their evening meal.

Rae closed her eyes and took in a deep breath. She smelled cumin and coriander in the steam rising from the hot trays, and for a moment she was back at the ashram in India thirty years ago. She remembered the long, dusty, rattling trip by train and bus from Bombay. There had been something earthy and freeing in all that poverty and chaos. She smiled, thinking about the other young Westerners she'd met making that trek, and the relaxed atmosphere created by all that strangeness. Friendships sprung up quickly as Western taboos were buried in a chaotic onslaught of unfamiliar smells, sights and sounds.

It had been a trip of firsts. Smoking ganja. Yoga. Meditation. Eastern religion. Losing her virginity.

Rae wistfully thought of Sudhir. He was two years older than she, his English formal and clipped with that delightful British pronunciation, his body long and sinewy. She suddenly felt warm and flushed and opened her eyes to steady herself.

Still thinking of Sudhir, she noticed a man in aviator glasses walking casually past the line. He stepped over the cordon, took a plate off the table and started to serve himself.

Someone in the front of the line must have said something. He turned around with a smile and said, "The food looks ready to me."

Two women wearing aprons came through the swinging kitchen door, carrying another hot tray between them. As they set it down on the table, the shorter woman brushed her bangs out of her eyes and said, "We're not serving yet."

"That's all right," the man replied, as he continued to spoon vegetables onto his plate. "I can help myself."

The young woman froze and blinked twice. Then her eyes narrowed.

With slow, perfect enunciation, she repeated, "We are not ready." When that had no effect she put her hands on her hips. "Please get back in line and wait for the gong."

"Well, I'm almost done. If you could just pass me those nuts ..."

A tall, solidly built, bow-legged man in the front of the line cleared his throat. "Son, the young lady would like you to wait."

Rae held her breath. The hum of conversation died away as the man in aviator glasses turned, still holding his plate, and looked the tall man over. He hesitated, then broke out in a smile.

"I had no intention of upsetting anyone." He took his plate and walked slowly back, past the long line and out the double doors at the back of the lodge.

Rae looked at David. "That was weird."

David frowned. "What a schmuck."

AT QUARTER AFTER SIX, Gil walked into the lodge and quickly served himself from the half-empty chafing dishes. He wandered back through the dining room and spotted Rae and David waving at him from the corner of a smaller table off to his left. He headed their way.

Gil slipped his leg over the bench seat and placed his plate on the table as he sat down next to Rae.

"Perfect timing," Rae smiled. "We were just talking about the outline for this evening and the wording of our three questions."

Gil noticed a yellow legal pad lying on the table. The top sheet was turned back and the open page was covered in David's scrawl. Gil took a mouthful of curry and said, "Not much to plan."

He turned the pad around and glanced over it. "Looks exactly like what we always do. The only thing I'd change is our introductions. We usually drone on way too long before giving the group a chance to speak…"

David cut him off. "Let's leave it as is. We need to model what we want from them."

David turned to Rae and continued working on the exact wording of the questions they would ask each participant. Gil lost interest and started looking around the dining room. He knew several workshops were offered that week and their participants would be scattered among those sitting around them. A large framed photograph hanging on the opposite wall caught his eye. It was a close-up of a condor in flight, soaring somewhere along the Big Sur coast. Gil was taken by the grandeur of its ten-foot wingspan surfing the steady updraft where sea breeze and mountain meet.

Rae nudged him. Gil broke his reverie and looked blankly at Rae for a split second.

"It's your turn to answer the three questions," Rae said.

"Let's see." Gil looked down at the questions scribbled on the notepad and went with the first thing that came to his mind. "Mostly, I'm comfortable in groups. I've discovered that comes as a result of just being myself. What I'd like to celebrate is being a real member of this team. It would be a miracle to really know what my calling is." Then he nodded at David.

While David was talking, Gil listened with one ear, while watching a thirty-something guy in pressed slacks and a dress shirt join the queue at the bar window. Gil noted the contrast to the room full of jeans, yoga outfits and outdoor wear and smiled to himself. *Must be his first time here.*

The guy was of average height and good-looking enough, except for his overly coiffed hair and a dour expression. He made it to the front of the line and pushed some money across the counter. The ponytailed barkeep handed him two Anchor Steam beers and one tall glass.

Gil thought, *Either he has a friend who drinks from the bottle, or this guy is serious about his beer.*

RAE LOOKED AT HER WATCH, 8:20 p.m. The workshop was scheduled to begin in ten minutes and she, David and Gil were sitting by themselves in the oval-shaped room with a dozen large cushions spread around in a circle. A young-looking woman with caramel skin and long black braids stood in the hallway and peeked in through the double doors. She asked softly, "Is this the Life Beyond Your Limitations workshop?"

Rae looked up and smiled. "Yes. Come in."

She watched as the woman bent down in the dark hallway and carefully untied one shoe, then the other, slipping them off and placing them neatly against the wall.

Rae wondered, *Would the group be appropriate for a teenager?* The woman walked gracefully into the alcove and stood at the edge of the room. Rae smiled warmly up at her and noticed the delicate bones of her narrow wrists.

"Welcome, you're the first one here. I'm Rae. This is David and Gil."

"I'm Carmen."

"Make a nametag for yourself and take a seat anywhere you like."

As Rae looked down at the roster and put a checkmark by Carmen's name, a bowlegged pair of Levi's passed in front of her. She looked up and recognized the tall, dark-haired man who had challenged the line crasher at dinner. She felt a little burst of warmth in her chest as her eyes followed him down the room to a pillow in the far corner. He sat down and, stretching his long legs out in front of him, folded his arms and leaned back against the ocean-side wall of glass.

Now several people were arriving. Rae noticed Gil paying particular attention to a man in pressed slacks, and wondered if Gil knew him. Others were quickly finding a cushion to sit on, but the man stood hesitating in the middle of the room in shined shoes and a crisp shirt. Something about his manner seemed awkward to Rae, as if he were uncertain whether he was really supposed to sit on the floor. Whatever his concern was, it seemed to resolve as he picked a spot and dropped himself onto a pillow.

AT 8:30 GIL NOTED all but one of the cushions were occupied and the room was quiet. David was lying against a backrest with his legs stretched out in front of him, looking around the room intently.

Rae was checking the roster, calling out each name and checking them off as each person responded. Todd was the only name that went unanswered.

"We're missing one person but we like to start on time. I'm Rae Milford. These are my co-leaders, David Levine and Gil Broadbent. If you haven't already done so, make a nametag for yourself and be sure to wear it for our first couple of sessions. There are tags and colored pens in the center of the circle."

Rae paused while several people put on their nametags. When everyone was back on their cushions, she said, "Gil will start us off with a few minutes of silent meditation."

Gil sat up straight, folded his legs and hooked his right foot over his left calf so that both knees pressed firmly against the floor. He leaned forward into the half-lotus posture, then settled back on his tailbone. "Find a comfortable position, relaxed but alert."

There was a stirring as people moved items of clothing and notebooks out of the way and adjusted themselves on their pillows. Gil said, "With eyes open or closed, simply follow your breath." The room fell quiet.

Gil counted his breaths, inhaling slowly, expanding his lungs down towards his abdomen and then up into his chest, holding it for a few seconds before exhaling slowly. He planned to sound the chime and end the meditation at thirty breaths.

At twenty-five breaths, he heard a door close in the outer hall. At twenty-seven breaths, the slap of hard-soled shoes reverberated across the stone alcove and a loud voice broke his concentration. "Boy, this place was hard to find."

Gil opened his eyes and saw a man standing by the hallway doors in cargo pants, a black T-shirt and aviator glasses. Gil said, "Just take a seat. We're doing a short meditation."

The man smiled, his expression vaguely indulgent. "Okay, no problem. I'm a big fan of Eastern mystical practices. Just go on doing whatever it was you were doing. Don't mind me."

Gil raised his eyebrows and looked at Rae, but she was sharing a look with David—some private recognition passing between them. She looked back at Gil and nodded.

Gil closed his eyes again and went back to the meditation. He decided to extend the time by ten breaths to give everyone a chance to settle back in after the interruption. As he counted, he thought about Rae and David's shared reaction. *What was that about?*

After a minute, Gil held up a small brass bowl and struck it twice with a wooden mallet, allowing the harmonious ringing to fade slowly away to silence.

David picked up a sheet of paper, cleared his throat and read:

> What would it be like if you lived each day,
>   each breath,
> As a work of art in progress?
> Imagine that you are a masterpiece unfolding
>   every second of every day,
> A work of art taking form with every breath.

He repeated the last two lines and added, "By Tom Crum." He put the paper down and looked towards Rae.

Rae said, "Welcome to Life Beyond Your Limitations. Take a look around you. These are your fellow travelers for the next five days. This evening, you will all have a chance to introduce yourselves and we'll go over the basic ground rules for the week."

As Rae spoke, Gil studied the tall man in jeans who sat with his legs straight out in front of him and his back leaning against the floor to ceiling window. He had crossed his arms before the meditation, stretching his light blue, long-sleeved shirt tight across his forearms and biceps. The sternness of his expression was counterbalanced by the levity of the white piping on his shirt, which scrolled casually across his shoulders and looped over the flaps of his snap-down chest pockets.

Next to Rae, Carmen sat with her legs folded neatly under her, very still. Gil had to look closely to track the slight movements of her shallow breaths. She had a delicate childlike face as if she hadn't yet grown into her adult features. She kept her eyes down.

It was a nice mix, five men and three women, most appeared to be in their thirties and forties except for the man to Gil's right. He was definitely older. His thick salt-and-pepper mustache and eyebrows had a jaunty, still-in-the-game look to them, but Gil guessed he was in his mid-sixties.

Rae said, "Gil, would you start?"

Startled, Gil took a moment to look around the circle and collect his thoughts. He was able to make eye contact with most of them, except the aviator glasses and the younger girl. He inhaled slowly and halfway through his exhale he began. "The others sitting in the room with you are strangers right now. Look at their faces. In only a few days, you will know them better than you know most of the people in your daily life, in some cases, better than you know your own family." Then he sat back.

Rae stared at Gil, but he wasn't sure what she wanted. After a long moment, she turned to David. "Would you like to introduce yourself?"

"My name is David and I'm co-leading this workshop. We are going to tell you a little about ourselves and the workshop. Then we want to hear from you."

Oh. Gil felt a pang of conscience about missing his cue.

David described his ordinary, middle-class childhood—ordinary except for his depression, which led to weekly psychotherapy sessions when he was just thirteen. He talked about the relationship he developed with his therapist, Dr. Hunt, which saw him through high school and college, fostered a deep appreciation for his inner experience and connection to others and led to his career in psychology.

BEFORE TAKING HER TURN, Rae briefly rested her eyes on an attractive woman with blonde hair sitting directly across from her. The woman looked shyly away. Rae noted her nametag. *Diane.*

"To sit in this room with you is to dwell in the sacred." Rae leaned forward. "You have all given up a week and traveled—some of you across the continent—to sit here with us and explore your inner resources and limitations."

Rae noticed Diane's eyes widening as if she wondered what she had gotten herself into.

Rae looked directly at Diane. "My goal for this week is to express what is true for me. I've often needed the same invitation we now offer you. There's no higher calling in this room than to be true to yourself. So when you disagree with someone in the group, when you disagree with the group leaders, when you're telling yourself your opinion doesn't matter, we invite you to speak up. Then be sure to watch how you're received. Make us earn your trust.

"In my first book, *The Road to Recovery*, I describe a process called share-check-share. I'd like you to practice it this week. Share a little, then notice how you feel about the response you receive before deciding whether to share more. If you feel good, you've probably been heard, valued, appreciated or supported. That's a sign that you might want to consider sharing a little bit more. Check each time for your reaction to how you are responded to. If you feel sad, scared, criticized or shamed, stop right there. By learning to build trust in yourself and opening up one small piece at a time, you will develop one of the most important relationship skills.

"If you were raised in a dysfunctional or alcoholic family, you learned to hide your feelings. And those habits don't go away when you grow up.

"David, Gil and I hope you'll find the freedom and courage this week to share who you really are: what you think, what you feel. That's the foundation for self-acceptance and the pathway for growing beyond your limitations."

Rae paused and looked at each person around the circle. She noted a quizzical expression on Diane's face. *I really have her attention.* "Now is the time for each of you to introduce yourselves. We'd like you to do this by answering three questions."

Rae stood up and walked over to the flip chart. With a magic marker she wrote in capital lettering on the chart:

1. WHAT BROUGHT YOU HERE?

2. WHAT OUTCOME DO YOU WANT TO
   CELEBRATE BY THE END OF THE WEEK?

3. WHAT WOULD BE A MIRACLE FOR YOU?

Rae turned back to the group. "Who would like to start?" Gil waved his hand. "First, I'd like to introduce myself." Rae felt embarrassed. "I'm sorry Gil, I thought you had."

With a straight face, Gil replied, "I'll forgive you this time." For a moment Rae was unsure how to take him. Then he broke into a broad grin and Rae shook her head at his tease.

Gil looked around the circle. "I always wondered what I would be when I grew up. And here I am sitting with you." He held a deadpan expression. "Not exactly the fame and fortune I'd imagined."

There were a couple of titters from the circle.

"But on the other hand, if my goal is to be myself and accept where I am, this room is a really good place to be.

"For years my relationship with alcohol distorted my experience. It took away my shyness, my vulnerability, my fear and my pain. I didn't have to work at it, I didn't have to wait, I didn't have to risk failing. All I had to do was take a drink and everything seemed better than it was before, especially me.

"The problem was I couldn't stay there. I kept waking up in this world. The one with nausea, headaches, dry heaves, depleted bank accounts, trashed relationships, broken trust and neglected responsibilities. I just couldn't get the two worlds to work together. In the end I knew I had to give one up.

"Then, like you, I came to this workshop. That experience, three and a half years ago, marked a watershed in my life. I uncovered feelings and memories that had been locked away for decades. I immediately saw that alcohol wasn't the solution, it was the problem."

Todd stood up and said to no one in particular, "Bathroom. Be right back," and walked out of the room.

Gil looked annoyed, but Rae was gratified to see him take a deep breath. After a moment he said, "Like a counter-intuitive Zen koan, I found what I sought by accepting who I already was."

Frank, the guy wearing slacks, and Diane both said, "What?" They looked at each other.

"I'm sorry," said Diane.

"No, go ahead."

Diane hesitated then looked at Gil. "Would you say that again?"

"Sure. I said that I could only get what I needed by appreciating what I already had."

Diane and Frank looked baffled.

Gil stopped talking and sat back.

Rae waited to see if he was done, then smiled at him and looked around the circle.

"Who's next?" No one stirred. Rae waited, then turned to her left. "Why don't you start?"

Carmen looked a little dazed and stared at Rae as if she must have meant someone else. When Rae nodded to her, Carmen said reluctantly, "I'm Carmen. I don't have a clue about my miracle, but I know I need something."

A long silence followed. The only sign of her discomfort was the redness moving from her neck into her cheeks, adding a schoolgirl charm to her youthful appearance. Rae became conscious of some rustling in the room, but continued to look at Carmen expectantly.

Just as Rae was about to say something, Todd returned from the bathroom and spoke up from the doorway.

"My turn?" he asked. Without waiting for an answer he said, "I'm glad to be here…"

"Todd," Rae interrupted, "would you mind waiting while Carmen finishes?"

Todd stared at Rae for a beat, then smiled and lowered himself onto his cushion.

"Carmen," Rae spoke softly, "what would you like for yourself?"

Carmen said slowly, "I'd like to know what's wrong with me; that would be a miracle. And it would be good for me to celebrate not being so scared around other people."

"Thanks, Carmen," Rae said. *She's older than she looks.* Turning to Todd, Rae added, "Thank you for waiting."

Todd looked over at Rae with pursed lips and raised eyebrows, as if he were studying her. Then he relaxed his expression and said, "A friend told me some wild stories about this place. I just finished a gig and was free this week, so I decided to check it out. They didn't have any openings in the other workshops, so here I am. I thought what the heck, I might even clear up a couple of things." Todd looked around the circle with a satisfied smile. Rae waited for Todd to continue.

After a moment, David said, "Why don't you name those things."

Todd gave David a questioning glance, then said in a condescending tone, "Like why I was let go from my day job for no good reason, and what my girlfriend's problem is."

"Thank you." David made a note on his legal pad.

"I'm glad you decided to come," Rae said. "In terms of a miracle, what have you been dreaming of that seems beyond your reach?"

Todd leaned back, settling himself into a more comfortable position and looking up at the ceiling. The group waited.

"Well, maybe something about my music. I love writing songs and performing. Although I majored in theater, I also studied music composition and theory in college, and I've been playing ever since. I started out with classical guitar, but recently I've been doing some great compositions in the neoceltic pagan style."

Here Todd paused and looked around the circle. "That may be a little esoteric for you. Let's just say I'm an artist and an academic."

Looking at Rae, he continued, "But right now I have to do other kinds of work to pay the bills, so I don't get to play as much as I want. So what would be worth celebrating would be to understand what's wrong with my girlfriend, my ex and some of my co-workers. They all let me down at some point. A miracle would be if they saw the light … or if I was able to get through to them … and be able to concentrate on my music as much as I want … and have an appreciative audience." He let out a short, snorting laugh.

"Todd," Rae said, "those are wonderful miracles." Rae turned her attention to the group. "As we go around, I would like all of you to write down your miracles, as well as what would be worth celebrating, so you can check back at the end of the week and see how far you've come."

After a short silence, the tall man in jeans and a cowboy shirt caught Rae's eye.

"Hi there, I'm Tex. I didn't really want to come here, but my marriage is in trouble and my wife wanted, well, she practically ordered, me to come. I'm here to see what I can do to make things better at home. I've been out of the winner's circle for too long and I'd sure like to get back in. If my wife somehow stopped being angry with me, now that would be something."

"Thanks, Tex, that's clear," said Rae, thinking, *I'd love it if Alan wasn't so angry with me.*

Frank straightened the crease in his slacks, sat forward and announced a little too loudly, "I'll go next. I'm Frank. I don't think I've ever worked so hard to get to a place that I felt so ambivalent about being at."

Several people chuckled.

"This is not the sort of thing I usually do. In fact, I've never done anything like this before. It's inconvenient to have to take the whole week off. I had to work all day Saturday, most of today, and drive like a madman to make it here on time." Frank stopped and looked at David. "Normally I like to go last. I like to get the lay of land, but with these butterflies doing the tango in my gut, I decided sooner would be better." There were a few more laughs around the circle.

"My problem is, I don't know what I should do with my career. I just lost the best job I've ever had. I mean it wasn't perfect, but I liked it. I felt important and recognized. Then they replaced me, not because I was doing a bad job, but because the law partners had this notion that they needed someone with a business background to help guide the firm through the changes going on in the industry.

"I was offered support to shape my position any way I want it. The partners made it clear they value me and want this to be a positive change. The thing is, I really don't know what to do next. I made lists of my options, of pros and cons, and of all the ancillary consequences but in the end, I'm no closer to deciding.

"The firm hired an executive coach for me. After working with me for several weeks and getting feedback from all my co-workers, she told me I actually had a much bigger choice to make. One of her clients had read your book, Rae, and attended this workshop. My coach recommended that I do the same. Now I'm here, and I don't really know what to expect. I'm more than a little nervous."

Frank paused and asked with a note of apology, "What else was I supposed to talk about?"

David responded, "Tell us an outcome you'd like by the end of the week, and what would be a miracle for you."

"Oh yeah, I guess I'd like to know what job to take. I mean, that would be enough," Frank concluded, with a slight smile and a shake of his head.

Rae noticed that Diane had listened to Frank with her mouth slightly open, as if she might interrupt him at any moment. As the room got quiet, Rae watched as she held her breath and sat motionless. No one spoke. Diane looked to her left at Gil. Her cheeks flushed as she raised her hand.

Gil nodded to her.

Avoiding eye contact, she began to speak haltingly in a soft voice.

"I'm Diane. I've never been in this kind of group before, either. Um, what's the first question?"

Gil repeated the first question, adding, "In here, you can always ask for something to be repeated as many times as you need."

"Oh yeah, what brought me here. Actually, my therapist also told me I should come here. She knows Rae, and said this would be a safe place where I could work on how uncomfortable I am around people. I get embarrassed and want to hide when I'm in social situations. I also have trouble knowing how I feel, and even if I know, I have trouble admitting it. Right now, this is kind of okay, but usually I wouldn't talk in front of people I don't know.

"My therapist thinks I have low self-esteem. I just don't like myself very much. And I end up in a lot of bad situations. Right now I'm seeing a man who rarely pays attention to me. I often feel more lonely when I'm with him than when I'm by myself." She stopped talking and stared at the carpet.

Rae was slightly alarmed by how red Diane's face had gotten. She continued to follow Diane's breathing, which slowed but remained shallow.

After a moment, Diane took a deep breath and then let it out. "What would be worth celebrating Friday would be if I could be comfortable being with you all, and not think I'm stupid when I say something. And maybe know what I want to do with my miserable relationship."

She paused. "A miracle? I don't know what a miracle would be. Can I pick anything?"

Gil responded, "Anything you want."

"Okay, a miracle would be if I really liked myself."

Diane sat back. Rae watched her face return to a normal color as her breathing slowed and deepened.

Gil cleared his throat. "Diane..."

Rae spoke over him. "Diane, I know how hard it is for you to say what you've just said. This is your first moment of healing in this room. Facing your fears and speaking the truth anyway, you have begun to break the chains that bind you. I know you're afraid, and I see you're courageous. I want you to know that it isn't courage if you aren't afraid."

Rae looked around. "This room is full of courageous hearts. You've left the familiar comfort of your home, to arrive at a strange new place. You're speaking out, breaking the rule of not trusting, of depending only on yourself.

"I…we…" Rae looked at David and then Gil, "acknowledge your courage."

Rae noticed Gil's closed expression and considered saying something as she rolled back onto her pillow. She took a deep breath and exhaled. *I'll let it go and give Diane some space to take in what I've said.*

The older fellow with the salt and pepper mustache raised his hand. "Hi, I'm Max and I'm excited to be here." He beamed. "I love all kinds of groups—classrooms, sports teams, book clubs, you name it—but I especially love this kind of workshop. I love the intimacy, the coming together, and the camaraderie. I'm always amazed at how quickly it happens. I'm already getting to know you.

"When Rose, my wife, and I were planning our retirement, we were living in Buffalo. We were bummed out about the gray, icy winters, so we went on the hunt for a small, warm-weather sunshine retreat. We found one in Sarasota, Florida. We've had a delightful time creating a second home there, where our snowbird bodies can thaw out from winter's freeze."

"So what would be worth celebrating, Max?" David asked. "And what is the miracle you want to have?"

"Well, I feel that I'm in a spiritual crisis. I'm struggling with fears and anxiety about my aging body and my growing awareness of death. I'm frightened about how long I have left. I'm not sure I understand my life or at least this part of it."

Max stopped himself, and looked directly at David. "When Social Security kicked in, I began collecting $1500 a month. Free money, I thought to myself, this getting older isn't such a bad deal. And I got Medicare. But then I realized that I'm heading into 'old age.' It's shocking. Where did the years ... the decades ... go? Looking in the mirror, I started to imagine myself as an old man ..."

Rae raised a hand to interrupt him and in a soft voice said, "Max, tonight we'd like you to keep your comments brief so everyone has time to introduce themselves. Maybe you can make a summary statement for now and then fill in more of this important information tomorrow?"

Max looked momentarily stunned. Rae also noted Carmen's flinch and Todd's unpleasant expression; was it disdain?

She was about to say something when Max said, "Okay, no problem. Sometimes when I think about this stuff, I can feel myself going on and on. I guess that sums up why I'm here. I would celebrate learning how to gracefully accept my aging. And a miracle would be to actually celebrate my life and welcome my death. That's it."

Rae thought Max had handled that well but there was still some tension in the room. She saw David raising his eyebrows expectantly at her and decided to address cutting Max off. Scanning the group and making eye contact with each person in turn she said, "Notice if you held your breath when I interrupted Max. Do you still feel a little unsettled?

"Many of us," she went on, "may have been raised in a household where disagreements led to anger, which sometimes led to violence. So as adults, we steel ourselves when even the smallest conflict appears. And often we pretend it's not happening. So let's name the event and discuss it."

"Max, how did you feel about me cutting you off?" Rae asked.

"I didn't like it, but I could understand it. I know I talk too much. I get wound up. My wife often has to make a 'T' with her hands to signal a 'time out' in our discussions. So I guess I'm used to it. I also want there to be time to hear from everyone tonight."

David asked, "What did others feel?"

Diane said in a small voice, "Scared."

Frank followed with, "On high alert."

"I thought it was rude," Todd said.

Carmen remained silent and shrunk back into her pillows.

Rae waited for any other comments, and continued. "It's important to notice that nothing bad happened. You can talk about how you feel. Let your nervous system register the safety you feel here in this room."

After several more comments the discussion died down and the introductions picked up where they left off, as others shared why they had come and what they wanted to achieve in the workshop.

THE SMALL DIGITAL CLOCK on the floor by David's side read 9:30. There was only a half-hour left to wrap up the introductions and he scanned the room to see who still hadn't spoken. David realized he'd overlooked the man sitting to his left. He was young, maybe in his early thirties, wearing a brown sweater and a pair of cords. David noticed nothing particularly remarkable about him, other than his ears, which looked out of place as if they might belong to a taller, heavier-set man who had gone a few rounds in the boxing ring. David read the nametag stuck insecurely on the man's fuzzy sweater.

"Ronald, we haven't heard from you yet."

Ronald nodded to David with a resigned look and turned to the group.

"Hi, I'm Ronald. I'm here because I've wanted to come to Esalen for a long time, and because I was intrigued by the title of this workshop. I'm not sure what I need to do, but I'd love to have more going on in my life. I'm here to learn about myself and the ways I might be holding myself back."

Ronald's voice was a little shaky. He took a deep breath.

"I got to tell you, even though I'm a therapist myself in 'real life'"—he said as he wiggled two fingers on both hands to signify a quote—"…this feels brand-new to me. I've never done anything like this and I'm a little nervous."

David noticed Ronald make eye contact with Diane and quickly look away.

"Let me see." Ronald lowered his eyes. "By the end of the week, I would like to celebrate getting clearer about how I get in the way of my being intimate with women. And as for my miracle? I want to meet the woman of my dreams here and live happily ever after."

Ronald looked up with a faint, somewhat rueful, smile.

"That's all for now."

"Thank you, Ronald, and welcome," said Gil.

Alison, an athletic looking woman in yoga pants and a fleece pullover, raised her hand.

"I'll go. I guess I'm last. My name is Alison, and I'm an alcoholic."

Gil and Rae responded in unison. "Hi, Alison."

Alison blushed. "Oops, wrong meeting." She smiled and said, "I might as well start by saying I have fifteen years' sobriety in AA. I'm used to being in rooms where people share their experience, but this format is different, and I'm feeling a little out of my element.

"I'm here because my husband and I planned to take this workshop together. We have busy lives, and we wanted to take time to renew our relationship. I was really looking forward to it but unfortunately, he had to cancel.

"I decided I needed to come anyway. I haven't been feeling comfortable in my own skin lately. I've been critical of my daughters... and my husband. I've started noticing I'm saying and doing things I haven't done since my drinking days. That worries me.

"I thought being sober was enough. But now I'm not so sure. I feel at a loss, and for once my AA sponsor doesn't seem to have the answers." Alison stopped for a moment. "It would be worth celebrating if I just knew why I feel so out of sorts." She seemed to consider this then added, "A miracle would be to get my old self back. My recovery self."

Gil sat up straight. "Congratulations on your sobriety. Say a little more about your old self. How will you recognize when she's back?"

"I was happy. I knew what I wanted, and why I was here. I wasn't second-guessing my husband, our choices or myself. I felt alive and engaged, part of the world."

"Thanks, that's clear." Gil paused.

David noticed a few downcast eyes. He considered the doubt and uncertainty that people might be feeling right now. Rae was busy making notes. He nodded to Gil.

Gil continued, "Thanks, everyone, for introducing yourselves."

Making eye contact around the circle, Gil said, "The first necessary condition for this journey is the experience of safety. To create a safe place, everyone needs to agree to ground rules for the next five days. These rules are simple and each one addresses an aspect of safety. I invite you to take charge of your own safety. Pay attention to your feelings and your needs. You always have the right to pass if you don't feel comfortable sharing.

"First, we ask each of you to agree not to use any mood-altering substances during the five days of this workshop. That means no alcohol, marijuana, or other drugs. This will allow you to be fully present, and to experience your time here without the distorting or masking effects of any drug. It also helps create safety for those in the group who've been in intimate relationships with active addicts. For people who've grown up with an alcoholic or are struggling with their own sobriety, just the smell of alcohol on someone, or even suspecting that others in the group may be drinking, can stop them cold. If you're taking prescription medication under a doctor's orders, we don't want you to stop. Just let one of us know about it after the meeting."

Gil saw Frank shift his position and look around. He remembered the two beers at the bar, and made a mental note to check Frank's relationship with alcohol. *I should mention it to Rae and David.*

Gil went around the room, asking each person to agree out loud to the rule. When it was Frank's turn, Gil was surprised to hear him say, "I agree not to drink, and I need to let you know I had two beers with my dinner tonight."

"Thanks for your honesty, Frank. Does going without alcohol the rest of the week sound difficult?"

Looking at Gil, Frank spoke with certainty, "No, not at all. I don't drink that much, except on special occasions."

"Great. So just notice—everyone notice—how you feel this week without alcohol. And I invite you to add cigarettes, caffeine, sugar or anything else you would like to try doing without this week. This is an opportunity to experience your natural energy levels. In this culture, when our bodies are tired, we think that means we need a stimulant. It actually means we need rest."

Several people chuckled.

"Alcohol and other drugs stay in the system for hours, sometimes days and weeks, and they limit access to a part of our experience that's important to this work—our deeper and subtler emotions." Gil continued around the room, monitoring each person's response, waiting for an objection.

Everyone nodded or said yes until it got to Tex. "I don't know about this. I planned to have a short shot with my meals, like at home. Don't see what the problem with that is. It'll be after group anyway."

"We already know from experience that you'll get more out of the week if you abstain. We want you to maximize your potential for growth."

Tex squinted one eye and set his jaw.

"What do you think about that?" Gil prodded.

"Well, I don't want to argue with you right out of the gate, but I don't see what's wrong with one shot. It's just a way to relax and it helps me sleep. Better than a tranquilizer, don't you think?"

The whole room went silent. Knowing it was the first challenge to the leaders and involved a central issue, Gil softened his gaze.

"Tex, what's your profession?"

"Horse trainer."

"Horse trainer," mused Gil. "So, Tex, let me ask you this. What if you told the new rider you'd just hired to stay off the rail because your horse seems to panic when he's caught against the fence. In fact, you've been working on that issue with the horse for several weeks, but just the other day the horse kicked the rail again. Fortunately, he didn't hurt his leg. Now, the new jockey tells you that he always rides close to the rail and he knows how to handle a horse there. Would you let the rider have his way, or trust your own knowledge of the situation?"

"Well, 'course I'd know the horse better, and so the rider would just have to follow my rules. It'd be my rules across the board."

"Exactly. So here we are. We've done this work for years and we've learned certain things. One is that you will not get where you want to go if you insist on doing it your way. You won't even be in the running. So I'm asking again, are you willing to not drink any alcohol during this workshop? It means trusting that we know this horse better than you do."

Tex's eyes burrowed into Gil's and Gil calmly returned his stare. After several seconds, Tex relaxed, his eyes sparkled and he barked out a short, coughing laugh. "That was some neat trick. I guess I know when I'm pinned to the rail." Tex smiled. "Okay, fella, five days of no drinking."

Gil smiled back at him.

David noted the group breathing audibly and shifting on their cushions as if needing to stretch after the tension of the last couple of minutes.

"Tex, I want to tell you that what you just did is critical to this work and important for the group," David said. "You spoke your truth and were willing to question what was being asked of you. Then you allowed yourself to be coached. You took the first step on the path of opening up to this work, this group, and yourself."

Tex looked intently at David, then nodded.

After Gil had gotten each person's agreement about alcohol and drugs, Rae laid out the second request. "The next commitment we're asking you to make is attending every group session, arriving on time and staying until the end. If you're upset and want to leave during a session, let one of the leaders know what you're doing."

Todd shook his head and said, "Wait a minute. The catalogue didn't say anything about mandatory attendance, and I don't plan to spend all my time in this room. I want to be out on the property ... at the baths, relaxing, enjoying myself. Maybe find some other musicians to jam with."

"I understand, Todd. That's a lovely way to spend time here at Esalen. Next time you might want to wait for a personal retreat reservation to become available instead of signing up for a workshop. In this workshop, we're asking that you come to every group session. You can go to the baths in the afternoons and evenings when we break. Are you willing to agree to that?"

Todd shook his head again and huffed. After a tense pause, he agreed. "Not that I have much choice."

"You do have a choice."

Todd simply shook his head.

"Okay. Thank you, Todd. Anyone else have a problem with this commitment?" No one responded.

Rae turned to David. "Would you address confidentiality?"

David began, "Our third ground rule is that everything done and said in this room stays here. You're certainly free to talk about your own experience with others, but we ask you not to discuss anyone else's work."

This one was easy. Everyone agreed without hesitation.

Rae continued, "The last request is, no violence. This includes both physical and verbal violence. And if you don't know what verbal violence is, it includes things like put-downs, name-calling and threats. Some of you have had more than your fair share of violence in your life already."

David watched for reactions around the room. Diane released an audible sigh. When Rae turned to look at her, Diane lowered her eyes and her face colored. As Rae began to ask each person in turn, Tex sat up and seemed to be carefully tracking each person's response.

After everyone had agreed to the guidelines, Rae continued, "Okay. Thank you. Welcome to all of you. As Gil said at the beginning of the session, by the end of the week, you'll have come to know each other in a very profound and intimate way.

"Right now it's time for us to stop for the night, and get some rest. Let's take a few moments in silence to note what we just experienced. Again, we recommend you write down what you said you're willing to celebrate, and what your miracle is. Now take a breath. Let go of your thoughts. And as you follow the next several breaths notice what's happening inside you."

Rae counted ten breaths and opened her eyes. "Thank you, everyone. You've come a long way to get here. Take good care of yourselves and get a good night's sleep."

David added, "See you in the morning at 9:30 sharp."

The room emptied as the workshop participants filed out, stooping to find their shoes and disappearing down the dimly lit entrance hall.

GIL OPENED A DOOR built into the curved wall of the meeting room and passed through into the adjacent master suite. Rae's clothes were draped over the desk chair and scattered on the bed so he flopped down onto the over-stuffed chair by the sliding glass door.

David followed him in, stopping just inside the door to grab a handful of macadamia nuts from an open jar on the small desk. Rae walked in and stepped around him, picking up her pile of clothes from the chair and adding them to the ones already spread across the bed. She made herself comfortable sitting cross-legged on the pillows and leaning back against the headboard. Rae picked up a stack of papers from the nightstand and shuffled through them. Pulling one out she said, "I have a reading for tomorrow, 'The Invitation' by Oriah Mountain Dreamer," and handed the poem to David.

Crunching away on his mouthful of nuts, he glanced over the first couple of lines. Then he handed the poem back to Rae. "That'll work."

Setting it on the bedside table she said. "I thought the session went well. Let's review their goals and call it a night."

Gil was listening quietly from the other side of the room. He felt vaguely dissatisfied but couldn't put his finger on exactly why.

David said, "I'll go down the list." He picked up his legal pad and skimmed the page. "Carmen said that she hopes not to be so scared of people. Her miracle is to figure out what's bothering her."

"Which one was she?" Gil said with a slight edge.

David peered over the top of his pad at Gil. "The young woman with braids." He continued reading, "Todd…" then looked up at Gil, "…the aspiring musician, wants to understand what's wrong with the people in his life." David continued reading, "His miracle is to be successful as a musician and have others, quote/unquote 'see the light,' whatever that means. Tex, the cowboy, said he was having problems in his marriage and would like his wife not to be so pissed off at him. Frank, the overdressed, good-looking guy, wants to know how to pick his next assignment at work. Diane, the shy blonde referred by her therapist, wants to celebrate being more okay with herself in relationships, and her miracle is to feel more confident."

Gil looked up from his own notes. "She wanted to like herself."

David retorted, "Same difference."

"Yeah, right." Gil rolled his eyes.

But David's nose was already back in his pad of paper. "Accepting aging and embracing death are the older guy, Max's, goals. Let's see…" David flipped the page. "That leaves Ronald and Alison. Ronald is the therapist who wants to understand his problem with intimacy, and his miracle is to live happily ever after with the woman of his dreams." David coughed a short chuckle. "And last but not least, Alison is the alcoholic in recovery. Her goal is to feel more comfortable in her recovery and life. And her miracle would be to re-connect with her old, happy self."

Rae said, "We have our work cut out for us."

"I don't know, it feels like a pretty solid group to me, though I couldn't get a fix on…" David consulted his notes, "Tex. He seemed to have a chip on his shoulder. I also wonder about tension between him and Todd over the dinner-line incident."

Gil's head popped up. "Incident?"

David continued, "And that thing with the alcohol…he might be a handful."

Gil turned to Rae. "What incident?"

Rae gave David a thoughtful look. "I think I understand Tex. He's more confused and hurt than anything, and I suspect he's an alcoholic. I'm more concerned about Todd. His behavior seems odd and he's arrogant. I have a hard time reading him."

Gil stood up. "What happened in the dinner line?"

Rae stared at him for a moment. "That's right, you weren't there. It was bizarre."

"This sounds like something you should have told me about." Gil looked back and forth from Rae to David.

"Not really, it was no big deal," said David. "Todd crashed the line, and started getting food before the bell rang. When a server came out and asked him to stop, he ignored her. Tex stepped in, told him to stop, and he did."

Rae gave David a questioning glance and added, "And Todd stalked out. The tension was pretty thick."

Gil frowned. "When were you two planning on telling me?"

Rae responded, "I thought they would say something in group but they didn't. In fact, they didn't really acknowledge each other. Tex looked self-contained most of the time, and Todd rarely made eye contact."

Gil shook his head. "I was wondering why they both seemed so awkward."

Rae said, "I think there's more going on for each of them than just the incident."

David looked at his watch. "Let's move on. What about tomorrow?"

Rae picked up a pen, slipped a notepad out from under her stack of paper and began to write. "I'll do the check-in. Gil, would you do the meditation again? And David, why don't you do the readings?" Rae looked up and smiled. "We've already picked the opener. You pick the closing reading but I reserve veto rights. I know how varied your tastes are when it comes to poetry."

Gil smiled. *Inappropriate is more like it.*

"Veto rights?" David laughed. "In your dreams! What about an exercise?"

Rae thought for a moment. "We can do the inner-child guided imagery."

"Good idea, who'll do the imagery?"

Rae looked at David. "Let's both do it."

"Okay, I love blending our voices."

"It adds a nice parental touch—mom, dad—for the regression-to-childhood experience."

Rae held her right hand above her head, palm out.

David slapped her hand with his own and exclaimed, "Yes!"

They laughed while Gil looked on in silence. The pleasure they took in each other was galling him.

"Okay," David added, "we're all set for tomorrow, 8 a.m., in the lodge."

"No." Gil folded his arms across his chest.

David and Rae turned in unison, as if surprised he was still there.

Gil looked at them both. "What's the point of our meeting tomorrow morning if you've already decided on the plan? All you're doing is wasting the time I would have had for a swim or a walk before group."

David looked thoughtfully at Gil. "It gives us a chance to make refinements and talk about any other thoughts we have before group."

"Ha," Gil snorted. "I know exactly how this is going to go. Between trips back and forth to the food bar, you'll make small talk until we're all done eating. Then, having frittered away an hour, you'll squeeze in a ten-minute check-in on your plan and end a good half-hour before group so Rae can go brush her teeth. You'll accomplish nothing except breaking up my free time into chunks too small for me to use. For what? For ten minutes of work that we could just as well do now or right before the session starts."

Rae sat quietly for a moment. "That's fine, Gil," she said, her voice soft and calm. "Why don't you do whatever you want tomorrow morning. Take care of yourself. David and I can meet over breakfast and we'll see you at group."

Gil squinted at her. *Am I being dismissed?* He was unsure of her intention and her soft expression made him hesitate. Torn for a moment he said, "Fine, I'll see you tomorrow," and stood up, turned and walked out.

DAVID LOOKED AT RAE. "What was that all about?"

"I don't know, but he didn't seem to like my answer."

"No he didn't. Let's check in with him tomorrow. For now, I'm ready to call it a night." David stretched and yawned. "I'm still on Indiana time."

Rae sighed, "I'm exhausted too."

David said goodnight and left Rae in her master suite, its long, vertical windows looking out on a black, star-encrusted sky.

3

Monday Morning

DAVID WAS IN THE LODGE BY 8 A.M., GATHERING HIS breakfast off the self-service tables and looking for Rae. He found her at their usual corner table. As they started to eat, they were surprised to see Gil entering the back door of the lodge. He waved to them and said, "I'll get something to eat and join you."

While Gil was off shopping the pots of hot cereals, David brought up the plan for the morning session. "They're done with group introductions and intentions for the week so we'll need to move right into the exercise."

Rae suggested, "Let's do our usual opening, and a one-word check-in. Then open the floor for anything that's come up so far."

"What could have come up? I want to get them warmed up with a longer check-in and then dive into the guided imagery."

"Okay, then let's do an open-ended check in. If anything is going on, it will show up there. And let's start with Gil's meditation."

Just then Gil walked up, arms laden with a plate, bowl, cup, silverware and a napkin.

Rae and David smiled up at him. "We've got the plan for the morning session," Rae announced.

Gil set his dishes down but didn't comment.

"Do you want to check-in?" asked Rae.

"Are you sure you want to hear what I have to say?" Gil squinted at her as he blew on a spoonful of steaming oatmeal.

Rae cocked her head slightly. "Gil, what's going on? Last night you seemed upset about something and decided not to have breakfast with us. Now you're here and seem unhappy about it"

Gil slowly took in the spoonful and swallowed. "I'm feeling left out."

"I'm sorry you're feeling that way. Do you want to talk about it?"

"Not really." Gil met her gaze for a moment then looked down and began stirring his cereal.

David thought, *Fine with me.* He turned to Rae and asked her about the seven a.m. movement class.

Rae hesitated for a moment, then started enthusiastically describing her adventures with this morning's community dance session.

Gil was silent for the rest of their breakfast together.

GIL, DAVID and several group members were already on their cushions when Rae entered the session room at 9:20 a.m. Rae took the same spot she had last night. She watched Diane come in and pause in front of Gil, who was seated on her cushion from the night before.

Gil looked up at her. "Would you like your seat back?"

"No, thanks," she said and sat in the spot Gil had abandoned. Diane looked around the room from this new vantage point and made eye contact with Rae.

Rae sensed Diane's vulnerability and gave her a smile. She watched Diane's shoulders drop as she settled in.

The others filed into the room.

Rae glanced at the tiny dial of the silver watch on her left wrist. *9:30.* "Good morning, everyone."

Rae counted heads and all eight participants were present. She gave Gil a nod.

Gil folded his legs underneath him and said, "We'll start with a short meditation."

Max and Alison were already sitting cross-legged, their eyes closed. Others quickly settled in.

"Find a comfortable position, upright and alert. Close your eyes or keep them open, whichever is most comfortable for you. Feel your seat on the cushion. Feel the floor supporting the cushion, the foundation supporting the floor, the ground supporting the foundation."

David shifted on his pillow and cleared his throat with a juicy stuttering cough.

Rae winced, *I hate it when he makes that sound,* but she resisted the urge to open her eyes and stare at him. Her mind went to Gil's anger at breakfast. *Had they really ignored him?*

"Notice your thoughts, feelings and sensations. Then let them go." Gil's voice, deep and slow, brought her back to the moment. "Just follow your breath, in and out ... in and out. I'll ring the bell at three minutes."

The room was still, except for the muted sound of waves rumbling as they broke on the rocks below. The whine of a car on the highway built and then faded away. Rae's breath slowed. Her mind quieted. The sounds stopped vying for her attention.

She heard the bell as if at a distance. *Is it time already?* She kept her eyes closed for a moment longer savoring the peace she felt.

"Thank you, Gil," David said, as he picked up a sheet of paper.

"This reading is an excerpt from 'The Invitation' by Oriah 'Mountain Dreamer'."

> *It doesn't interest me if the story you are telling me is true. I want to know if you can disappoint another to be true to yourself; if you can bear the accusation of betrayal and not betray your own soul; if you can be faithless and therefore trustworthy.*
>
> *I want to know if you can see beauty, even when it is not pretty, every day, and if you can source your own life from its presence.*
>
> *I want to know if you can live with failure, yours and mine, and still stand at the edge of the lake and shout to the silver of the full moon, "Yes!"*
>
> *It doesn't interest me to know where you live or how much money you have. I want to know if you can get up, after the night of grief and despair, weary and bruised to the bone, and do what needs to be done to feed the children.*
>
> *It doesn't interest me who you know or how you came to be here. I want to know if you will stand in the center of the fire with me and not shrink back.*

*It doesn't interest me where or what or with whom
you have studied. I want to know what sustains you,
from the inside when all else falls away.*
*I want to know if you can be alone with
yourself and if you truly like the company you
keep in the empty moments.*

David set down the piece of paper and looked around the circle. Everyone was still. After a moment, Alison spoke up from across the circle. "Can I get a copy of that?"

"Sure, Alison. Does anyone else want a copy?"

Several people raised their hands.

"Okay, is there anyone willing to make copies of this at the office?"

Diane raised her hand. "I will."

"Thanks." Rae started to explain the next section. "We'd like everyone to give a brief check-in. Just finish this sentence stem: 'Right now, I feel…' with a single word. I'll start, and we'll go around to our left quickly, without thinking about it too much. Right now, I feel peaceful," Rae smiled and looked to her left, at David.

"Right now, I feel confused," David said with a straight face. "I thought we agreed to do a longer check-in."

"That's more than one word." Rae smiled. "Max you're next."

Max looked back and forth between David and Rae before starting. "I tossed and turned all last night; a lot of fear and excitement. I want to open up and also run away as fast as I can. Impossible to do both at the same time—like a clam on hot wheels. So I'm going to sit with myself and you, and try to be as open as possible." Max took a breath.

"Thanks, Max," Rae cut in before he could start up again. "Tex, you're next; keep it to one word."

Tex said, "Fine."

Rae waited for Tex's word. Then she realized, *That was it.*

And so she continued around the circle. "Tired." "Nervous." "Anticipating." "Calm." "Waiting." "Watchful." "Eager."

When everyone had spoken, Rae said, "Now it would be helpful if each of you would share what you got from our session last night." No one spoke.

Rae looked around the room. Frank's right leg was bouncing nervously. Rae thought, *Flight response.* "Frank, why don't you go first?" Rae thought she caught a flash of anxiety as he looked up at her.

"I'm not sure what to say."

"Start with the first thing that comes to mind."

"Really?"

"Yes, really."

Frank cleared his throat. "Well, I woke up this morning wondering where I was and what I was doing here. I'm not even sure exactly how I ended up here." Frank paused. "I mean I'm a normal person, and this is not a normal place." Several titters interrupted him. "But I know I can get through this week. I just need to stay alert."

"Alert for what, Frank?" Rae asked.

Frank thought for a second. "I'm not sure."

"Okay. I invite you to be curious about what you need to be on alert for. Watch and see. And what did you get last night?"

"Oh, yeah ... people were amazingly honest. I liked that."

After a moment, Max raised his hand and started talking at the same time. "I already feel part of this group. People were more open with us last night than most of my friends are with me back home. And I have great friends.

"I want to be open and tell you everything about myself…without holding back." Catching Rae's eye, Max coughed out a one-syllable laugh. "Don't worry, Rae, I don't mean right now."

Several people joined in the laughter as Rae pantomimed her relief by wiping the back of her hand across her forehead. Then she smiled. "Thanks, Max. And while we're still getting to know each other, everyone please start by giving us your first name."

No one volunteered. Rae looked around the circle to pick someone but before she could Diane half raised her hand.

"Hi, I'm Diane. I walked in last night totally scared, but as I listened to others I began to feel like I might belong and started to think it would be all right—that *I* would be all right. I really liked the rules."

Several others made similar comments, but when it came to Tex, all he said was, "I'm Tex."

"Anything else, Tex? Anything you noticed last night?" Rae prompted.

"Nice people."

Todd was also brief. "I'm Todd. I guess we got to know each other a little bit last night."

After everyone had spoken, Rae said to the group, "We have an exercise for you this morning, a guided meditation. Is there anything else that needs to be said before we begin?" Rae looked from person to person in the circle. No response.

"All right then, please find a comfortable position. You can lie on the floor or rest against your pillow. Rae waited until everyone had settled in and the room was silent. "You may want to close your eyes. Allow yourself to relax, starting at the top of your head, relaxing your scalp, your eyes, your ears, the back of your head..."

Rae slowed her speech and continued softly, "...your mouth...your jaw...your shoulders...chest...back...arms. Now allow that wave of relaxation to flow on down your body through your abdomen...hips...legs...ankles...right to the tips of your toes."

Gil stood up and Rae looked over at him and nodded. He walked over to the stereo in the wall cabinet and turned on the CD player. As the light, dreamy music of Mike Roland's "Fairy Ring" began, Gil slowly brought the volume up to a quiet background level.

David and Rae were now both standing and moving slowly about the room. They began to alternate short phrases of instruction and suggestion, Rae's tone and voice blending in with David's, their words overlapping.

"Each breath an invitation to drop deeper into yourself."

"Notice the sounds in the room, the music, the rustling of bodies on the floor settling in...

"...the sound of waves breaking in the distance. Know there is nothing you need to do." David paused. "Notice your thoughts and let them go."

"Think of a safe place, a place you would like to be."

"A special place. It might be somewhere you loved to go as a child. Or it might be somewhere you have always dreamed of going. Or it might be somewhere you imagine, somewhere peaceful."

"You might be high on a mountain top."

"Or a sunny beach."

"I want you to imagine yourself sitting there comfortably, without a care in the world." After allowing time for everyone to take that in, Rae added, "Now a child appears in the distance, and as you watch, he or she begins walking toward you." She saw Todd's body visibly stiffen.

"There is nothing you need to do, except be there for the child." Rae noticed tears streaking Diane's cheeks and scanned the room for other reactions. Tex was watching her, Todd's posture continued to be unnaturally rigid, and Ronald was snoring quietly. The others lay breathing calmly, eyes closed.

She noticed Gil sitting by the stereo, busily writing in his notebook. It seemed odd to her that he would be so disengaged.

David and Rae were now speaking closely in turn, completing each other's sentences. David said, "Spend time with this precious child..."

Rae said, "...and notice what he or she has to say."

"This child may have a special message for you..."

"...or the child may be silent, or shy, or frightened..."

"However he is ..."

"She is..."

"...is how he needs to be..."

"...she needs to be. For the next 60 seconds, just listen." Rae paused and, looking at David, put her finger to her lips.

They waited quietly and when the minute was up, she said, "Take a moment to say goodbye to this precious child."

"Reassure him..."

"Reassure her..."

"... that you want to stay in contact with him."

"... in contact with her."

Rae began to lead the participants out of the guided imagery, bringing their attention slowly back to the room. "Notice the sensations in your body ..."

David continued her sentence, "... notice the sounds in the room ..."

Rae tapped Gil's foot with hers and nodded toward the stereo. Gil rose slowly and turned to switch off the music. In the silence, the only sound that remained was the soft rhythm of the surf breaking far below.

"And when you're ready, become fully present to this room ... right ... now." Rae walked over to her cushion and sat down as people begin to stir.

The group remained silent as people began sitting up and looking around. Diane was crying softly and looking down. Ronald was now wide awake, smiling and making eye contact around the room. Several others met his gaze. Tex had his eyes on Rae, and Todd was staring out the window.

After a few moments, Rae said, "What we'd like you to do next is to pair up with someone else in the group and share your experience. We will be joining you to listen in."

There was a muted hubbub in the room as people found partners and began to talk. Max had gone to sit with Diane, who was still crying. Alison paired with Carmen, who had said little in the check-ins and had avoided eye contact.

David, noticing both Todd and Tex sitting by themselves, beckoned Todd to join Tex. With a shrug, Todd stood up and walked over to him.

Rae waited until everyone was settled, then said, "Okay. Please look at your partner. Decide who will go first. Good … now look into their eyes and know that it has taken commitment and courage to get this far, to be here with you now. See the hero in that person. That's right. Now take turns and share what just happened in the guided imagery. You have five minutes each."

GIL SAT IN on Frank's conversation with Ronald.

Frank glanced briefly at Gil and continued. "I was feeling really relaxed and just following the words. I was on a deserted beach I'd never been to before, with white sand, palm trees, tropical blue water and a cloudless sky. I was startled when I saw a small boy walking toward me. It was the strangest thing. He just appeared, and walked toward me as if someone else was imagining him for me. I wondered what I should do. Then I heard Rae's voice telling us to just sit and notice the child. So I sat there, amazed and excited and scared. It was like being in a movie.

"The boy seemed shy and sad. He stopped a few feet away and just looked at me. I wanted to reach out towards him but I was afraid of frightening him away. After a while, he came over and sat in my lap. He just seemed to want to be close to me. Somehow I knew he'd been through a lot and needed my attention. I felt really sad for him."

Rae's voice broke in. "It's been five minutes. Please switch roles. It's your partner's turn to speak."

Frank continued over Rae's announcement. "Then, before I knew it, the time was up, and he was getting ready to leave. I told him that I loved him, that I would come back and visit him, and that I wanted him to stay close to me. I promised that I would be there for him when he needed me. I really felt he was hearing me. I hugged him and watched as he walked back across the sand and disappeared."

Gil took advantage of Frank's pause and interjected, "It's time to switch."

Ronald looked at Gil and asked, "Can I give Frank some feedback?"

"Not now; it's your turn to share your experience."

"I don't have much to say. I drifted off. I think I fell asleep. I remember hearing Rae say I should go to a safe place. I thought of my room back home, the house I grew up in. I liked that room. I spent a lot of time there. It was fun to picture it and see how much I could remember. I thought about my toys and my books. I relaxed and I don't remember anything else until the music stopped playing. I guess I'm tired after traveling all day yesterday and then staying up late at the baths last night. I ended up in a tub with a bunch of people and got into a long conversation. There's something really freeing about sitting naked in the dark and talking to complete strangers about whatever comes up. I'm thinking about going back there again tonight."

Ronald continued on about his hot tub experience until Rae spoke up from across the room. "That's five minutes. Please finish up in your pairs and join the circle."

ALISON GOT UP and returned to her seat. Several others broke off and did the same. Rae watched as Todd walked out into the corridor toward the bathroom.

After a couple of minutes, everyone was settled in. David asked, "Does anyone have anything they would like to share with the group?"

No one said anything. The room stayed quiet for awhile, then Tex half raised his hand and said, "I didn't get anything out of that."

"Would you like to say more about that?" David said.

"No."

Rae watched as both David and Gil seemed to assess this response. Rae guessed that they were each debating taking it further with Tex, inviting him to learn about his sense of separation or shutdown. Gil looked over at her and she discouraged him with a subtle shake of her head.

Gil turned back to Tex. "We always honor your right to choose when you want to continue and when you don't."

Looking around the circle, David asked, "Does anyone else have anything they would like to share with the group?"

Just then, Todd walked back in through the door. "That exercise might be useful for some people but I'm more focused on the here and now. That's what I'm wanting to work on."

Rae looked back over her shoulder at him and frowned. She knew better than to take the bait but her words were flowing before she could stop them. "The here and now becomes more accessible when we examine our past. We are a combination of past experiences and natural capacities. As George Santayana wrote, 'Those who do not remember the past are doomed to repeat it.'"

Rae thought, *That was a little harsh.* She paused while Todd took his seat. "Todd, is there anything that you would like to share about your experience?"

"I'm good."

I doubt it. "Okay. Who's next?"

Diane raised her hand. All eyes turned to her.

"Well, I don't know exactly what I got," she said, looking sideways at Tex, "but I had a lot of feelings. Mostly sadness."

"Can you tell us what happened?"

"Well, as soon as I saw the child, well, um, I just started crying. I guess I felt what it was really like to be that age. I mean, she looked just like I used to look. She had pigtails—really light blonde, almost white—and was dressed in my old cowgirl outfit, my favorite thing to wear when I was that age."

Rae asked, "How old were you?"

"Seven. I was seven years old and I wasn't happy. My family was really awful." Here Diane began to cry again; she stopped speaking and seemed to be holding her breath.

"What was awful, Diane?"

More tears. Diane seemed not to notice. Across the room, Alison reached for the Kleenex as if to pass it to Diane. Rae caught her eye and gave Alison a brief shake of her head to stop her. Alison lowered her hand and dropped her eyes. A flush rose to her cheeks.

Rae brought her attention back to Diane. She was crying more freely now. Then words followed. "My father used to get angry and hit us," Diane said, her voice barely audible above the sobs.

Rae saw the subtle straightening of spines and increased alertness in the others. Carmen's hand flew to her mouth.

Rae gently placed her hand on Diane's hand and said nothing.

"He used to hit us with belts, even a horsewhip—whatever was handy. I hated him. But mostly I was afraid of him. I used to pray that the horsewhip would disappear off the mantle. I never had the courage to take it, but I prayed that God would!"

Rae tightened her grip on Diane's hand.

"And when I saw that little girl—me—I remembered how awful it was. It makes me sick." She removed her hand from under Rae's and crossed both arms over her belly, leaning forward as if to protect her midsection.

Rae hesitated, and then rested her hand gently on Diane's back between her shoulder blades.

Rae held it there until she felt the warmth radiating from the contact. Then she said quietly, "It's over. You're safe now. You can weep for the child. You can imagine gathering her in your arms and holding her against the pain. You can do that … now."

Diane drew in a long breath and seemed to hold it.

"Breathe," Rae whispered.

Diane released the breath and gathered in another. She began to sway forward and backward.

Rae slipped her arm around Diane's shoulder and held her as she rocked.

Gil scanned the room. Tex's face was set in hard lines. Carmen had shrunk even further into the corner; her eyes were closed, her brow tightly furrowed. Ronald and Max were sitting with their backs straight, eyes riveted on Diane. Only Todd seemed unaffected as he sat with his head back and a small smile on his face.

Diane gasped. The sudden intake of air was followed by a howl, another howl, moans, and finally sobbing. Diane shifted her body pressing into Rae's chest and belly as if she were burrowing into her. Rae wrapped herself around Diane and tightened her hold.

After a while, Rae started to speak slowly with a reassuring cadence. "It happened ... it's over ... you survived ... it wasn't your fault ... you were just a child ... you're safe now."

Rae noticed Diane's sobs becoming ragged and shallow. "Breathe." Then Rae bent her head and began whispering in Diane's ear as she gently rocked her.

Eventually Diane's sobbing slowed, then stopped. Her breathing evened out. She became quiet. Still. Rae matched Diane's breathing. They both ignored the snotty wet on Rae's shirt and on Diane's face. More time crawled by, as if seconds were mysteriously expanding. And then Rae finally felt what she was waiting for. Diane's entire body relaxed in Rae's arms like a deflating balloon. Diane rested quietly for several minutes, breathing into Rae's shirt. Then she lifted her head, aiming her lips at Rae's ears.

"Are people staring?"

Rae made an exaggerated gesture, swiveling her head to look all around the room, then lowering her mouth to Diane's ear, she stage-whispered "Yes!"

They both giggled.

Rae kept her head bent low over Diane's.

"You don't have to look at them until you're ready."

Diane nodded her head, still wrapped in Rae's arms.

Rae continued to talk quietly. "While you take your time, is it all right if we check in with others and see how they're doing?"

Diane nodded again.

Rae raised her head and made eye contact with David and Gil. Both had moved to sit next to participants with tear-streaked faces. Alison was leaning against Gil, whose arm was protectively around her. David sat next to Carmen with a look of somber anger, an expression Rae had seen before when the issue of child abuse came up.

Gil roused himself and cleared his throat. "Pay attention to your thoughts and feelings, and let's go around the room and say one word that describes what this experience has been like for you. Please don't give your analysis of what happened for Diane. Focus on yourself and your own feelings." Pausing, he gave David an inquiring glance to see if he had anything to add.

"I'll start," David said. "I want you to complete this sentence stem: Right now, I feel..." He paused. "Right now I feel outrage. I'm not a physical person, but I would have liked to turn that horsewhip on your father."

"That's more than one word," Gil said with mild irritation. He turned to Max. "Stick to the assignment."

Max nodded to Gil and said, "Sad."

Tex sat erect and kept his eyes on Diane. "I'm angry."

Ronald and Frank were "concerned" and "disturbed."

Carmen said, "Scared."

Gil thought for a moment. "Protective."

Todd was slouched back against the glass behind him. "Pass."

"Sad," said Alison.

During the go-round, Diane had shifted incrementally until she was able to peek out at each person who spoke while continuing to lean against Rae.

Rae gently unwrapped herself from Diane. "Diane, are you ready to say something?"

Squaring her shoulders, Diane replied, "I have two words. Exhausted and excited."

"Would you be willing to say more about what just happened for you?"

Diane took a breath.

"Thanks … for helping me … I haven't cried like that for a long, long time. It feels like a huge load has been lifted … I don't really want to say much else about it right now." Diane looked around from person to person. "Thank you." She looked back at Rae. "I'm finished now."

Rae smiled at her. "I see that. That was a courageous piece of work and I invite you to continue noticing how you feel, asking for what you want and taking care of yourself the way you have been."

Gil waited a moment, then looking around the room said, "We have fifteen minutes left before we break for lunch. Look at what's going on for you. Notice how you feel. I'd like you to turn to the person next to you and take a minute to say what's on your heart."

He moved around the room while people connected with a partner. Diane stayed next to Rae and chose not to do the exercise. Soon a murmur filled the room as people eagerly started to share their experience.

David paired up with Carmen. "I'll partner with you since Diane is sitting this one out."

Gil settled next to them and listened in. After David went on at great length about his feelings of admiration for Diane, his outrage at her father and his protectiveness towards her, Gil called out to the room that it was time for your partner to share.

Carmen sat silently looking at David for most of the remaining time. Then as if she had been turning something over in her head and finally come to a decision, she softly said, "What Diane said, about her father, that was a lot like my home."

It was the first time Carmen had said anything about violence in her childhood, but Gil wasn't surprised. He had suspected something was going on from her lack of eye contact and her hunched shoulders during Diane's sharing.

Gil called everyone back to the group, and invited each person to make a brief statement about how he or she was doing.

Gil led off. "I'm really impressed with the level of work already occurring in this room. I feel so grateful to be with you on this journey."

Several people directed their comments to Diane, acknowledging her courage and openness.

Carmen shared, "That was really upsetting."

Tex's jaw stuck out and his energy gave emphasis to his words. "Well, I said I was angry, and I still am. I'd like to hog-tie your dad and give him a taste of his own medicine!"

Diane smiled.

Todd said matter-of-factly, "I'm practicing patience," and drew some odd looks from around the circle.

Alison got up, approached Diane, and gave her a hug.

Gil wrapped up the meeting by saying, "This was an intense session. Take good care of yourselves until we get together again."

GIL, DAVID AND RAE gathered in Rae's bedroom. Gil flopped down on the bed, while David reached once more for the can of macadamia nuts sitting on the bureau. With his hand already inside the container, David asked, "May I have some of these?"

Despite the tightness in her stomach, Rae said, "Okay." She tried to tune out the annoying sound of David's munching as she sorted through her collection of poetry readings. When she looked up, David was actually tilting the can of nuts into his open mouth. "Don't eat them all," she snapped. Then, in a milder tone, she explained, "I use the nuts to manage my blood sugar."

Gil lay on the bed, looking at the rough wood ceiling. "Wow. That was really something. I didn't expect the work to go so deep so soon." He turned to look at Rae. "You were wonderful with Diane. It was a joy to watch you work."

Rae glowed. "Thank you. She's such a sweet woman. And she was ready to work. I think you're right, this group is dropping in quickly."

David sat on the bed, still chewing nuts. "Where do we want go with the afternoon session?"

"First I have something to ask you," Rae said. "Why did you put Tex and Todd together on the debrief of the guided imagery? We haven't dealt with their dining room confrontation and they're both still sitting on their stuff."

"Yeah," snorted Gil. "I noticed it too. David, didn't you say last night that you thought Tex might be difficult? It's like the blind leading the blind."

David's expression went deadpan and without affect he said, "It made perfect sense to me. It's been a long time since we had two people show up in a workshop so unprepared.

And because of the dining room incident, not in spite of it, I wanted them to acknowledge each other. Do you have any other ideas about how to handle them?"

"They are taking a little longer to get comfortable with the group," Rae responded. "I'm glad you both took my cue to back off on Tex. But as closed lipped as he is, he is far more present and direct than Todd. We need to find a way to bring Todd into the room. The next time he makes a deflecting, judgmental comment like, 'I'm just interested in the here and now,' we need to get curious and explore it with him.

"I'd also like to get to our 'Draw a Child' exercise today," Rae continued. "What do you think?"

Gil stood up. "I think the rest of the group is ready. But after all that happened this morning, we may need to take care of some clean-up work first."

"Okay, if someone brings something up in check-in, we will attend to that first. Meanwhile, I'm hungry. Who wants to join me for lunch?" Rae looked expectantly at Gil.

Gil grinned. "I'm going for a hike and then a quick swim." He dropped the grin and said, "I'll meet you at 3 o'clock and we can finish planning the next session."

"I'd like to eat with you, Rae," David offered. "Can you wait a minute while I call Joann?"

"Sure."

They walked down the dirt road to the phone booths and Rae waited outside, half-eavesdropping and half-musing, while David talked to his wife. Rae felt a faint jealousy listening to his laughter and easy banter. The contrast to her conversations with Alan was stark.

———

RAE AND DAVID sat at a glass table on the sunny deck at the back of the lodge with their freshly served lunch spread out before them untouched. They held hands and closed their eyes. David began reciting the mealtime blessing in Hebrew. *"Barukh ata Adonoi..."* Rae closed her eyes and did her best to mumble along behind him.

When the prayer was over, she opened her eyes and was struck by the contrast between their plates of food. Her plate featured a variety of colors: bright orange sautéed carrots, deep red beets nestling against a spiked light green artichoke and a dark green spinach salad. The white baked sea bass alongside macaroni and cheese on David's plate reminded Rae of the bland fare at her mother's table.

Colorless.

David looked up, speaking as he chewed. "What do you think about the older guy, Max?"

"What do you mean?"

"He seems preoccupied with death, but he looks fit to me. I wonder what he's so anxious about. Maybe there's something he's not telling us."

Rae was holding a napkin in front of her plate to protect her lunch from the tiny bits of food occasionally flying out of David's mouth. "Swallow your food before you talk, please."

"Sorry," David said as he covered his mouth and chewed.

Rae thought about David's question. "I've no idea if there's something else going on with Max, but his fears seem normal to me. I'm more concerned about Gil. He doesn't feel like an equal member of the team."

"He does seem irritated." David looked thoughtful. "Maybe it's fear. Not too long ago he was a participant, and now he's leading. I felt the same way twenty years ago, the first time I led a group with you."

"God, I remember, you were positively weird," Rae laughed. "You hated my structure so much you grabbed my notes for the opening session and stuffed them in your mouth!"

David started laughing. "If you weren't such a control freak, I wouldn't have had to go to such lengths to get your attention."

"Touché." Rae paused for a moment. "So, let's have Gil lead the next exercise. It's simple enough, and he's been through it lots of times."

"Good idea."

"Let's stop here. I'm tired and need to lie down for an hour. We can take it up again with Gil at three o'clock."

Rae waved goodbye to David and walked back up the steep hill to her room. The building was quiet and the meeting room was empty. Alone with the view, the silence and an hour to herself, she closed the door behind her and breathed a deep sigh.

She spent five minutes in the "legs up the wall" yoga position hoping to dispel her lethargy. Rae's legs did feel lighter, but the posture hadn't lessened the increased gravitational pull on her mood. She sat up, stacked three pillows behind her, and picked up Ann Patchett's novel *Bel Canto* opening to her bookmark. Normally she luxuriated in an escape into fiction, but today her heart wasn't in it. She felt a chill despite the sun pouring through the glass doors. Wrapping a wool blanket around her shoulders, she forced herself to read another page.

4

Monday Afternoon

OUT ON THE SLOPING LAWN BELOW THE LODGE, David sat in an Adirondack chair twenty feet from the cliff's edge. The day had started fair, but the wind blowing whitecaps out at sea all morning had finally arrived ashore. David put his hood up and was leaning away from the sea blast, engrossed in his book, *Prayers for Rain*. He loved the moral complexity and ambiguity of Dennis Lehane's stories. Laughing at yet another pithy line, he turned the page and the alarm on his phone went off. He pulled it out of his pocket and looked at the time.

"Damn."

He marked his place in the book and stood up quickly. A buzzing, pulsating sound drowned out all thought. His vision tunneled and his body went slack. The solid thump as his side hit the ground registered as if from a great distance. He came to with his cheek pressed against the damp ground wondering why he was staring sideways at blades of grass. He noticed his left shoulder was hurting, then he remembered where he was.

Sitting up next to his toppled chair, David started down the list of his usual fears—heart attack, stroke, and brain cancer—before it occurred to him that he had fainted. It hadn't happened for a long time, but he knew the feeling. Maybe he'd eaten too much at lunch, or he'd sat still too long.

SITTING AT A HEAVY wooden dining table in the lodge, Gil impatiently looked at his watch. It was ten after three. "Where is he?"

Rae smiled at Gil. "Oh, that David!"

Gil didn't appreciate her levity. He had the chronically late person's bad habit of resenting it when he had to wait for others and this was just one more in a string of perceived slights he'd been ruminating on.

David approached the table from behind Gil and, seeing Rae's smiling face, quipped, "I thought if I enjoyed the fresh air a little longer, the two of you might get all the work done and I could just breeze in and sign on the dotted line."

Gil turned and gave David a withering look.

David smiled, "Sorry I'm late. I just had..."

Gil interrupted him. "I cut my walk short to be here."

David's expression turned serious. "I passed out on the lawn."

"So you were sleeping in the sun when you should have been meeting with us?"

"Not exactly." David paused, his expression blank.

"So what kept you?"

"I stood up and keeled over."

Gil gave David a puzzled look.

Rae tilted her head and looked up at David touching his arm. "Are you all right?" Rae's voice was half an octave higher than usual.

"I don't know. Something like this happened to me a long time ago. I fainted at a Louisville restaurant and ended up in the ER. The doctors called it syncope, not enough oxygen in the brain, but I have no idea why I passed out just now. It's a little unnerving."

"Have you been to the tubs?" Gil asked.

"Yeah, I went down for an hour right after lunch."

"You're just dehydrated. Drink some water."

David looked surprised. "Really?"

"It happens all the time. Go drink a couple of glasses of water, then we'll get started."

When David returned, the three of them discussed their plan to have each workshop participant draw the child he or she had met in the guided meditation.

"The last time we did this exercise, the work that followed filled the rest of the week," David observed. "That exercise was like a Pac-Man, devouring all the available time."

Gil and Rae smiled at the dated analogy. Rae acknowledged, "Our plans really are more important, aren't they?" She continued with a feigned grim look, "We've got to stop the group from following its own agenda. We have to control the process. After all, we know what's best for them, don't we."

"Yeah!" David laughed. "What do they know about what they need?"

Gil weighed in, "All right, all right, keep your voices down. I know you're kidding, but someone overhearing us could think you're serious. In any case, our first priority should be to make room for the issues that are already up."

"I know, I know" said Rae, still chuckling. "We're just kidding. I trust that whatever needs to come up, will. We'll allow as much time as it takes. The process comes first. May the Force be with us." She giggled.

Gil didn't smile.

Rae gave Gil a long appraising look. "Gil, do you want to tell us what's going on with you?"

Gil was caught off guard. His eyes moved from Rae to David and back again. Maybe it was the place or the nature of their work, but he was suddenly willing to be honest about it. He dropped his chin and took a deep breath.

"I'm sorry but I'm not getting the consideration or sensitivity I expect from you two. I'm uncomfortable and I feel out of place in group and I'm angry about it."

Rae nodded. "You might be feeling a little insecure considering this is your first time co-leading. Is there something I can do?" Rae glanced at David. "Either of us can do?"

"I would like to feel more included and consulted. I haven't been leading this work for twenty years like you, but you must think I have something to contribute or you wouldn't have asked me to join you."

"I do think you have a lot to offer the group and that's a clear request. Do you agree, David?"

"I do."

"Thanks." Gil looked at Rae, then David. "Both of you."

"We want this to work," Rae said.

A FEW MINUTES LATER, they walked up the winding steps to their workshop room. Once there, shoes off, they spread out to find seats around the room. Everyone but Todd was already on a cushion. Rae made a quick scan of each person's affect.

Diane met Rae's gaze squarely. Rae noticed something different about her, a new sense of comfort or ease maybe.

Tex sat sullenly, as if he didn't want to be here.

Rae began the meditation and found it calming. She lost track and had to force herself back from timeless drifting to open her eyes and check her watch. *Five minutes are up already.*

She took a breath. "When you're ready, allow your eyes to open and bring your attention back into the room."

Rae luxuriated in the in-between moment as everyone began sitting up and looking around.

Then David's voice broke the stillness.

This being human is a guest house.
Every morning a new arrival.

A joy, a depression, a meanness,
some momentary awareness comes
as an unexpected visitor.

Welcome and entertain them all!
Even if they are a crowd of sorrows,
who violently sweep your house
empty of its furniture,
still treat each guest honorably.
He may be clearing you out
for some new delight.

The dark thought, the shame, the malice,
meet them at the door laughing,
and invite them in.

Be grateful for whoever comes,
because each has been sent
as a guide from beyond.

David closed the book. Rae sat still, allowing the powerful words to sink in while she looked around the circle once
more before starting. "Thank you for that Rumi poem. Let's
do a brief check-in." She thought for a moment. "Please share
about anything that's keeping you from being fully present."

"I feel funny starting without Todd," Diane blurted out.
"Do we know where he is?"

Everyone looked around, but no one spoke.

"He didn't say anything to me," Rae said.

Just then, heavy footsteps sounded from the hallway and
Todd stepped into the room. Waving his pad of paper, he
said, "Forgot my notes. Had to go all the way back to my
room." He took the empty seat next to Alison and sat back
with a complacent grin.

Frank raised his hand. "I'll go."

Rae was annoyed with Todd but turned her attention to
Frank. Despite his brand-new jeans and a bright polo shirt,
he looked a little disheveled. His hair, normally carefully
combed, had a distinct hedgehog-like quality.

"I just woke up from a nap and I remembered this crazy
dream." Frank's words tumbled out as if he were eager to
get rid of them. "I was going scuba diving with my brother.
We were on a steep cobble beach next to a bottomless
ocean. I was worrying about what we'd find in the depths.
I knew I didn't have my equipment together but I'd have to
make do if I wanted to go. My brother was suited-up, and
already heading out. I had to make up my mind. I knew

there were monsters out there and the thought of all that deep water gave me vertigo. I was afraid. But somehow I knew I couldn't put it off any longer. Then I woke up."

Rae said, "Frank, I would like to give you an opportunity to work with this as soon as we finish the check-ins. Are you willing to put a bookmark here and we'll come back to it."

Frank looked a little uncertain as he nodded and said, "Okay."

"Good."

Rae turned to Ronald and said, "You're next."

Ronald froze for a second, then looked around. "Well, to tell you the truth, I'm really not sure I belong here. I'm moved by everyone's honesty and courage." Ronald turned to Diane. "I was really touched by what you shared this morning."

Rae saw Diane flush and look away as Ronald continued.

"I think to myself, what do I have to be upset about? My parents weren't alcoholics. I wasn't physically or emotionally abused. I didn't experience neglect … in fact, quite opposite.

"It seems like many of you have had hurdles to overcome. I feel inadequate precisely because my life hasn't been difficult. It's true I haven't achieved what I thought I would by now, but I don't have any excuses. As a teen, I dreamed about being a great philosopher or a famous professor. Instead, so far … nothing.

"I think I'm a good enough psychotherapist, but that doesn't feel like enough. I'm not living up to my expectations. For one thing, I'm in my thirties and I'm still not married."

Gil interrupted him. "It sounds like you're clear on where you are. What would interest me more specifically is what are you willing to do about it. Think about that while we continue with the check-ins."

Rae noticed Ronald staring at Gil as the last few people checked in. *Is that hostility or just surprise?*

After everyone had spoken, Rae turned to Frank. "Thanks for being patient. Let's continue with your dream, and then we'll check back with you, Ronald.

"Frank, I want you to remember your dream and take a deep breath, then let it out slowly and tell me what you notice."

Frank closed his eyes and took a deep breath, then another and another. He opened his eyes. "I have butterflies in my stomach."

"Can I come over and sit by you?"

Frank stiffened. "No, thanks, I'm fine."

Rae decided to push back. "I didn't ask how you were. I asked if it would be all right if I came over and sat next to you."

"I don't understand."

Rae could sense Frank's dream receding. It was as if an impenetrable fog had arisen between them. *I should have stayed with his sensation of butterflies.*

"I am offering to go a little further with the dream you had."

"I'll pass."

"Okay," Rae said lowering her chin in resignation. "You have an open invitation to come back to the dream anytime you're ready."

David bent forward and made eye contact with Rae. She raised her eyebrows to let him know she was stuck. David nodded then looked down the room at Ronald. "Would you like to answer the question Gil asked about what you want to do?"

Rae saw Gil shift forward on his cushion as if he were going to say something.

"Yes," Ronald said, speaking in an unnatural monotone. "I want to be in an intimate relationship. I want to learn how to share myself and my life with someone I love. I'm thirty-five years old and I've never lived with anyone." Ronald paused as if daunted by the enormity of his confession. His eyes cleared. "That's what I want," he said. "I want to be in a relationship." He paused and lowered his voice. "But I don't know how to get there."

Rae watched the lines on Ronald's forehead disappear as his breath slowed and deepened. A slight, perplexed smile broke across Ronald's face, like the first, faint glimpse of recognition.

"That's all for now," Ronald concluded, folding his arms. "It feels good just to be clear."

David glanced upwards as if formulating a response.

Gil reached over and put his hand on Ronald's knee. "You say you want a healthy, intimate relationship. Are you willing to take a small step towards that right now?"

David looked at Rae. She read the surprise in his expression and frowned to convey her concern, then turned back to see where Gil was going to take it.

"I don't know," Ronald responded hesitantly looking back and forth between David and Gil. "I feel good about saying I want a relationship."

"You've just taken a big step." Gil paused as if considering how hard to push. "You can stop there if you want."

"Or what?"

"Or take the next step by picking someone here who you're willing to practice with."

"Right now?" Ronald asked with rising pitch.

"Yep."

Ronald didn't look completely comfortable with this suggestion.

Gil said, "Take a risk."

Ronald closed his eyes for a moment as if gathering himself, then turning his head slowly he looked around the entire circle. His gaze settled on Diane three cushions to his left.

Ronald turned back to Gil. "Now what?"

"Have you chosen someone?"

"Yes … Diane."

"Good. Now find out if Diane is available to do this piece of work with you."

Ronald looked at her. "Well?"

Diane turned to Gil. "What do I have to do?"

"Just listen."

"That's all?"

"That's all."

"Okay." Diane sat up straight and lowered her chin slightly.

Gil said, "Ronald, I want you to sit in front of Diane."

Ronald moved into the middle of the circle, sat down and crossed his legs. Gil registered both the distance and the awkwardness of Ronald's choice, but decided against asking him to move closer. Gil turned to Diane. "Your job is to listen and say back as accurately as possible what you've heard. When you're done, you can check with Ronald to see if you missed anything."

Diane gave a half-smile and a nod.

Gil smiled at Ronald and said, "It's all yours."

Ronald looked at Diane and shrugged. "I'm not much good at this, but this is just an exercise, isn't it?" Ronald waited as if expecting an answer.

Diane shifted on her pillow and glanced at Gil, who shook his head slightly. Diane looked back at Ronald.

Looking back and forth between the two of them but getting no response from either, Ronald settled his gaze on Diane. As he exhaled his shoulders dropped slightly. "Okay." He took another breath. "I'm attracted to you."

The room went dead silent. A moment passed. "Not that you have to do anything about it. I mean this is just my assignment, isn't it?" Ronald was talking fast. "It's just that you have a way of saying things out loud that I'm already thinking but would never say. Of course, you're gorgeous, and that makes you seem unapproachable, and I imagine you're not interested anyway so I haven't said anything. I mean if you wanted to get to know me, you'd have sat with me at lunch today instead of walking past and sitting by yourself..."

"Ronald, take a breath," Gil interjected. "You've made a good start; now let's give Diane a chance to respond."

Diane turned to Gil. "I'm just listening, right?"

"Yes, just paraphrase what you heard Ronald say."

"He said he finds me attractive."

"Tell him directly."

Diane turned to Ronald. "You find me attractive."

Ronald blushed and looked down.

Gil prompted Diane, "Anything else?"

Diane thought about it. "He thinks I seem stuck-up."

Ronald looked up. "Uninterested."

"Uninterested," Diane repeated.

Gil leaned toward Ronald. "Did she get it?"

Ronald seemed to be considering the question as he continued his unfocused stare in Diane's direction. "Yes," he said quietly.

"Good. Now you can respond, Diane."

"Respond how?"

"Start with how you feel about what Ronald said."

Diane frowned. "I thought I just had to listen."

"Letting Ronald know something about how it landed with you is the next step."

Diane looked at Ronald. "I'm feeling a little nervous. I don't want to hurt your feelings. I think you're a nice guy, and I'm flattered that you find me attractive."

Ronald adopted a lopsided smile somewhere between a grin and a wince. "I guess that would be a no."

Diane looked at Ronald. "Yeah, it's a no." She smiled and Ronald gave a single explosive laugh.

Gil felt the tension break, and saw relief on several faces as he looked around the room. He came back to Diane. "Is there anything else you want to say?"

"No."

"Ronald?"

"Not really."

"Ronald, are you open to feedback?"

"Not right now."

Gil waited for Ronald to move back to his pillow. But Ronald stayed where he was. The room was quiet.

"How are you feeling?" Gil asked.

"I don't feel much of anything right now."

Gil scooted forward a couple of feet and sat cross-legged facing Ronald. Mirroring Ronald's posture, he rounded his shoulders forward and hollowed his chest as he stared fixedly on the middle distance. He kept pace with Ronald's breathing, shallow and slow. Numbness began to settle over Gil. He echoed, "I don't feel much of anything right now."

Ronald looked intently at Gil. Gil met his stare blankly, keeping his focus on the lack of emotion and sensation he was experiencing. Slowly, Ronald's expression softened and his shoulders dropped. Then he turned away.

Gil became aware of an overwhelming sadness rising from deep in his abdomen, spreading upwards and engulfing him in a gelatinous mass. He sank into the feeling until he was completely submerged in a thick, black ocean, breathing viscous darkness in and out.

Again Ronald glanced over at Gil. When their eyes met this time, Gil could see the sadness. As he felt the connection, the rest of the room dropped away. A long time seemed to pass.

Ronald took in a deep breath and let it out. "When I was maybe three or four, I walked in on my mom taking a bath. The door was behind the tub, and all I could see was red, wavy hair above a long, smooth, freckled back. Her skin was glistening with soap and water as she worked the washcloth over her shoulders and down her sides. I reached out to the glistening soapsuds sliding down her back, but when I touched her skin, she jumped. Her whole body twisted around. I saw her breasts. Her face was big and red as she yelled at me. I ran out of the bathroom crying. After that, the door was always locked when she took her bath."

Ronald closed his eyes.

Gil sat and said nothing.

Ronald opened his eyes. "What now?"

Gil took a deep breath and let it out while he looked Ronald in the eye. "How are you feeling right now?"

Before he could answer a voice broke in on them. "Ronald, is it okay if I touch you?" Rae said, kneeling next to Gil.

Gil was startled. *What's going on?*

Ronald seemed surprised as well, and looked back at Gil.

Despite his annoyance, Gil found himself nodding encouragingly at Ronald, as if giving him permission to answer Rae's question.

Ronald turned to Rae. "Okay."

Rae moved past Gil without making eye contact, and gently placed her arms around Ronald's shoulders from the back. Ronald didn't move. Rae began humming a lullaby from her childhood.

Gil felt hijacked, but his anger quickly gave way to embarrassment as he watched Ronald stiffen. *Ronald isn't relating to this.* But before Gil could think of a way of intervening, Ronald began to slowly sink into Rae's arms. He still didn't look at ease but finally one tear rolled out and down his cheek, then another and another.

After a while, Rae's humming stopped. Gil waited a beat, then asked, "Diane, is there anything else you'd like to say to Ronald?" Rae turned and frowned at Gil, and shook her head.

Diane didn't answer.

Rae held Gil's gaze a few moments, then leaning forward next to Ronald's ear, she quietly asked, "Is there anything you want to say?"

Ronald shook his head.

"Are you open for feedback now?"

"Yes."

Rae stayed behind Ronald and raised her eyebrows at Gil.

Looking around the circle, Gil said, "Whoever would like to share, just tell Ronald what you're feeling right now."

Tex spoke up. "Listen, what just happened, and what happened to Diane before… I mean all this stuff. I've hardly ever seen a man cry. Certainly not my father. And not me. If I cried in front of him, he would have smacked me good!"

Gil waited for more, but Tex was done. "Tex, when we finish with the feedback for Ronald, I'd like to come back to what you just said. Is that okay with you?"

"Well, I guess so but I don't have anything else to say."

Gil waited while several people expressed how affected they were by Ronald's tears, even if they weren't sure what the tears were about. Ronald's eyes sparkled as he listened to the feedback.

Alison was the last to speak. "Ronald, you seemed so young and so vulnerable. I wanted to come over there and take care of you. I just wanted you to stop hurting."

Ronald sat quietly with a smile for a moment, then he thanked Rae and turned to Gil. "I think I have a lot more to learn about my relationships with women."

Gil laughed out loud and said, "Me, too."

While they continued laughing together, Gil snuck a glance at Rae but she was looking around at the others.

As their laughter subsided, Rae said, "Good work, Ronald. And thank you, Diane, for your willingness to listen, and your honesty."

Rae moved back to her seat and turned to Tex. "I'd like to hear what you were thinking and feeling as you watched Ronald work."

"Well, it's just that I was taught men don't cry. Ronald seems like an okay guy and yet he really cut loose. I don't get it."

Rae asked, "Would you like to hear from Ronald about crying?"

"Why not."

"Ronald, could you tell Tex what that was like for you?"

"Sure." Ronald turned to look at Tex. "It was a relief. I guess I've been holding those tears in for a long time, maybe in part for the reason you mentioned." Almost as an afterthought, Ronald added, "And it's a little weird, as a therapist, to realize that about myself."

Tex spoke directly to Ronald, as if the others weren't in the room. "I remember the last time I cried. I got in trouble for something and Dad whipped me. I went to bed and was crying in my room, when the door burst open and my dad yelled, 'Shut up right now!' He was carrying his leather belt, and when he slapped it together, it sounded like a gunshot. I think I was eight years old. I stopped crying then, and I don't think I've cried since."

"Tex, what do you see in people's faces?" Rae asked.

Tex looked surprised to find out he and Ronald weren't alone. All eyes were on him. He turned and looked around the room. In a softer, thoughtful voice, he said, "I see Diane has tears in her eyes. It looks like … it looks like people are feeling sorry for me."

"Yes, and how does that feel?"

"Well, I don't like that feeling."

"Would you be willing to tell each person what you see in their faces?"

"No. I wouldn't."

"Okay, Tex. As we've said, you can pass. But as we move along, I invite you to keep track of your feelings and notice that your father can no longer threaten the little boy you were." Rae paused to allow space between Ronald's work, Tex's sharing, and whatever came next.

After a minute she asked, "What else is in the room?"

Alison raised her hand. She was sitting tall on her cushion in the center of the wall of windows. Rae gave her an appraising look-over. Rae guessed she was in her late forties, but her body was svelte and had the youthful suppleness of a steady yoga practice. Her skin was bright and her eyes clear. She was sitting upright and her legs were tucked under her in a meditation posture. Rae nodded to her.

Alison took a breath as if to center herself and started talking about her own childhood. She described her wild teens and early twenties, her drinking and the recovery she found in Alcoholics Anonymous. Rae noticed Alison's smooth delivery had the ease of an often practiced disclosure. It left Rae feeling a bit disengaged. *Stale and dry,* Rae thought, *like old bread.*

As Gil listened and watched, he recognized the outlines of an AA share: her experience, strength and hope. He felt buoyed, connected to Alison and his own gratitude for the program. Alison's belief in a Higher Power and her reliance on her program and her sponsor shone through in the uplifting tale of her turnaround from her disaffected and dissolute years to the present comfort she experienced with herself and her joy in being of service to others. She radiated her gratitude for the miraculous changes in her life.

Then Alison's brow furrowed, she looked at the floor and her voice faded.

"After all these years in recovery and all the gains I've made in my life, I feel I'm right back where I started, and I don't know why. I've started lying to my husband and my children … little things mostly. Things I could just as easily tell the truth about, but some voice inside me says, 'You don't need to say that. They won't know the difference.' Like the other day, my husband asked if I had seen his non-alcoholic beer in the refrigerator. I told him no, knowing full well I drank it with lunch. There's nothing wrong with me drinking a non-alcoholic beer, but not everyone in the program thinks so, and I don't want to get into a discussion about it. Least of all with my husband. It's better left unsaid.

"Now I'm embarrassed about it. I wonder about my need to hide it. Am I going to drink again? What would it be like? I know I'm an alcoholic and I can't drink, but I have those thoughts anyway.

"I have to admit, the lying really gets to me. I used to lie all the time when I was drinking. I'd lie about where I'd been, who I was with, what we had done. I lied to avoid conflict. I lied to get what I wanted. I lied to cover up. But most of all, I lied to protect the most important thing in my life, alcohol. Then I got sober and started telling the truth. God, it was sweet … just the simple truth. No lies to remember, no different stories to different people, no complications, contradictions, embarrassing traps to fall into.

"Then about a year and a half ago, I noticed I was starting to exaggerate some things, minimize others and tell small white lies on occasion. At first it seemed innocuous enough. I told myself it was normal, just part of the way everyone talks. But it didn't stop there. I began to fabricate to put myself in a better light or to protect myself from criticism and judgment. The weird thing is I knew I'd eventually have to tell my sponsor about it.

"I don't know what's wrong. What happened to all my confidence and success? I'm going right back to those feelings of self-loathing that led me to drink and use in the first place. I don't drink. I don't use. I go to meetings. I should be doing better than this. Right now, I'm not feeling my recovery and it scares me." She stopped abruptly.

Rae smiled. *Now that's real.*

The room was still.

Gil shifted in his seat. "Alison, may I give you some feedback?"

Alison turned to look at him and nodded.

"What you just described, the isolation and lying and not talking to your sponsor, these sound serious to me, maybe more serious than you're aware. Your sobriety is at risk, maybe not today but someday, and very likely sooner than you think. This is especially true because you don't think you need to worry about drinking again. I'd like you to take advantage of this week to really examine what's bothering you. You might start tonight with an inventory of your fears and resentments."

Alison's shoulders squared for a moment, then relaxed. "Okay."

Gil continued, "Would you let us know when we get back together in the morning what you discover?"

"I will."

Rae made a slight bow of her head to Gil, and then checked her watch. She could see that if there were going to be enough time for the "Draw a Child" exercise, they would need to start now. Her mind started sorting through options for how to make the transition.

As if reading her mind, David spoke up, "Does anyone have anything else to bring up? Any unfinished business?" No one spoke up so David pointed to Gil while Rae stood up and walked to the small cupboard in the side wall.

While Rae was laying out flipchart paper and dumping a bucket of crayons in the center of the circle, Gil said, "We'd like you to take a large sheet of paper and a handful of the crayons and draw a picture of yourself as a child. Draw whatever comes to mind. The child might be 4 or 9 or 12. Whatever age comes to you. You might choose to draw the child who appeared in the guided imagery. Just allow whatever image comes to you.

"Be sure and draw with your non-dominant hand. If you're right-handed, draw with your left, and vice versa." There were several moans from around the circle. "Don't worry, this is not an art contest. We'll give you fifteen minutes to complete your drawing. Then we'll break into groups."

Diane sat frozen in her seat as others reached towards the pens and crayons in the center of the circle. When most of them were working and Diane was still sitting there, Rae asked, "Diane, what's the matter?"

"Uh, I don't think I can do this. Is it okay if I just sit here? Or maybe take a walk?"

"What is it you don't think you can do?"

"I don't think I can draw a picture of myself as a child. I don't remember a whole lot. Mostly what I talked about this morning, and I don't know what to draw. I'd rather just sit here, okay?"

"You look frightened."

Tears welled up in Diane's eyes, and she dropped her head.

"Would you like some help with this?"

Diane looked at Rae. "It's too hard," she said softly.

"Right, Diane, it's hard because the little girl that you once were is in urgent need of your attention and comfort. I think she's been waiting for you a long time. I imagine you lived a lot of your childhood relying only on yourself, without much support from your mom and with lots of fear of your dad. It's time to deal with this. You don't have to do this alone. I'm here to help you."

"I don't know where to start."

"Just try it and see what happens."

Diane looked puzzled.

Rae nodded. "Just pick up a crayon and make a line."

"Diane stretched forward and chose a black crayon. Transferring it to her left hand, she made a tentative line. She paused and looked at Rae.

Rae smiled. "Now let the crayon take over."

Diane's hand began moving, adding another line and another until a box house and a peaked roof took shape in the center of the page. She began to bend over the paper in earnest and press harder with the crayon. Soon dark stick figures appeared.

Rae moved away from Diane and noticed David earnestly engaged with Tex. She joined them.

Tex said, "Playing with crayons is ridiculous. I came here because I'm having problems in my marriage. I don't need to mess around with my past; I'm trying to deal with now."

"I hear this seems unrelated to you," David said, "but the events of your childhood may be directly related to the problems you're experiencing with your wife. Deciding to stop crying at the age of eight may have had ramifications you aren't aware of."

"That sounds like psychological bullshit!" Tex glanced at Rae. "Pardon my French."

David tried a different tact. "How about if you do it as an experiment? Perhaps it won't mean anything to you, but are you willing to find out if there's something important for you to learn from this?"

David watched as Tex lowered his chin and paused, pursing his lips into a thin line. David thought of Gil's conversation with Tex last night about drinking this week. He wondered if Tex was thinking the same thing.

Tex remained silent.

Before David could try again, Rae said, "Tex, you bet good money on us when you signed up for this course. Are you willing to let us run it?"

Tex gave Rae an assessing look and she met his gaze. Finally he broke his stare and said, "What were the instructions again?"

Todd let out a barking laugh. Tex turned and gave him a hard look. Todd was suddenly very busy reaching for the crayons and concentrating on his selection of colors.

Meanwhile Rae repeated the directions for Tex. Soon Tex was working and Rae looked up to scan the room. Everyone seemed busy on their drawings. She watched as Todd slashed away at his page then abruptly stopped. Next he grabbed a handful of crayons and held them in his fist as he dragged the bunch of them along the four edges of the sheet. Nodding with apparent satisfaction, he put down the crayons, shoved the sheet of paper behind him and turned to look out the tall windows.

GIL WAS SITTING next to Frank, who was slumped back into his pillow and showing no sign of participating. Gil reached over and handed him a sheet of paper.

Frank took it and smiled. "Thanks."

Frank bent forward to gather up a fistful of various colored crayons. He carefully picked through them, putting some back and replacing them with others. Apparently satisfied with his selection, he shifted back to his pillow and sat staring at the large blank sheet.

He held a salmon crayon in his left hand and leaned over the empty sheet. His hand began moving in circles as he pressed the crayon onto the paper. Deep circles of peachy pigment colored in a small space in the center of the sheet.

Gil knew he ought to check on the progress of others around the room but he was enjoying watching Frank draw.

Next, Frank selected a blue crayon and, with rapid back and forth strokes, made a curved line like the bill of a baseball cap over the salmon-colored circles. His hand moved quickly and confidently like an inspired artist but what was going down on paper looked more like the work of a seven year old. The juxtaposition of bold strokes and childish results left Gil a little amused.

Frank filled in the bill of the cap in pink, and then drew a brown outline for the figure's shoulders, and black-and-brown stripes for a shirt. Frank's whole arm was in motion now, using strong strokes. He frowned in concentration, and his left cheek bulged as he bit his tongue. His hand whipped back and forth over the page, strengthening the lines, filling in the colors. He scrawled in a pair of pants, bent at the knees as if the legs were in motion, and two arms, one reaching forward, one backward. A boy was taking shape, dashing across the sheet.

Frank's eyes lit up and he grinned. "This is great!"

With the black crayon, he scratched in a dark patch of clouds above the child, then drew the trunks of tall trees, a winding blue creek, brown mountains, a yellow sun, black V-wings of birds, and behind the child, a pursuing animal—all rough black lines of wild, unkempt fur and a long snout with sharp teeth and a big red tongue lolling out one side of its mouth.

Gil, still watching Frank, noticed wetness spreading underneath Frank's armpits and dampness along his hairline. The drawing was coming alive. Nothing like the child's scrawl that Gil originally saw in it. Simple, yes, but there was a quality of raw energy, color and motion that animated it.

Frank looked up at Gil. "I've never drawn anything like this before."

Frank ran his finger along the edge of the tongue dangling sloppily out of the beast's mouth. "That tongue reminds me of my dad, when he'd been drinking." Gil shivered. "He had a way of sticking it out in a leering, open-mouthed yawn, his watery eyes staring blankly at something in the middle distance."

Gil noted Frank's rapid, shallow breathing.

"I need some air," Frank whispered, standing up and walking around Rae to the sliding glass door.

Gil followed him out, nodding to Rae to let her know he was watching him.

Frank walked to the edge of the deck, grabbed the wooden rail and was pushing up and down off the balls of his feet. Gil walked over and stood beside him, placing his own hands on the railing but keeping his feet on the deck. Frank's gyrations slowed and Gil calmed down as he felt Frank's center of gravity settle safely on the deck side of the rail. Exhaling, Gil looked down at the baths, two hundred feet below.

Frank continued staring southeast, towards the horizon. "All of a sudden the room felt stuffy. Everyone seemed distant and unfamiliar."

Gil matched Frank's shallow breathing. As they stood there side by side, Frank's breathing began to deepen. Gil continued to match his posture and breath.

After a while, Gil asked, "Better?"

Frank let out a long exhale. "What's happening to me?"

"You were triggered. That memory blindsided you."

"What does that mean?"

"It probably means you were in touch with some part of your experience that you normally aren't aware of." Gil paused. "We should go back in when you're ready."

Frank still looked shaken but said, "Okay."

They walked back inside and took their seats. A few people were still working on their drawings. Gil looked over at Rae and their eyes met. Rae pointed to her wristwatch. Gil turned back to the group.

"Take another minute to complete your drawing. Then, still with your non-dominant hand, in the lower right corner write your child's age and what nickname or whatever you were called back then."

Rae saw Diane bite her tongue as she concentrated on scratching a "5" and "Dee Dee" across the bottom of her sheet in childlike print. She closed her eyes and smiled slightly.

"Please finish up. We'll get in two groups of three and one group of two. As soon as you form your group, decide who'll discuss their drawing first."

Gil watched to see how people sorted themselves out. Ronald was the first one up, walking directly across to Diane and asking, "Mind if I join you?"

Diane looked a little taken aback but nodded okay, then leaned toward Carmen with a smile and invited her over.

Gil caught a look of relief cross Carmen's face as she pulled her pillow around to face Diane and Ronald.

Rae put a pillow down next to Diane. David stayed next to Todd as Max joined them. Alison scooted her cushion up to Frank and Gil.

Tex, who was sitting alone, frowned and looked around. Gil waved him over to join him, Alison and Frank. With a sharp upward tilt of his head, Tex acknowledged the invitation and got up. Alison moved to make room for him on the floor beside her.

Gil announced, "Describe your drawing to your partners. You'll each get five minutes, and then we'll switch. At the end of each presentation, the listeners can give any feedback you have, especially how the drawing and the story affected you. Start now."

Turning to the small group around her, Rae asked in a low voice, "Have you decided who's going first?"

After a short pause, Diane said to Ronald, "I'll go. This exercise was really hard for me. I didn't want to do it."

"Diane, show us what you drew," Ronald said gently.

"Well, this is the home I grew up in. It always felt like there was a cloud hovering over it. Everything was dark and closed-in. The windows were always covered, so light could hardly penetrate. Inside the house you see everyone in my family. I'm the little figure over there in the corner. I tried to not be noticed; that was the safest way. You can see how big my father is ... was.

"I remember how weird it was in my twenties to realize that my dad was only five feet eight inches tall. I had always thought he was well over six feet. Anyway, you can see how big he seemed to me. That's a horsewhip in his hand. The one he used to hit us with."

Carmen drew an audible intake of breath.

Turning to Carmen, Diane continued, "Actually, he beat my sister more than me. She was older and stood up to him more often." Her voice caught. "But it was hard to watch." Tears began sliding down Diane's cheeks. She quickly covered her eyes with her hands, her shoulders trembled.

Rae leaned over and whispered gently in her ear.

"Diane, remember, it's over. It was awful. You survived. You're safe now. You don't have to carry this alone anymore."

ACROSS THE ROOM, Gil's small group sat for a moment in silence. Frank was looking down. Alison looked back and forth between Tex and Frank. Tex, not looking at anyone, finally spoke up.

"Might as well get this over with. The whole thing seems silly to me." He pulled the large sheet of paper from behind him and dropped it down unceremoniously in front of his crossed legs. "This is what I drew."

Gil took it in and realized that Tex had artistic skill, even drawing opposite-handed. Using a minimum of line and color, the drawing etched a large field, verdant and enticing. A small figure stood alone on the left, while a dark, shadowed house loomed on the right.

Frank and Alison both leaned into the scene, as if pulled by gravity, and looked up inquiringly at Tex.

"That's me. That's my family house. And this is the acreage where I spent every moment I could." Tex ended the sentence with emphasis, as if he were done, and sat back.

Alison asked Gil, "Is it okay if we share some things with Tex?"

"If it's okay with Tex."

Tex shrugged.

Alison reached over the drawing to point at the frightening shape of the dark house. "Tex, this house looks so scary."

Tex glanced down. "That's just how it was. I was supposed to stick around and take it but I left whenever I could."

"Take what?" Frank asked.

"My dad's anger."

Tex's stoic restraint communicated more about that anger than his words. Gil felt a shiver run through him.

"I'm so sorry." Alison reached out impulsively, her hand making it halfway to Tex's bare forearm before she caught herself and paused. Looking at Tex's set face, she dropped her hand back in her lap. Gil, Alison and Frank studied the drawing while Tex stared straight ahead.

Rae announced from the other end of the room, "Okay, finish up with the first person and move on to the next."

"Is there anything else you'd like to tell us about this drawing, Tex?" Gil asked.

"No."

"Tex," Gil looked him in the eye. "I hope you take time this week to look at what your home was like for the little boy you were. I agree with Alison. It looks scary."

The group was silent for a moment, and then Frank placed his drawing down in front of Tex and Alison.

"This is me running towards the hills. Growing up, I spent a lot of time in the undeveloped hills around our suburban house. I liked it out there. It was another world ... a different life. I felt happy when I was in the hills."

Frank frowned and pointed to the dark storm above the hills.

"Then there are these dark clouds. I don't know what they are; I just drew them. Last of all, I drew this black dog. He's chasing me, I think. I've been running my whole life, but I've always thought I was running towards something, like the green hills in the drawing. The feeling I have looking at this picture is 'get me out of here!' I don't want to be anywhere near that dog or those threatening clouds. I want out. I've always been a runner. As a kid, I could outrun the bullies. In high school, I ran cross-country. I wasn't the fastest on the short course, but I could keep it up longer than most. Now I run to stay in shape and because I like the way I feel afterwards."

He paused. "That's it."

Alison and Tex looked at Frank and then at the drawing. After a moment Alison said, "That dog scares me. He looks deranged. And I notice he's right on the heels of the child, but the child seems to be looking ahead towards the hills, not back at the dog. I worry about the child. I'm afraid he isn't paying attention."

Tex suggested, "Maybe he ought to turn around and chase that dog."

The tension broke and Frank laughed. "That's something my Uncle Harry would have said. He never ran anywhere unless it was towards a fight."

WHEN EVERYONE had shared in Rae's small group, she made eye contact with both Gil and David. Responding to their head nods, she asked the groups to finish their feedback and then return to the larger circle. The loud buzz of conversations from all sides slowly died down and people moved back to their original seats. Rae stayed where she was, next to Diane. The room became quiet.

Gil slowly looked around the room, taking in each person. "Who would like to share with the larger group?"

Diane raised her hand as she stared at the floor. "This exercise was hard for me. I don't like thinking about what happened when I was a kid."

Gil said, "Hold up your drawing so everyone can see it."

Diane held the drawing in front of her and slowly rotated it. Then she laid it on the floor and pointed to a dark stick figure in the corner of the picture. "This is me. I'm really scared. My dad is standing with a horsewhip in his hand here." She pointed to a figure in the center of the drawing. "He's getting ready to beat someone. I was scared all the time when he was in that mood. I remember the time he tried to kill my sister. My mom jumped on him to stop him, but he just threw her off." Diane paused. "I don't like to think about this stuff."

"Diane," Rae asked, "would you be willing to work on your relationship with your father?"

"He's dead."

"Death doesn't end a relationship. You can still do the work. You can still heal."

"I can?"

"Yes, you can."

"If you really think it'll help. Even with my father dead, I'm still afraid."

Rae placed a pillow out in front of Diane. "This is your father.

"Diane, what would you like to say to him?"

"I don't know."

"I'm here with you. Your father can't talk back. This is your chance to say whatever you feel like saying."

"Well, if I could tell him how I felt without having an anxiety attack, that would be amazing."

"This is your chance."

Diane took a moment, staring at the pillow.

"Okay. Here goes... Dad, I want you to know that I was scared of you." She paused to look at Rae. Then she swallowed. "I was always afraid you were going to hit me. Or Sis. Or Mom. You wouldn't even let us laugh! I felt I couldn't breathe around you. Everything I did was wrong. You never said anything nice to me. You just hit me when I did something you didn't like."

Diane got louder.

"That night you beat Sis... Do you remember? I thought you were crazy. You didn't stop until you were too tired to hit her anymore. How could you do that? What's wrong with you?"

She paused, lowered her voice and spoke with emphasis.

I'm never going to let someone else hurt me like you did. I won't let anyone get that close. I won't tell anyone what I'm feeling or who I am. It's too dangerous."

Tears ran down her face.

Rae sat erect and calm. "Diane, stay with telling him how it felt to be his daughter. You don't need to understand him. You need to tell him what it was like for you."

"It was awful! I wanted the police to come and take you away. I wanted to hide the horsewhip."

Diane was weeping openly and her voice got small.

"Please don't hurt us anymore! Please!"

Rae whispered in her ear: "Tell him how much you hated it, and that he has to stop. That he can't do it anymore. He can't hurt you like that anymore."

With surprising energy and force, Diane spat out, "Dad! Stop hurting us! You can't do that anymore! Stop hitting us. No belts. No horsewhip. No hitting. No more!"

The room was dead quiet. Slowly Diane looked around.

Seeing Diane was done, David invited the group to give her feedback.

Alison whispered earnestly, "That sounds like my childhood. Not the horsewhip, but my dad was always angry and we were all afraid of him. Thank you for doing that work. I feel stronger and not alone."

In a flat, emphatic voice, Tex pronounced, "Any man who hits a woman isn't a man, in my book."

When everyone, except Carmen and Todd, had shared how they felt listening to Diane's story, David opened the floor again. "Who would like to talk about their drawing next?"

Frank's hand shot into the air.

"I felt more like someone watching than someone drawing. I just watched while my hand knew what to do. I drew this black dog chasing me. When I realized it reminded me of how I felt when my parents were drinking when I was really little, I got short of breath. My heart was racing. It's starting to beat faster now, just talking about it."

Gil watched Frank and followed his breaths. "Would you like to explore this?"

Frank looked at him, a little startled, and said, "What do you mean?"

"May I sit beside you?"

"Sure."

Gil moved next to Frank, facing into the circle. He got settled and looked over at Frank, mimicking his posture and following his breathing.

"Just relax and follow your next breath in. Bring your awareness to your body. Notice any sensations." Gil continued to watch Frank's chest rise and fall, breathing slower now, and deeper. "Describe what you notice."

Frank sat there silently for a moment with his eyes closed. "I feel tight in my chest."

"I feel tight in my chest." Gil repeated Frank's words without changing their pitch or inflection, like an echo of Frank's voice coming back to him.

"My whole body feels tight, actually."

"My body feels tight." Gil repeated the phrase and then decided to take Frank deeper. "Go back in time to when you first felt this tightness in your body."

Frank's eyes opened. He looked at Gil. "It was my parents' fighting. I used to hear them battling late at night down the hall. It was like some awful sitcom." Frank smiled.

Gil was puzzled. "So, your parents' fighting caused the constriction you're feeling?"

"No, it wasn't the fights, it was afterwards. Mom always ended up crying in my room. After Dad would storm out, she'd come into my room, lock the door and ask me to hold her. Sitting together on my bed, I'd put my arms around her and try to comfort her."

Gil felt his insides turn over. He remembered his own father sitting on his bed late at night, drunk and wanting to talk and how horrible it was. Frank was sitting there calmly describing it while Gil was having all the feelings. Gil was having a hard time thinking straight. He could feel the sweat dripping down his sides as he looked over at Rae and David, unsure what to do next.

Rae waited for Gil to say something. When he didn't, she leaned forward and softly said to Frank, "I noticed you smiled as you described what happened after your parents fought. Would you tell Gil what you're feeling right now?"

"Sure." Facing Gil directly, Frank continued, "I'm feeling a little … I don't know … out of body."

Gil just nodded, then looked back at Rae.

"Help him breathe into it, Gil."

Gil placed his hand tentatively on Frank's back as they sat side by side. He could feel the rising and falling of Frank's ribs and began to match his breathing. They sat silently for several seconds.

Finally Frank said, "I get upset when I hear people fight. That's all."

Rae stepped in again. "Anything else right now, Frank?"

Frank shook his head.

Rae asked, "Would you like to get some feedback from others about how they felt while you were working with Gil?"

Frank smiled. "Okay."

Ronald sat, legs crossed on the edge of his pillow. "Frank, that was no way for your mother to behave. I'm sorry you had to experience that. I'm angry that your mother and father didn't work it out between them and that you were dragged into their issues. A little boy shouldn't have to take care of his mother."

"Keep the feedback to your own feelings," David interrupted.

"Okay." Ronald grimaced. "Frank, I'm sad and I'm angry."

Diane raised her hand. "I felt really sorry for your mom having such a difficult marriage. And for you having to do the clean-up."

David frowned. "Just your feelings please."

Todd put his hands behind his head and looked up at the ceiling. "I feel you were too easy on your mom; you should have thrown her out."

Rae raised her hands, palms facing out. "Okay, I see many of you want to protect Frank. And it's hard to stick to just feelings without giving advice. Let's move on."

Gil felt confused. *I thought I was facilitating this.*

Rae continued. "With less than ten minutes remaining, we don't have time for another share. For those who haven't shared their drawing with the larger group, we'll complete this work tomorrow." She reached for her stack of poetry, pulled out a sheet and read a short poem that was untitled and unattributed. At the end, she repeated the last line, "Only a person who risks is free."

David closed the session by urging everyone to take good care of themselves and get a good night's sleep.

Rae noticed Tex leaving the meeting room quickly and thought he looked stressed. *The last few hours have been jarring for him. He's not used to expressing feelings and talking about childhood. But he did make a couple of connections in the room and he seemed engaged until the last few pieces of work.*

———

AS GIL REACHED DOWN to help Rae up off her cushion he said, "Let's meet now." Rae agreed and held on to Gil as she turned to give David a hand up. They lifted David and Gil dragged them both, laughing, into the bedroom.

"Whew!" Gil dropped heavily into the cushions of the only chair as he splayed out his arms and legs.

Rae and David fell onto opposite sides of the queen bed. Rae propped up the pillows behind her. David reached back over his shoulders to stuff a pillow under his head. The three exchanged glances.

"That was some group!" exclaimed David. Rae and Gil nodded. "Gil, that was good work you did with Frank. He's going to be a tough nut to crack, but at least you got him talking. The feelings will follow. And Rae, your work with Diane was beautiful."

Before Rae could say thanks, Gil said, "I don't think I can work with him."

Rae and David said simultaneously, "With Frank? Why not?"

"I got angry. I was experiencing all the feelings Frank wasn't owning. I was triggered and couldn't stay centered."

"I have a date to call home in ten minutes," David said. "Why don't we meet after dinner and talk about this?"

Rae frowned at David, then turned back to Gil.

"Whether you held onto your own feelings or not, your work with Frank was good."

Gil gave Rae a half-hearted smile and shook his head.

"I need to walk down to the phone booths to call Joann," David said, getting up and looking at his watch. "I'll meet you in the lodge at 7:30."

Gil stood up. "I'm going for a walk."

"Say hi to Joann for me," said Rae.

David said, "Okay," as he walked out the door.

Rae looked at Gil. "I'm going to rest. See you at 7:30."

Gil walked out of the room, not sure exactly why he felt so let down.

DAVID WONDERED if the Institute would ever get cell reception as he took the shortcut down the dirt road to the phone booths. He was pleased with himself. Knowing his way around gave him a sense of belonging, a kind of ownership. This was his home turf, much like the block by block delineations of the Detroit neighborhoods where he grew up.

He felt the same way about his marriage to Joann. It was home. His highest aspiration in life was to be a good husband and a father. He loved that he and Joann had worked hard and hung in there over the decades. It wasn't easy being married to Joann but it was the most rewarding thing he'd ever done. David was proud of how much he had grown. Making a family with Joann and helping to raise their two boys brought him a deep sense of satisfaction and joy.

He couldn't wait to hear her voice. That slight huskiness at the beginning of her sentences as her vocal cords warmed up reminded him of Janis Joplin's vocal in "Piece of My Heart." It was a romantic association for him, evocative of the yearning and angst of his younger years.

As he approached the phone booths, he spotted someone leaning under the lid of an open car trunk. Something awkward about the posture caused him to take a second look. It was Tex. Through the angled opening between the car and the lid David saw him put a bottle to his lips and tilt his head back. It was over in a second. Tex capped and returned the bottle to the trunk. David thought it was odd but he was running late. He shifted his attention to the open booth and went in to make his call.

GIL WALKED INTO the lodge at 7:35. The servers were already clearing away the food, so he grabbed a plate and walked into the kitchen. The lodge keeper and a couple of the kitchen staff were hustling back and forth, carrying large chafing dishes and platters from the dining room to the kitchen and setting them down on a long stainless steel table. Gil traded his plate for a small serving bowl from a stack under the table and quickly served himself a large helping of pasta primavera and some tossed salad before they were whisked away to be washed.

Gil took his rescued dinner back to the crowded dining room and looked around. He finally spotted David and Rae leaning over their empty plates and laughing. As Gil set his bowl down and pulled the bench out from the long table, David stood up and asked, "What's for dessert?"

"Cookies," Gil said, stepping over the bench and sitting down. "You'd better hurry, they're clearing everything."

As David rushed off, Rae took a sip of her herbal tea. "You're late."

"Fashionably late." Gil smiled at her across the varnished wood table, but Rae didn't smile back.

Gil asked, "What's on the agenda, or have you and David sorted it all out already?"

David came back with three dessert dishes each stacked with homemade tollhouse cookies. He corralled them all in front of him, grinning. "These are all for me, so don't get any ideas."

"Oh, David, that's so thoughtful of you," Rae said laughing as she took a cookie off one of the dishes.

"Hey!" David leaned over his cookies like a mother hen and glared at Rae.

Gil reached in from the side and nabbed another cookie.

"Hey!" David's voice shot up an octave.

They broke out laughing, so long and hard Gil thought it a little odd.

"Now, are we ready to work?" Rae asked.

David let out a long breath. "Okay, I'm ready."

Gil nodded and Rae said, "I'd like to start with where we are. Who wants to go first?"

"I'll go." David put the uneaten half of his cookie back on the plate. "I'm feeling good about being here. It's always good to see you both, and good to have you leading with us, Gil. I'm enjoying the group, especially Max, and I think this is a particularly easy group to run. Most everyone seems engaged and willing to put themselves out there."

David turned his head to look at Gil. "And there's something I need to address with you, Gil." He looked back at Rae. "That's all."

"Before we do that, let's finish our check-ins. Is that okay?" Rae looked at Gil and he nodded. "I also want to talk to you, Gil. You've made a couple of comments about feeling insecure, and your participation in group has puzzled me. Otherwise, I'm doing well, considering how concerned I am about being away from home right now. Alan never likes it when I spend time away, and we had a blowup just before I left. I plan to call him later, but I dread it. He's been leaving message after message for me. I can't walk by the bulletin board outside the office without finding another pink slip with my name on it."

Rae took a long sip from her mug of tea. "I'm also concerned about Tex. He's in denial about his drinking, and he's keeping a pretty tight lid on his feelings. Something has to give."

David observed, "I saw Tex down by the phone booths, drinking something out of his car trunk."

Gil straightened up. "What?"

"I didn't think about it at the time, but I wonder what he was up to."

Gil snorted a laugh. "I don't. Not after what a big deal not drinking was for him."

Rae looked at David. "I agree, but I'm not sure how to handle it."

David said, "Let's ask the whole group to check in about how they're doing with their commitments and see if he owns up to it."

Rae agreed and said to Gil, "Your turn to check in."

Gil raised his eyebrows. "Wait a minute. That sounds like a set-up. We ask Tex to confess, then we confront him with what David saw?"

"No, no, no… we need to check in with everyone anyway. It will be the right time for David to clear it up with Tex if he needs to." Rae looked to David. "Do you agree?"

"Yep."

Gil shrugged "Okay."

"That's settled then."

Gil said, "Now about my participation: I just don't feel like I'm part of the team. Like the decision you just made now. I wasn't asked for my input. I don't agree, yet we moved on anyway. It's two against one. I'm not really your co-leader. I'm a student with privileges, or an assistant. I feel that in group all the time, undercut or overridden by both of you. I don't feel confident about my work. I get lost and need your help. I really don't know why I'm here, or what I'm trying to prove.

"Don't get me wrong. I love you guys and I love this work. I just don't feel at home in my role. And it's freaking me out, because this is what I'm hoping to do with my life. I walked out on my lab job. What I would do if I wasn't doing this, I have no idea."

David waited a moment to see if there was more, then softly said, "Gil… listen… you do great work. You were very supportive of Frank during the Draw-a-Child piece. When you jumped into my work with Ronald, I have to admit I was annoyed. But you took him in a direction I didn't anticipate, deeper into exploring his wanting to be in a relationship. Then you skillfully facilitated his dialogue with Diane. You're a valuable member of this team."

Rae watched Gil's reaction and thought about what she could add that might help.

"Gil, I hear you don't feel treated like an equal, you feel left out and not part of the team. I'm sad about that. But it's not how I see you. And I invite you to keep letting us know, anytime these feelings come up for you."

She sat for a moment, letting that settle.

"Anything else you'd like to say?" Rae asked Gil.

"No," Gil replied.

"Okay, let's leave it as an open, important topic, and plan tomorrow morning's session."

THE HANDCRAFTED wood planks of the spacious phone booth smelled of tannin and varnish. Rae sat there staring at the archaic black-and-chrome phone box fastened to the wall. She read the sequence of dialing instructions and codes on the back of her phone card.

Rae couldn't remember anywhere she had seen a pay phone recently except here. The contrast between the cutting-edge workshops and this anachronistic phone struck her. Definitely not convenient but still she hoped it would stay this way. There were more important things to do here than to stay connected to the outside world.

When she got her courage up, she entered the numbers that would make this call three cents a minute instead of a dollar and waited for the dial tone. Then she called home.

Rae took a long, slow breath as the phone rang three times.

Her husband's voice, businesslike and a little aggressive, barked at her. "Alan Rabinowitz here."

Why couldn't he just say hello, like everyone else? she wondered.

"Hi, honey. Sorry I'm a little early." Rae forced a lilt into her voice. "It's been a long day, and I didn't think I'd make it till nine." She held her breath. She knew that his next words would tell her how the conversation was going to go.

"As long as it pleases you." His tone was cold and acerbic.

It's going to be one of those calls, she thought. "I've been worried about you. I know you don't like it when I leave to come up here for a week. How are you doing?"

There was a pause on the other end of the line.

"Well, since you ask, I'm hurt and disappointed. It doesn't seem to matter to you that I'm fighting for my life here. I should be very angry, but I'm mostly sad. Sad that you're so self-absorbed and callous that you could jet from one end of the country to the other, immersing yourself in the adulation of your fans and cavorting with all your paramours, while I'm left here on my own to face my death."

"Yes, yes, yes, Alan, you're dying. You've been dying ever since I met you. And you're very likely to go on dying long after I'm laid to rest in the family plot in Avila."

Rae regretted her outburst. This wasn't going to be a fight because in fights, there were winners and losers. This was going to be Armageddon. There would be no winners.

5

Tuesday Morning

S THE MORNING SESSION BEGAN, DAVID SAT, EYES closed, his back against the propped-up pillow and his legs straight out in front of him. A bag of ice was resting on his right ankle, which had begun to bother him yesterday after the steep uphill climb from the baths. At the moment he was enjoying the ritual of counting his breaths and allowing his mind to wander.

David's reverie was interrupted by the sound of Gil's voice.

"With your next breath, bring your awareness back into the room and when you're ready, open your eyes. Look around and see who's with you this morning."

David picked up his quote by Patrick Overton and read aloud.

FAITH

When we walk to the edge of all the light we have
and take that first step into the darkness of
* the unknown*
we must believe that one of two things will happen—

* There will be something solid for us to stand on*
* or, we will be taught how to fly.*

As David finished, Rae held back, letting the words settle on the room like leaves settling after a gust of wind.

"This morning when you check in, please include a statement about what yesterday was like for you, and how you're doing with your commitments concerning alcohol and other drugs. I'll go first.

"I'm still feeling very tender about what you shared yesterday and the work you did. I feel so privileged to be present to such open, beautiful hearts. Not using alcohol hasn't been an issue for me for many years. Sugar is my, quote unquote, drug of choice, and I've been really good about not over-doing it this week."

Diane, seated next to Rae, spoke up next.

"I've had an amazing morning. I feel excited and shy about it, all at the same time." She glanced around the circle, her large, sea-green eyes peering through the strands of blonde hair falling across her face.

"I woke up thinking about my drawing from yesterday. That little girl I drew, that was me, and she's been so sad … I've been so sad. I don't know the difference between me as a child and me as an adult."

Her voice cracked and her lips trembled. Rae continued to give Diane her full attention, but decided not to reach out and touch her.

Rae smiled. "Your little girl is right here with us, isn't she?"

"Yeah." Diane blushed and smiled.

"Well, I want her to know that she's welcome here. As we continue with check-ins, I want you to imagine holding her in your lap. Let her know that you're a grown woman and you'll look after her and keep her safe."

Diane folded her arms over her stomach and nodded.

"And how are you doing with your commitments?"

"Oh yes, I haven't had a drink. I haven't even thought of it."

"Who's next?" Rae inquired.

Todd sat up. He was wearing a black tee shirt with the sleeves cut off. He smiled at the group.

"I had a great morning. I went up on the road and walked for an hour. I feel terrific. This sitting around gazing at your navel is hard for me. It felt good to do something physical. I'm eager to get to the real work. I came here to figure out how to help my old girlfriend and straighten out the people at work." He leaned forward and made eye contact with Tex. "I'm wondering when we'll look at the current obstacles in our lives."

"And how are you doing with the ground rules? Especially the requests for being here on time and not drinking?"

"Well, I'm usually here on time, and I haven't had a drink."

Rae noticed her tightened belly and the sudden lack of oxygen in the room as the others stared at Todd.

"Todd, this is our fourth meeting, and you've been late twice. Are you willing to re-commit to being here on time?"

"I told you what happened last night. It couldn't be helped. And I don't remember another time. Even though I thought I'd spend part of the week here just soaking in the tubs and hanging out, I have no problem with coming on time. Except when something unexpected comes up."

"Do you see where you might have avoided being late last night?"

"I guess I could have come without my notebook."

"Yes. What about that?"

"I really need my notebook to keep track of my insights."

"Todd, we're going to complete go-rounds. I'd like you to think about the choices you're making. Are you willing to do that?" When Todd nodded with a slight shrug, Rae looked at Alison, who was sitting next to Todd.

Alison looked over at Gil and began speaking.

"I've kept the commitments and I haven't had a drink, but I also haven't done my assignment. I thought about it on the walk over here this morning. I thought of all the reasons it's the wrong assignment. You missed the point. You gave me the same old, tired AA solution without understanding the nature of my problem. My husband and kids need to make some changes too. I mean, I have a problem with drinking, but that doesn't mean they don't have problems too. It takes two to tango."

Alison stared at Gil. He met her gaze, but didn't say anything.

"Look, I don't want to drink, but that doesn't mean I buy into all that stuff you hear in AA. Why should I believe in a program invented by a Christian stock speculator and a drug-addict doctor?" Alison's eyes were bright and her voice was quite loud.

Rae, sitting tall, glanced at Gil briefly, as if expecting him to say something, then turned back to Alison.

"I'm sure your family has problems. They wouldn't be human if they didn't, but they aren't here. You are. So the question is, what are you going to do about it? Your choices got you here."

Alison lowered her chin and kept eye contact with Rae, but said nothing.

"AA has worked for millions of people." Rae continued. "It's the treatment of choice for addiction. The social model for recovery is the best we have to offer today."

As Rae pushed the program at Alison, Gil was thinking of sharing similar thoughts. But something started to shift inside him as he listened to Rae pile it on, and watched Alison grow more distant and withdrawn. *What happened to the fire in Alison's eyes? She seemed so alive a minute ago, and now, with all of Rae's best intentions and absolutely solid advice, she was shutting down.*

"I know all that. That's what everyone in AA tells me. Sometimes I think they're all brainwashed."

Just like you are, Rae. Gil finished the sentence for Alison in his mind. He could feel the tension in the room. It was clear Rae wasn't reaching her. No one else spoke up. Everyone was waiting.

Gil felt the pressure building inside him. He knew what he needed to say and it was heretical, yet he didn't want to quash it. He was scared and excited at the same time.

"Alison, I want you to know I support you." Gil's voice was deep, resonant and shot through with the inflection of strong emotion. "Don't give in. Hold on to your position." Gil could feel the energy of his words cutting right through everything Rae had just said. He was way out on a limb, and he knew it. But the moment it was said, he could see the shift in Alison. Her body relaxed, she smiled, her eyes went wide with surprise and shone with appreciation. He knew the feeling. She'd been seen. She'd been met, she'd been accepted, right where she was. And that was what needed to happen if she was going to do any meaningful work this week.

"Thanks," Alison said. I know I need to work AA. I just don't accept the God thing and I don't like being told what to do."

"Hold on to your convictions as long as you can." Gil noticed uncertainty flicker in her eyes.

"Okay." Alison said hesitantly, then sat silent.

Gil could see she was already beginning to question herself. *Good.*

Gil took in the questioning glances from Rae and David, but he didn't care. The whole room felt more alive to him.

Rae turned to Tex. "You're next."

"I'll take a rain check."

Rae gave Tex an appraising look. His eyes were narrowed and his jaw muscles stood out below his temples. "That's fine; we'll come back to you."

"No."

"No, what?"

"No, don't come back to me. I pass."

"That's fine, Tex, you always have the right to skip a check-in or an invitation to work." Rae let that sink in. "So just answer the question about your commitments."

Tex's chin jutted forward and his eyes narrowed as he looked straight at Rae. "I decided that having a drink was my own business."

Rae took a deep breath and let it out slowly. She noticed several others were holding their breath.

"Breathe."

She heard the exhales around the room as she took another long breath. "Tex, what you just shared is very important. I'll finish doing check-ins, then come back to you."

Tex shrugged.

The remaining group members spoke briefly, and the tension in the room remained high. After everyone had checked in, Rae turned back to Tex. He met her eyes with a hard stare.

"Tex, you said drinking was your own business. Did you take a drink?"

"Yeah, I took a drink."

"What happened?"

"Nothing happened. I was near my car, where I have a bottle, and I took a swig."

Rae waited. The room was still. Max coughed discreetly.

Tex sat, his arms folded in stoic silence.

"Tex," she began slowly, "something did happen."

"Nothing happened."

"Here's what happened, Tex. On Sunday night, you gave your word you would not use alcohol, and less than twenty-four hours later you drank."

Glaring at Rae, Tex remained resolutely silent.

"When you give your word, are you usually trustworthy? Does a gentleman's agreement carry weight with you?"

His nostrils widened and the right corner of his mouth twitched twice.

"I always keep my word, but that was a ridiculous agreement."

Tension drained from Rae. She knew Tex had just turned a corner, and she could sense exactly how this conversation would play out.

"I don't want to argue the merits of the agreement, I just invite you to look at your behavior. You're a man who is as good as his word. You gave your word, and broke it. What does that mean?

"In other arenas I imagine I could count on you. Your colleagues could count on you. Your horses could count on you. But here, with this particular agreement, I see you couldn't be counted on. What do you make of that?" Rae paused for effect. "I'm inviting you to be curious. I'm inviting you to examine your behavior."

Tex slumped, his lips tightened and he shook his head slowly. He inhaled and exhaled hard.

"I knew I was going back on my word. Not just to you, but to the whole group. I knew it as I took that slug, and yet I did it anyway."

Rae's out-breath whistled gently through her slightly parted lips. "Tex, you're a very courageous man. In this very moment, you're living that courage. Thank you for honoring me and the group and yourself by telling the truth. Now we can look together at what it is about your promise about alcohol that was different from other promises."

"The only difference is that I didn't keep my word."

"Yes. So the question is, why? What was different about this particular promise? What is the power alcohol has in your life?"

"Booze is just booze. There's nothing special about it."

"Okay. Are you willing to explore that with us? Here? Now?"

"I guess so."

"Great!" Rae sat back and let out another big breath, then turned to David and Gil. "I'd like to get your help with this."

Gil, his eyes bright, asked, "Tex, why don't you start by telling us how much you drink and how often."

"I don't drink that much. No more than other guys."

"How much is that?"

"Look, I know what heavy drinking is. My father was a drinker. I mean, a real drinker, a fifth-a-day man. I don't drink anything like he did." Tex paused and fidgeted. "I see that I broke my word. But that doesn't make me a problem drinker. I'm nothing like my old man."

"Tex, this isn't about your dad. I believe you when you say you don't drink anything like him. But the important piece here is how alcohol affects your life, not your dad's life."

David cleared his throat and took over. "For instance, how does your drinking play into the problem you came here for—your marriage?"

Gil shot a questioning look at Rae, who was completely focused on Tex.

David glanced down at his notes. "What's your wife's name?"

Tex's eyebrows knotted up. "Sherri..."

David proceeded methodically in an even tone. "Has Sherri ever said anything to you about your drinking?"

Tex locked eyes with David, but didn't respond. Tex's right hand beat a drum pattern on his thigh.

David, seeing that his question had hit home with Tex, decided to let this go for now. "Tex, our only goal is to support you in seeing if this drug plays any part in the trouble you've run into. I don't have any investment in giving you a diagnosis around alcohol, but you agreed not to drink and you drank."

There was no response from Tex, just a fixed stare.

"So will you re-commit to not drinking, and report back what you see about the role of drinking in your life?"

"Also," Gil said, forcing himself to ignore his anger of being elbowed aside in the middle of his work again, "there's a Twelve Step meeting on Wednesday night that we encourage everyone to attend. It's at 7, and it's open to anyone and any program. I suggest you check it out."

Tex was quiet for a moment. Then with a head shake of surrender, he said, "Okay."

David and Rae exhaled and exchanged glances. Gil held his temper.

Before the check-ins could resume, Alison spoke up. "I'd like to say something to Tex if that's all right."

"If it's all right with Tex," David and Gil said in unison. They looked at each other and smiled. "Great minds," quipped Gil.

Tex dipped his head toward Alison, indicating he was listening.

"Tex, you remind me of myself, the first time I really saw what my drinking was doing. I didn't want to admit it, but I finally had to. Don't let this go on until you've lost Sherri. Or your health. Or your self-respect."

There was a long silence. Everyone seemed to be holding their breath. Finally Tex nodded, touching his forehead as if tipping a hat.

The check-ins continued. Rae noticed Diane sitting up straight and looking intently at each person as they shared. *This week is already making a difference for her,* Rae thought, and made a mental note to be alert for opportunities to affirm her.

There were no more issues with the ground rules in general, or alcohol in particular. David looked around the circle.

"We're going to finish presenting the drawings. Who hasn't shared?"

Max raised his hand.

"Max. Anyone else? Todd, you haven't shared with the larger group about your drawing, have you?"

"I guess not."

"Okay. Well, we'd like to hear from both of you."

Max held up a drawing of a lone figure, a five-year-old boy, wearing short pants and suspenders, his hair slicked back.

"I was very lonely as a boy. My parents were first-generation immigrants. My mother's entire family was killed in Europe before my father could arrange for them to leave." Max paused and his voice dropped a notch. "And they weren't taken by the Nazis, they were murdered by their own neighbors." Max's eyes glistened as he took a deep breath.

"When my mother was pregnant with me, she received a telegram telling her about her parents' deaths. From that day on, she grieved. She was in mourning every day of my childhood. She had nothing to give and left me on my own. I learned not to count on her. But how I longed for her to take care of me. I often joke that I became a teacher by the age of five so I could teach my mother how to overcome her depression. I was totally unsuccessful. That remains the greatest failure of my life."

No one said a word, as Max paused for a moment to take a deep breath before continuing.

"She blamed my father for not sending for her family sooner. And my father drowned in the ocean of my mother's bitterness. I became afraid to make the wrong move, of not getting enough done, or not getting it right, or ... whatever. I still try to do everything perfectly, worrying that somehow I won't get done whatever it is that needs to be done."

The last words were spoken in a rush. Again Max stopped to catch his breath.

"For many years, I felt there was something wrong with me. Why couldn't I make my mother happy? I wondered if it was something about me that made her sad, something I was supposed to do or be.

"I've worked so hard on believing that I have a right to be here. It later became my life's work as a special education teacher to help young people understand the world and themselves. I want everyone to feel they belong! In my drawing, this little five-year-old boy is standing alone, frightened and confused."

David's eyes were filled with tears. "Max, I'd like to give you a hug ... I need a hug too. May I come over and hug you?"

David stood up right away and took a couple of steps forward. Max looked uncertain, but got up and accepted David's hug. David embraced him ferociously and Max tentatively squeezed back.

David thought, *Two aging Jewish men sharing our grief,* and he cried all the harder.

Gil did not like David's hyper-emotionalism, but he was impressed with the all-in quality of his embrace.

Rae felt warm and loving towards them both, particularly David. She admired his willingness to put his feelings out there. She made a quick scan of the room and saw few dry eyes. Even Todd looked uncomfortable and embarrassed. And Tex was staring curiously at Max and David. Diane and Alison were holding hands.

Rae rose and moved toward the two men. She reached her arms around both of them and leaned into the hug.

Gil felt compelled to support her. He couldn't leave her out there in the middle of the room, glued to David and Max's hug all alone. So despite his better judgment, he quickly joined her, enfolding the other side of the two men in his arms.

Several others quickly piled on, forming a rugby scrum with David and Max at the center. Tex, Todd and Carmen stayed seated.

David felt panic rising up through the overwhelming warmth and safety he was experiencing. He needed air. Finally there was a shift in pressure as the outer edge of the group dropped their arms and stepped back. Everyone quietly melted away as quickly as they had joined, and soon all were back on their cushions.

David broke the silence.

"Max, would you like to say what that was like for you?"

A deep sigh escaped Max.

"I'm relieved ... I've carried all of that for a long time. I've always felt so different from others." Max looked at each person in the circle. "I'm so grateful to have finally said it aloud. That was a first. Thank you all for listening."

David paused to let Max have this moment of gratitude.

"Would anyone share with Max what it was like for you?"

"God, Max!" Diane's words tumbled over David's. "I've heard about the Holocaust, but never from anyone personally affected by it."

AFTER AN EXTENDED "debriefing" period, with several people sharing their feelings, David said with sincerity, "Max, I want to thank you for sharing."

Tears welled up in David's eyes again. "I, too, grew up feeling deep inside that, as a Jew, I was vulnerable in a way others weren't. I always wondered who would take me in if the Nazis came for me."

Gil felt the weight of silence pressing down on the group. *Where the hell is he going with this?*

"David, would you like to ask that question now?" Rae's voice was soft and loving.

Without hesitation, David turned to Gil. "Gil, if they come for me, will you take me in?"

Gil hesitated caught between the only answer he could give and his aversion to what David was doing. "Of course I would." Gil felt slightly nauseous.

David's tears started to fall freely. He continued, "Rae, would you take me in? Could I count on you?"

Rae was stunned by the power and the history of the question, by the voices in the past that had answered "Yes," and by the many more voices that had emphatically said "No." For several seconds, she simply stared into David's vulnerable eyes.

"David, my home is always open to you. If they come and you can't find me, just know that my home is yours. Walk right in. You can count on me."

Gil's nausea took a violent twist and he gagged. He quickly glanced at Rae, afraid that she had heard him, and was relieved to see she was still staring into David's eyes.

Rae knew it was unusual for leaders to do their own work, but she had no doubt about the rightness of David asking this existential question and receiving the answer every heart longs for and deserves.

Gil felt betrayed, not by David's inappropriate and dramatic intrusion into the work being done, but rather by Rae's abandonment of all the principles she'd ever taught him. *Where was the container that leaders were supposed to provide for this work? Where was the authenticity of present-moment, first-person reality?* More than ever, Gil felt the ground of this work, this calling, crumbling beneath him.

In the next few minutes, Max, Ronald and Diane all vowed to be there if ever such a time should come again. Gil felt more and more isolated from the group, like he was the only one who hadn't drunk the Kool-Aid. He didn't like the feeling.

David remained emotional and grateful through it all. At the end he cried again, thanking everyone for their support and telling them all how much their generosity meant to him. "I think we're healing something bigger than our individual grief here. My pain goes back three generations and across many families. For all of them, I thank you."

I don't believe this. Gil felt trapped. If he said anything real, he'd hurt David's feelings and look like a jerk. If he didn't say anything, he'd be complicit in this farce and abandon his principles. For the first time, he felt something like a dawning awareness of his kinship with Todd.

David paused and said, "Let's take a ten-minute break."

Gil threw David a look and, failing to get his attention, saw that Rae was already starting to stand up.

"Hold on a moment." Gil was surprised to hear how loud and forceful he sounded.

David looked up, eyebrows slightly raised. Rae watched. Everyone froze.

Gil was sitting up ramrod-straight. His voice dropped a half-octave and projected out to the corners of the room.

"I don't think this is a good time to defuse the energy."

David hesitated for a second. He felt the need to step aside from the intensity of the last twenty minutes and set a clear boundary between his personal work and the facilitator role he was re-entering. But he understood Gil wanting to keep the group focused. He made a quick decision.

"Okay. Let's all stand up and form a circle. We'll do an exercise in giving and receiving nonverbal communication. One person will act out how he or she is feeling without words, and the rest of us will mimic them. Okay, Gil?"

"Great." Gil felt like he was back again and participating.

People immediately shifted about and got up from their pillows. The mood in the room was suddenly light. People laughed and threw themselves into the pantomime. David led off by playfully exaggerating his display of grief and they all mimicked him. Then he turned to Frank next to him and said, "Just act out what you're feeling."

Frank held his stomach and rocked silently with belly laughter. Everyone joined in.

When the exercise had gone all the way around the circle, the energy in the room was high and Gil had to admit he felt refreshed.

As people took their seats, Rae noticed how comfortable she was letting David and Gil do more of the leading. Turning her attention back to the room, she said, "Gil, thanks for speaking up, and David, thanks for your creative response to Gil's concern." She was glad to accept the change in her role and had a sudden realization. *We are working together in ways that surpass the sum of our individual abilities.*

"You're welcome." David turned to Todd. "Todd, are you ready to tell us about your drawing?"

Todd appeared distracted. "I don't know where the drawing went."

"Here it is." Diane smiled and, reaching behind her, picked up a drawing from the raised hearth. "You left it there last night."

Frowning, Todd took the sheet of paper and laid it on the carpet.

The picture showed a dark, thick line down the center of the newsprint sheet. On one side were two stick figures, one tall, one short. A similar sketch was mirrored on the other side, with one short figure and two larger figures, one with long scribbled hair. Todd stared at it silently for a moment.

"This side is me and my mother and my grandmother. This side is me with my dad. That's after my parents divorced."

"What was it like to be you back then?" David asked.

"Great. I won races on the cross-country team and I was good with the girls." Todd grinned.

"I remember you said Sunday night that the miracle you wanted was to work things out with your girlfriend. Can you see anything about your childhood that seems relevant to your issues with your girlfriend?"

"Nah. My childhood is done and gone. And even though my mom and dad divorced, I still got to see my dad whenever I wanted. He was a real happy guy. Did what he wanted." Here Todd paused for a brief moment. "He and I used to run together sometimes."

"And your mother?"

"Well, she wasn't so happy. Had to work too hard. I guess Dad didn't give her and Gram much money. But what could he do? He had to support himself."

"Did that ever bother you?" Gil asked.

"What?" Todd looked over at Gil as if confused about which leader he should address.

"That your father took care of himself, while you and your mother and grandmother went without enough child support?"

Todd's eyes narrowed for a moment, and then he shrugged and said with an exaggerated calm, "Whatever." He looked back at David. "Okay, I'm done."

Rae asked Todd, "Do you have a response to Gil's question?"

"What question?"

"About your dad."

"What Gil said about my dad wasn't right."

"So, Todd, what did you hear Gil say that wasn't right?" Rae kept pushing.

"He called my father a deadbeat in so many words."

Gil's chin dropped and his brow furrowed. He felt an immediate charge in the room.

Rae didn't miss a beat. "Todd, clearly you have some feelings about what Gil said. Are you willing to discuss this with Gil?"

"There's nothing to discuss."

"Well, you heard Gil say something that didn't sound right to you. Do you want to just drop that?"

Todd glanced over at Gil, then shrugged and looked away.

"Todd, I saw Gil's surprise and I watched you withdraw. Did you notice his reaction? Because it's really important when you want to improve relationships that you be aware of how others are responding to you. So, are you willing to explore what just happened?"

"Sure," he said, leaning further back into his pillow.

"Okay, good. Here's what I'd like you to do. Both you and Gil move your pillows into the center of the room and adjust your pillows so that the distance between you feels comfortable."

Both men stood up and reached down for the giant overstuffed pillows they had been resting on. Gil plopped his pillow down in the center of the room. Todd kicked his pillow about three feet in front of Gil's. Gil looked at Todd, squared his shoulders, and leaned forward and then back. He got up, shifted his pillow back a foot, then sat down again. Todd met Gil's gaze and then turned to watch Rae.

"Thank you. Todd, who in this room do you feel most comfortable with, or trust the most? Invite them to come sit with you. They'll be your support team."

Todd, observing the group, replied, "I trust everyone here. Everyone can be my support team, if that's what you think I need."

"Okay. What I would like now is for you to tell Gil what you heard him say. Don't give him your response, just reflect back as best you can what you heard him say. Can you do that, or do you need some coaching?"

"Oh, I can do it, all right."

Gil nodded his head.

Todd started with measured coldness in his voice. "Gil, you put my father down. That's not right. I don't like it. I..."

Rae immediately interrupted him. "Hold on, Todd."

Todd pivoted toward her.

"Thank you. I want to clarify your task here. All you need to do initially is say what you think Gil said. You might say something like, 'I heard you say my father didn't pay enough support and kept mom and me poor.' You'll have a chance to share your feelings in just a minute. Is that clear?"

Todd stared a moment longer, seeming to struggle with an internal dialogue.

"Yeah, I can do that."

"Good. After you've accurately stated what Gil said, you'll have a turn to say what you think or feel about it. So first paraphrase what you heard, and then ask Gil if you got it right."

"Okay, okay. I heard Gil... I heard you, Gil, say my father was a deadbeat. And he wasn't..."

"Todd, stop there. Now check with Gil to see if that's what he said."

"Well? Isn't that what you said?"

"I asked how you felt. You said your father didn't give your mother enough money to take care of you. I asked how that felt for you." Gil paused. "I wasn't calling your father a deadbeat."

Todd sat rigidly for a moment. His dark eyes moved around as if looking for something to fix on. Turning toward Rae with his eyebrows still furrowed, he asked, "Well, what do you think? What's the difference between what he's saying and what I'm saying?"

"The only difference I can hear is that Gil didn't make a judgment about your father, but rather wondered if *you* have, or had, any feelings about the situation."

Todd sighed a long audible release of breath as he turned back to Gil.

"Did you hear me say my dad was a deadbeat?"

"No, I heard you say that he didn't provide enough money for you or your mother."

Todd squinted and tilted his head. "Well, okay then, but I won't have anyone calling my dad a deadbeat."

"I was simply asking about your feelings."

"Okay."

Gil sat quietly, allowing space for Todd to go on. The silence extended.

Rae's gentle voice intervened.

"Todd, would you go further and tell Gil more about how you felt when you thought he called your dad a deadbeat?"

"Well, Gil, I just misunderstood you, and I guess you misunderstood me. There's nothing else to be said."

After the room sat silently for a while, Gil stirred. "Todd, is it possible that your father was a good man, and at the same time he didn't give your mother enough child support?"

A slight shake of the head accompanied Todd's examination of Gil's expression.

"I don't know."

From the side, Rae prompted, "If you did know ..."

"Sure, I guess it's possible. He could be, in fact he was, a good man."

"Todd, do you have any feelings about the idea that although he was a good man, maybe he didn't pay enough child support?"

"No. No. Just glad to see how you misunderstood me, and to get that cleared up."

"Does it mean anything to you personally about your own life that your dad could be both a good man and imperfect?"

"I don't know."

"Look and see."

Todd furrowed his brows in thought. His head shook slightly.

"I guess it could mean that when I make a mistake, it doesn't mean I'm a bad person. Or any of us, for that matter."

Gil's face broke into a huge grin. He held his right hand up, palm facing Todd. With a perplexed look, Todd lightly touched Gil's hand in a high-five.

Gil settled back.

By a slight shake of her head, Rae indicated to David that something was still missing. Todd had said the words, yes, but they didn't seem to connect to his feelings.

Rae thought sadly, *What a lovely gift Todd could have given himself, self-acceptance—that would be invaluable.*

This exchange had the potential for impacting Todd's whole life, but I just don't think he got it.

"Todd," Rae asked, "can you tell me, Gil and the group what you got from looking at this issue about your father?"

"Just what I said. We all make mistakes."

"Anything else?"

"Nope."

"Is there anything else either one of you would like to say before we turn back to the full group?"

Todd shook his head.

"Yes." Gil drew a long breath and closed his eyes, then looked at Todd. "What you said about being good whether or not you make mistakes is a great insight."

Rae involuntarily held her breath and willed Todd to take this second opportunity to get it.

"Yes. Yes, it was a good thing to see," Todd replied without enthusiasm.

Then he dipped his head in finality and rose to return to his original place, and Gil followed suit.

David suggested they go around the room for any feedback for Todd. Several people spoke then the room got quiet.

Tex took a deep breath. "What you just said was big. Makes me think about horses. They make lots of mistakes, and a good trainer just brings their attention back to the task without breaking their spirit. It's not about the mistake; it's about a horse's spirit. I could use the same medicine."

David said, "What do you mean?"

"I'm clear about my feelings toward Sherri. I can see that I've made mistakes. It's hard to look at."

"Maybe this is an opportunity to do just that, look at it."

"And since Sherri isn't here, someone else could sit in for her and you could talk to her."

Tex laughed. "I'll have the real thing tomorrow. Sherri's meeting me for lunch at Nepenthe."

"What if we had her join us for a session to do some work with you? Would that be all right?" David asked.

Gil winced. Rae stared at David with a perplexed expression.

Tex stirred. But before he could answer, Gil said, "I'm not open to bringing in someone new at this point."

David's expression didn't change. He turned to Rae.

Rae said, "I would only support it if everyone in the group agrees. And I think we need to discuss this first ourselves."

"I'm willing to talk about it," Gil said, "but I'm not interested in inviting the group to vote on it."

The room went dead quiet.

Tex broke the silence. "I'm not sure I even want do this."

"Tex," Rae cut in, "while you're considering the question, would it be all right if we address Gil's concern? Does that work for you?"

Tex nodded.

Rae turned to David. "Would you like to respond to Gil?"

"I suggest we talk about this after the session and then check in with Tex before the afternoon meeting. I'd like to know right now if Tex is willing to work on his relationship with Sherri and whether the group is open, as one possibility, to inviting Sherri to join us just for that purpose."

Gil frowned. "I just said I don't want the group voting on it. I think we should talk about this outside the group."

Todd's voice broke in from across the room. "I want to make sure we have enough time for those of us who paid to be here. We still haven't got to the important issues."

Rae ignored Todd and said to Gil, "So you're uncomfortable with the proposal?"

"Yeah."

"Okay," David cut in, "let's finish with our closing reading. Then we'll see you all back here at 4 o'clock. Tex, we'll check back with you then."

GIL CLOSED THE DOOR to Rae's room and threw his papers on the bed. "That was a surprise!"

David stood by the window looking out. He turned around. "Before we talk about Tex, I just want to say that was a powerful session. I was really moved by both of your responses to my Holocaust question." David's eyes filled with tears. "I can't tell you how healing that was for me. I had no idea what a weight of fear I carried about what happened to my people."

Rae smiled at David and said, without missing a beat, "I meant what I said. I would take you in without question." David's eyes overflowed as he reached out and took Rae's hand, then Gil's. Gil looked away. Rae reached for Gil's other hand to complete the circle. She squeezed it and Gil looked back towards her. They stood in silence. David looked at each of them in turn, while Gil kept his eyes lowered.

Once again Gil felt and fought the gag response. David's dramatically asking people to take him in if there were another Holocaust just didn't ring true for Gil, and this work was supposed to be about truth. *But what can I say? I mean really, the Holocaust?*

Rae was radiating, as if a light source beyond her was shining through. David was smiling. Gil took it in and held on to their hands all the harder as he struggled to contain a sensation of dizzy swirling inside. David was so moved by the intensity of Gil's grip, a fresh tear was running down his cheek.

Rae smiled at both of them and let go of their hands. Then Rae lay down on the bed, David sat next to her, and Gil sank into the wicker easy chair in the corner.

"It was a critical session," Rae led off. "Tex turned a corner with his willingness to admit what's going on, and Todd did his first piece of work. Both of those things needed to happen. I've been feeling held at arm's length by Tex and completely at a loss with Todd."

Gil finally found his tongue. "I think you're both deluded."

Rae and David both exploded in short barking laughs.

"Why do you say that?" David asked, still chuckling.

"Todd was completely unaffected by the work I did with him, Tex is still in denial, the group was put off and confused by your emphasis on the Holocaust, and, other than Diane, no one has really felt safe enough to take any big risks."

"Whoa, that's a mouthful. Let's take it one piece at a time, okay?" Rae waited for Gil's nod of agreement, and then turned to David. "Are you open to us talking about this?"

"Sure."

Rae said to Gil, "What Tex did was huge. It opens the door for him to look at his core issue, alcohol. And you did great work with Todd. He's difficult, but it's early in the week, and you have no way of knowing where this will lead him. All you, or we, can do is what you did today. Keep inviting him to look at himself.

"But what I really want you to hear is that David's work was moving for me and others in the room, had meaning for him, and offered a small piece of healing for everyone."

Rae waited to see how this was landing with Gil.

Gil frowned and shook his head slightly. "Fine. Let's talk about Tex and Sherri so I can get a swim in before they stop serving lunch." He added, turning to David, "Frankly, though, I was shocked at how you rode right over me when I was working with Tex earlier in the session."

"I'm not sure what you mean," David said. "All three of us were questioning him about his drinking."

Gil shook his head. "Let's drop it. I want to move on to Tex and Sherri. I'm pretty clear that bringing in someone new would disrupt the work for others and take precious time. This group has been struggling with the issues of safety and trust, waiting to see how we would handle our more reluctant participants. There are people in the room who had alcoholic or abusive parents, and there is no way they're going to feel safe or commit themselves until they see that we can handle those issues first."

"Look," David responded, "Tex's got a problem in his relationship. This is a rare opportunity. I'd like to shake things up and have Sherri come in. Other participants could benefit from seeing a guided couple's conversation." David looked at Rae to see whether he could count on her support.

"That's not the point," Gil said. "I think it will interrupt our progress to bring in someone new. The group will get sidetracked. Plus, I think it's irresponsible to work with her and then just have her walk away without the container or support that the group offers."

"Why not let Sherri and Tex decide that, and let the group decide if they want to invite her in?"

Rae intervened, "I don't think we should spend any more time on this. Gil's against it, and I'm not willing to go forward unless everyone agrees. Sherri's not in the workshop, and she's not our concern at the moment. Anyway, I'm tired and I need to eat. Sorry, David." Rae picked up her scarf and walked toward the door.

"Let's offer to work with Tex in group and take it from there." As she opened the door, she looked back. "Now, are either of you going to walk with me to lunch?"

Gil smiled. "I'm with you as far as the pool."

"Let's go," David said, and the three of them walked through the meeting room and out into the ocean-reflected sunlight of Big Sur.

6

Tuesday Afternoon

RAE SAT ALONE OUTSIDE, HER BACK TO THE WARM wood of the solarium wall. The evidence of her lunch was on the table in front of her: fragments of beets and green lettuce on a plate, a ring of yellow squash soup in a bowl and a half-empty glass of tea with a Hibiscus infusion.

She broke off her distant gaze and took in the lodge deck, the boughs of cypress, the receding coastline and the wide blue edge of the Pacific. Most of the tables were empty. Max and Diane were sitting in the shade of the cypress on a fixed bench that rimmed the edge of the deck. Their heads were together and Max was holding Diane's hand. Rae was struck by the intimacy of their posture. She smiled and thought, *Tuesday and the group is starting to bond.*

Rae felt a pang of jealousy. *Where had her bond with Alan gone?*

She leaned back and closed her eyes, hoping in vain to regain her sense of peace.

GIL BEGAN THE SESSION with a meditation that he consciously extended by two minutes.

The group will be meditating 15 minutes by the end of the week, he thought with satisfaction.

Silence followed the closing sound of the Tibetan chimes. Rae read aloud from Jean-Paul Sartre,

Freedom is what you do with what's been done
to you.

"Let's check in." David looked around the circle. "I'll start. I continue to be profoundly moved by the deep level of work being done here. This morning was a real gift to me—the piece about taking me in. I feel safer in this world now."

As others checked in, Rae noticed Diane starting to fidget.

When it was her turn, Diane stared at the carpet in front of her. She cleared her throat. "I've been talking to Max about my dad and how scared I was as a little girl. Max encouraged me bring it up in here." Diane shook a little and took a deep breath. She looked toward Max, who nodded approvingly. "So if it's all right, I'd like some time later."

Diane turned toward Alison, indicating she was done with her check-in.

Alison looked at Gil. "I did my assignment over the break." She held up her notebook and waved it.

Gil smiled back at her in recognition. He noticed the warmth rising in his chest. "I'd like you to share it with the group later if you're willing."

"Sure." Alison turned to her left and made eye contact with Carmen.

Carmen hesitated, and then looked over at Rae.

"I had a very hard afternoon. I've been feeling like I don't really belong here." She looked down at her hands.

Rae was taking a moment to choose between reassuring Carmen and empathizing with her when Todd's voice interrupted.

"I'm doing fine." Todd leaned back and crossed his arms behind his head. "I'm eager to see what you've planned for this afternoon. I'd like to get right to work."

Ronald was the last person to check in. He looked at Todd, then sat up and cleared his throat.

"Something's been on my mind since lunch yesterday. I've tried ignoring it, but it's taking up space in my head. I'm having a hard time being present."

He looked over at David. "This involves someone else in group, and I'm not sure what to do."

"Okay," David said. "Just tell us what you're thinking."

Ronald, looking a bit confused, took a deep breath.

"I was sitting with Diane at dinner and Frank walked up..."

David interrupted him. "Don't get into the story. Just tell us how you're feeling right now and we'll do some work on it later."

"Uh..." Ronald stopped. "Okay. I feel anxious and concerned, and I'd like some time."

"Thanks," David said. "Now, we have some unfinished business from this morning..."

"Wait a minute." Diane sat up straight, brushing back a stray lock of blonde hair that fell across her face. "Ronald just put some real feelings out there, and we're going on like nothing happened." She blushed a little from her vehemence and glanced at Rae for reassurance.

Rae's face lit up with a warm smile. "I know how difficult speaking up is for you, Diane. No one did that for you in your chaotic family. Good work."

"I kind of surprised myself." Diane smiled. "I don't feel scared now."

"No, you don't, do you?" Rae laughed.

David interjected, "Diane, I think it's great…"

"Just a moment, David." Rae kept her eyes on Diane. "I'd like to let Diane take this in.

"Are you open to feedback?" Rae asked.

Diane said, "Yes."

David continued, "I'm proud of you for speaking up." He appeared concerned. "I'm also protective of your little girl self, and I'm happy that she has such a strong woman to take care of her now."

Diane stared thoughtfully at David.

"Excellent, Diane, I can see you're really taking that in." Rae continued to monitor Diane's posture and expression. "Pay attention to what it feels like right now. Breathe it in. This is how it feels when people really see and appreciate you. This is how you want to feel when you're in an intimate relationship. Would you like to say anything else?"

"No." Diane lowered her head. "But I'd still like Ronald to finish what he brought up."

David exchanged a glance with Rae. A bit chagrined, he thought, *Diane had to ask us twice to clean up this issue.* "At the end of last session we committed to Tex to work on his marriage if he wanted to. That commitment comes first.

We'll get to Ronald later in the session. Is that okay with you, Ronald?"

"That's fine with me." Ronald looked at Diane and she nodded yes.

David addressed Tex next. "All right, then, back to where we left off. We talked it over and decided that it would be too disruptive to invite Sherri in for a session. So, Tex, if you want to work on this, we'll ask you to choose someone to sit in for Sherri."

"Anything else you want to say about that, David?" Rae asked.

David gave her a blank stare.

Gil leaned towards David, grinning. "Anything personal you want to add?"

"No, certainly not." David exaggerated his frown, and then broke into a laugh. "Oh, you mean the part where I apologize to the group."

"You mean to Gil and me," Rae smiled.

"Yes. All right. I shouldn't have suggested bringing Sherri into group without first consulting with you two. I'm enthusiastic and I don't always consider the consequences to others. My wife Joann is on me all the time about that. I'm sorry for any anxiety I might have caused any of you." There were some puzzled faces and some nods.

"Okay." David turned to Tex. "You brought up your concerns about your relationship with Sherri more than once. Would you like to work on that now?"

"Well, I don't know what the point is, since she's not here."

"This isn't about her; it's about you."

"I still don't get it."

"Okay, even without Sherri, you can learn more about what's going on, get clearer, and change your part in what's problematic in your relationship."

David wasn't sure how this was landing with Tex. "Let me rephrase the question. Are you willing to do something that may help you?"

Tex sat with his arms folded and a wary expression.

"I guess so."

"Good. The first thing to do is to choose someone to sit in for Sherri."

"I don't know who would want to do that."

"Just ask."

"Okay." Tex looked at the women in the group and stopped at Alison. "You don't seem to have any trouble getting on me about my drinking. Would you be Sherri?"

David saw Alison's hesitation.

"It's up to you, Alison. Tex and I will help you play the part of Sherri if you're willing."

"That's what I get for my confronting you," Alison laughed, and Tex smiled. "Okay, I'll give it a shot," she agreed.

"Thanks, Alison. How about the two of you sitting down in the middle here?" David threw two pillows into the center of the room.

David coached Tex, "Give Alison some guidance about how Sherri responds during heated exchanges with you."

"Well, Sherri is a real spitfire," Tex said to Alison. "She pulls no punches. She's quick to tell me exactly what she thinks, and that often includes what I'm doing wrong, and what I should be doing instead." Tex's eyes widened as his words tripped over each other. "She interrupts me. I never seem to be able to get anything right. She blows things out of proportion."

Tex paused to catch his breath.

"Oh yeah, and she says she'd be happy if I was half as caring with her as I am with my horses," Tex smiled.

David watched Alison listening. "Alison, do you have any questions for Tex?"

Alison shook her head no.

"Okay, Tex, here's what I'd like you to do. After 'Sherri' speaks, just repeat what you've heard. And the same goes for you, 'Sherri'."

Alison nodded.

Tex sat in silence, his eyes narrowed.

"What's going on, Tex?" asked David.

Shaking his head, Tex looked irritated. "This saying back what I've heard seems like a waste of time. Sherri speaks in plain English. I can understand her words perfectly."

"You're annoyed that I've asked you to work on your communication by repeating what's been said, since you already understand what she's saying."

"You got that right."

"How did that feel to you just now, when I said back what I just heard?"

"Um … well, that seemed okay. But this is different. I don't want to parrot 'Sherri' over and over."

"So are you saying that you won't try this method of communication?"

"No. I just don't want to waste time. I'd just like to get this whole thing over with."

"Okay, Tex, when you and Sherri get into an argument, what communication tools do the two of you usually use to resolve the conflict?"

"What do you mean, 'tools'?"

"When you're upset with each other, how do you try to resolve it? Do you communicate your feelings and listen to each other?"

"I never thought about it. We just get pissed off. She yells, and then I shut up."

"So, Tex, how is that working for you?"

Tex chuckled. "Speaks for itself, doesn't it?"

"Well, if it doesn't work, why not try a different way of talking with each other?"

"Well…"

Alison turned to Tex. "I'm willing to do it David's way. I could use some practice for my own marriage."

"Okay, okay," said Tex, "but all this parroting is retarded, no offense intended."

"That's a judgment, but let's not get derailed. So Tex, will you mirror back to 'Sherri' what she says to you?"

"I think it'll be a waste of time, but what the hell."

"Good. Thanks for being willing to try something new. It looks like you have some things to say to 'Sherri' and she probably has some things to say to you. So one of you begin."

Tex and Alison looked at each other warily; a silence filled the space between them.

"You go first," Tex said quietly.

"No way. You always want me to open up first, and then you cut me off."

David watched Tex react, as if the words had come from Sherri herself.

"There you go again. It's 'always' this and 'always' that; or 'never' this, or 'never' that." Tex glared at Alison.

"Tex, you agreed to say back to 'Sherri' what she says to you. Give it a try."

"I'm sick of her saying 'always' this and 'always' that."

"You'll have a chance to say what you're feeling, Tex, but you invited 'Sherri' to speak first, and she has. So it's your job to mirror back what you've heard."

"But I don't agree with her."

"It's not about agreeing or not, Tex," David said. "It's letting 'Sherri' know you heard what she said."

"But that just reinforces her view."

"Instead of trying something different, you're reverting back to how you usually respond to her. I ask you again, Tex, is that working for you?"

"Well, no, but I don't agree with what's she's saying."

"Mirroring back to the other person doesn't mean you agree with her; it's simply letting her know that she's been heard. So, try again."

"Well, I don't even remember what she said."

"Then ask her. It's hard to listen to someone else when you're upset and anxious to jump in and say what you're thinking or feeling."

"Okay. Sherri, what did you say to me?"

Alison's face grimaced momentarily, as if she were shaking off an angry response.

"When I open up to you, I feel like you take advantage of my vulnerability. Then I end up feeling hurt and angry."

"Good," said David. "Now take your time, Tex, and only tell Sherri what you heard."

Slowly, with a pause between each word, Tex said, "You feel that I hurt you when you open up to me."

Alison's eyes began to tear up. "I don't know why I'm crying. I'm not Sherri!" She wiped her eyes with the back of her hand and looked at David.

"Give it a shot, Alison. Use your feelings as if they were hers. Complete this sentence: 'Tex, I'm crying because…'"

"Tex, I'm crying because you heard that I felt unsafe with you, and you didn't attack me."

Tex looked puzzled.

"I don't get it. What'd I do to make her cry?"

"Just say back to her what you heard."

"Okay. You felt safe with me because I didn't attack you when you expressed your feelings."

"That's partly right, Tex. I…I felt safe with you because I let you know that I was vulnerable and you didn't hurt me. I feel unsafe when you hold that against me. It felt so much better when you let me know that you had heard me."

"Why would you feel unsafe? I've never laid a finger on you. You know I would never hit you after the way I grew up. It really burns me that you don't feel safe with me. You don't know what unsafe is! I am not my father, damn it."

"Tex, I never said you were."

David stopped her.

"Now it's your turn to tell Tex what you heard him say to you."

"But I feel falsely accused," Alison objected.

"I know. You'll get a chance to clear that up after you mirror back to Tex, just as he did to you."

"Tex, you felt hurt that I said I felt unsafe with you. You felt unsafe as a kid, and you'd never hurt me like your father hurt you."

"Damn straight! And I have never, ever, laid a finger on you, even when I was furious with you. Never." A barely perceptible tear appeared in the corner of Tex's eyes above his tightened jaw as a reddish hue spread across his face.

"You've never physically hurt me, even when you were very angry with me."

"That's right. But I get blamed for everything anyway, and never get any credit. That really hurts. I can't seem to do anything right."

"You feel blamed by me, and don't feel I give you credit for your good qualities."

Tex nodded.

Alison looked at Tex.

"I'm terribly sorry. You're right. I'm in so much pain that it's hard for me to see beyond it. Even when you're gentle and loving with me, I can't seem to let the love in. So it's as if you never treat me lovingly. And when I'm upset or angry, I really let you have it."

"Yeah, that's what it's like, and I hate it. I feel like a total failure with Sherri … I mean you, and I hate to fail."

"The truth is, I have more positive feelings for you than I show. I'm afraid you'll hurt me, so I go on the offensive. I wish I could just be honest with you and say how I really feel—the good and the bad. That way, you wouldn't think everything you do is wrong."

"I'd like that. I need to know you care about me."

"And I need that from you too, Tex."

As they came closer to reaching an understanding, David did not ask them to mirror each other any more. "Tex, Sherri, you're doing just great. When you're ready, say what you love so much about each other."

Tex shifted about on his pillow and appeared uncomfortable. Alison seemed to be searching for how Sherri might feel towards Tex.

Tex spoke first. "You go. I'm no good at this kind of thing."

Alison said to David, "I'm not sure how to do this."

"Just think about what you've experienced and learned about Tex this week, and imagine what attracts Sherri to him."

Then Alison smiled and turned confidently to Tex.

"I love how smart you are. You're knowledgeable about so many things. I see how loving you can be, particularly with your horses. So much so, that I find myself jealous of them from time to time. And when you're in a good mood, you have an incredibly wicked sense of humor. You make me laugh. You also have amazing energy." Alison paused, and then added, "Tex, my life is never boring with you."

Tex looked stunned.

"Let that sink in." David paused. "When you're ready, tell 'Sherri' what you love about her."

Tex took his time then cleared his throat. "You're brave. You're willing to try anything. You're really competent. It seems there's nothing you can't do. I love how you're so affectionate with me. I never know what you're going to say next. You're always surprising me."

Tex and Alison smiled at each other.

David waited a moment, then asked, "Does this feel complete for you, Tex?"

"Yes."

"Alison, is there anything else you would like to say as Sherri?"

"No. That was great!"

"Okay. What do you both take away from what just happened?"

"Am I done as Sherri, so I can answer as myself?" Alison asked David.

"Yes."

"You go first," she told Tex.

"It was good to hear nice things from Sherri, and I felt good saying nice things to her as well."

"Expressing to Tex what made me upset allowed me to get in touch with positive emotions towards him. I wasn't just stuck in the negative," Alison responded.

"Is there anything else either of you would like to say?" David asked.

"Tex, some of what you said hit home with my own marriage. Frankly, I was amazed at how much I felt like your wife!"

Tex smiled. "There were moments I forgot who I was talking to because you sounded so much like 'Sherri'. Thanks for helping me do this."

"Thanks, both of you," said David as he picked up his yellow pad. "We have three who asked to work, and time is short. So, if you have feedback, you can talk to Tex and Sherri after group." There were lots of smiles and Gil laughed out loud. "What's so funny?" David asked.

Diane clued David in. "You said Sherri instead of Alison."

"Ha!" David let out an explosive laugh. "Alison, you were obviously convincing in your role. Okay, who's next, Diane or Ronald?"

Diane looked surprised. "I'm not ready."

"Okay, Diane. How about taking up Ronald's issue, Gil?"

Gil was caught off guard and felt his anger rising. He was already overshadowed by David, and now David was giving him assignments.

With only a slight hesitation, Gil asked, "So, Ronald, who do you need to talk to?"

"Frank," said Ronald.

"Ask him if he's open to discussing this with you."

Ronald asked Frank, "Are you?"

"I don't know. Do we need to?"

"Frank, Ronald is asking if you are willing, not if you think it's necessary," Gil said a little more vehemently than he intended.

Frank raised his eyebrows. "Okay, I'm willing."

Rae gave Gil an appraising look.

"Good." Gil slid forward off his pillow and sat cross-legged in the center of the circle, patting his palm on the carpet in front of him. "Ronald and Frank—come here and sit facing each other."

Ronald pulled his pillow to the center. Frank crawled forward on his hands and knees and sat back on his heels.

"Ronald, now's your chance to talk to Frank."

Ronald looked at Gil. "When Diane and I were at dinner yesterday..."

Gil interrupted him. "Talk directly to Frank."

Ronald turned to Frank, "... Frank walked up."

"*You* walked up," said Gil.

Ronald frowned. "You walked up and asked if you could join us. But as you started to slide your leg over the bench, I said to you, 'Diane and I are having a private conversation.' You looked embarrassed and angry.

"After you left, Diane told me she had invited you and was concerned that I might have offended you. I felt guilty. I had no idea that Diane had asked you to join us. I feel awkward about it and I'm concerned you may be angry with me."

Ronald gave Gil a nod. "That's it."

Gil smiled briefly.

Rae watched Frank as he shifted on his pillow. Then she noticed Todd. He was lying back against the cushions and staring out the window, even as several others were leaning forward, intently focusing on Ronald and Frank.

Frank continued to shift his weight but remained silent.

Ronald looked uncomfortable. "You seem annoyed, Frank, and I'm concerned you're holding a grudge against me."

Frank glanced at Gil.

Frank said. "I want to tell Ronald not to worry about it."

"Reflect back to Ronald what you heard him say."

"You said you didn't want to be interrupted, and didn't know Diane had invited me. That's fine with me. The last thing I wanted was to butt in. I hate feeling awkward."

"Whoa, you need to slow down," Gil instructed Frank, "Just repeat what you heard and then ask if you missed anything."

"Did I get it right, Ronald?"

"Almost. I also said that you acted annoyed and that I was worried you were holding a grudge against me."

Frank asked Gil, "Why would I hold a grudge? It's no big deal."

"Just repeat what you heard."

"I seemed to be put out, and you thought I was mad at you."

Gil questioned Ronald, "Did he get it?"

"Yeah."

"Okay, Frank, now you can respond."

"I'm fine."

Gil murmured, "Hmmm."

Frank swiveled his head toward Gil, "What?"

"You say you're fine, but you sound annoyed."

"Well, yeah, I don't know how this whole thing got blown so far out of proportion. It's really no big deal."

"Apparently it's important enough for you to be annoyed about."

Frank shook his head. "I don't get it."

"Turn that into an 'I' statement, Frank, and talk to Ronald directly."

"I think what happened was nothing, and I don't know why you're making a big deal out of it."

"Keep looking at him and tell him exactly how you feel about it," said Gil.

"I feel like this is no big deal."

Gil kept his gaze on Frank. "That's a thought, not a feeling."

Frank frowned at Gil, then turned back to Ronald. "I feel you're making a big deal out of…"

Gil interrupted him. "Sad, mad, glad—those are feelings."

Frank raised his voice, "I feel sorry this whole thing even came up."

"Okay. Good. Now say that to Ronald."

Frank rolled his eyes. "I'm sorry this came up."

Gil looked at Ronald and nodded.

Ronald said, "You're annoyed that this got blown so far out of proportion. Did I get that right?"

"That's right." Frank smiled wearily.

Ronald continued, "I didn't mean to make a big deal out of it, but I did want to know where I stood with you. I like you, and would like to get to know you better."

Frank blushed slightly and glanced away for a moment, then at Ronald.

"I'd like that, too."

Gil smiled. "Do you need anything else?"

Ronald said, "No." Frank shook his head. Gil shuttled back to his pillow as they returned to their original places.

Gil scanned the circle and saw lots of smiling faces. The reduced tension was palpable. *Everyone now knows that differences and concerns will be respected and addressed. And they've seen how to do it.* Gil felt competent for the first time since he'd arrived two days ago.

He turned to Diane. "I want to check in with you now. Is this what you were hoping for?"

Before Diane could answer, David turned to Frank and asked, "You mentioned not wanting to feel awkward; would you like to say more about that?"

Diane looked confused. Gil frowned but said nothing.

Frank hesitated. "No, not really. I was just explaining why I left abruptly."

David nodded. "And..."

Gil said, "Frank, consider David's question and let us know if you find anything more that you'd like to explore. Right now, I'd like to hear from Diane."

Diane paused and seemed uncertain about what had just happened. She looked at Gil. "What were you asking me?"

"You asked to hear from Ronald. Is there anything else you want to say about that?"

Diane looked first at Ronald and then at Frank. "It meant a lot to me to see the two of you work it out. I'm not used to seeing that and it certainly wasn't how my family resolved things. But watching you, I realize that's what I want for myself and I want to be with someone who wants that as well."

The room was quiet.

Ronald's eyes glistened as he looked at Diane while Frank gave her a brief smile. Gil looked at the two of them and thought the contrast was telling. Ronald definitely had a crush on Diane.

After a few moments, Gil opened the floor for feedback. "Keep your comments only to how it was for you to witness Ronald and Frank. Please avoid advice or analysis."

Rae stepped in quickly, ignoring Gil's directions. "I want to acknowledge you both for sticking with it. It was difficult for you, Frank, to understand that even if the issue was not important for you, it was definitely important for Ronald. That's why he kept at it, and, to your credit, you were will-ing to keep going until he was satisfied."

A number of others shared, and when everyone was done, David looked at his watch. "There's an hour left, and we still have an exercise we want to get to."

Rae raised her eyebrows.

Gil sat up and cleared his throat. "Right now we still have work that's up."

David looked down at his sheet.

"Diane, would you be willing to wait until our next session?"

Diane seemed torn between disappointment and anxiety. "I can wait if I have to… I don't want to take up the time you have set aside for the exercise."

Rae put her hand on Diane's arm and whispered, "Sweetie, are you answering that way just for David's benefit?"

Diane burst into tears and nodded her head, then choked out in a child's voice, "I really don't want to wait. Why do I always have to wait?"

Gil sat bolt upright. Rae moved a little closer and spoke quietly to Diane. "That's right, you don't want to wait any longer, do you?"

Diane's tears poured forth again.

Rae continued. "Why don't you tell David what you do want?"

"I'm scared."

"Who are you afraid of?"

"David." Diane's voice trailed off into a whisper.

"How old are you right now, Diane?"

"Five. "

"You need the help of an adult right now, don't you?"

"Yes," Diane whispered.

"I invite you to ask your adult self to help. She isn't helpless the way your five-year-old was."

After a pause, Diane's eyes opened. She glanced around the circle and focused on Rae.

"You're right. My adult self can take care of this. I can speak up and protect myself. Nothing bad will happen."

"That's right. What could your adult self say to David that would be clear and satisfying to you?"

Diane's back straightened.

"David, I don't want to wait until after the planned exercise. I'd like to work on my piece right now."

David smiled broadly and congratulated Diane. "Of course. Thanks for being so clear."

A silence settled over the group. Diane looked thoughtful.

Todd cleared his throat.

"Well, you know, actually," Diane said slowly, "I think I just did the work I needed to do."

Whoops and cheers broke out around the room and a huge grin spread across Diane's face.

"I saw that I was safe with all of you, and I stood up for myself. Thanks!"

Gil looked around at the smiling faces and relaxed postures and sensed a big shift in energy. But Alison was fidgeting as if she were unable to share this moment with the others.

David glanced at his notes and then announced, "We have time for one more short piece of work. Who would like to go next?"

Alison raised her hand. "I don't want to."

David looked confused, uncertain how to take the conflicting signal. Gil smiled.

Alison addressed Diane. "I'd like to be more like you, the way you said what you thought just now." To Gil she said, "When I'm at an AA meeting, I notice myself wanting to sit in the back to avoid being called on, although I know I really need to walk up to the first row and sit right in front of the secretary. And when the time comes, I need to raise my hand and share."

Alison closed her eyes and paused for a second. "Shit. I hate looking at what I don't want to see. You all are being so fucking courageous and I'm sitting here thinking, 'I don't care what you all do; I'm not going there.' But I know I can't stay sober if I don't do the fucking work." She opened her eyes and stared straight at Gil. "I want to stay sober. I want it more than anything."

Gil gently nodded, both as recognition and encouragement.

Taking a deep breath, Alison continued, "So... here's what I saw when I talked with Tex this morning about his drinking, and what I felt when I was doing the writing assignment this afternoon.

"I'm angry."

David cocked his head to one side. "Angry at? Angry about?"

Gil kept his focus on Alison and spoke out quietly and precisely. "Not now, David." As Alison brought her attention back to him, Gil gave her a nod. "Please ignore David and continue."

David's eyebrows shot up, "What..."

Rae smiled at David. "I think Gil has this piece."

"I'm sober, but I'm not a happy camper." As if those were the magic words, Alison's face flushed and her words tumbled out. "I resent my husband and all his needs. I resent my family and their expectations—that I'm going to take care of everything, organize family gatherings, be the go-between in squabbles, solve everyone's problems and make everyone happy."

She paused as if considering what she had just said. Her eyes were tearing up. "I'm constantly putting my needs and feelings aside. I'm a person too!"

Gil could hear and see both the anger and the sadness.

Suddenly she faced Gil. "So what the hell do I do now?"

So it's anger, then, that's bothering you most, Gil thought. *The sadness will have to wait.* "You're working your program so let me ask you something. Do you want direct feedback?"

"I sure do."

"Okay, here goes…" Gil said to Rae and then to David, "Please add anything I miss."

"Alison, you're doing good work right now. You're on Step Ten, 'Continued to take personal inventory and, when we were wrong, promptly admitted it.' So even as you speak, you're working your program and shoring up your sobriety."

Alison's shoulders relaxed.

Gil took a breath while he held Alison's attention.

"You've been worried and upset about your marriage and your family, and now you're seeing the resentments you've been building, brick by brick, like a wall between you and them. What's obvious to others is often not obvious to us. So here's what I see… and this is really familiar to me. One, make a list of your resentments and deal with them. Look at your part, own that and make amends. Two, beyond that, what might not be obvious to you yet is that you need to be going to Al-Anon."

Alison's chin stuck out and her brow furrowed. "What the heck do you mean by that?" she asked somewhat belligerently. "Al-Anon is for the family, not the alcoholic."

Gil registered Alison's use of the word "heck" instead of the cursing she had used in describing her upset. Although the response was sharp, she seemed to be connecting with her resources.

"It happens to the best of us. Underneath our addiction is our codependence. As if it's really about them, not us. If only they would act differently, then I'd be better. That's what Al-Anon addresses."

Alison looked stunned, staring into Gil's eyes. Everyone waited.

Rae beamed her approval and tapped her wrist. Gil knew that meant they were running out of time. He had to close the session.

Gil cleared his throat.

"Alison, that's a lot to digest. And there's more to be examined. I'd like to invite you to sit with this over the break, and let's come back to revisit it in the next session."

Alison blinked, still dazed. "What?"

"We're out of time, and need to wrap this up."

"No, no, no. You're not leaving me here wondering what the fuck you just said."

"That's it. That's exactly the point!" Gil nearly shouted, smiling. "You're speaking up for yourself and stating what you need, instead of walking out of here harboring a resentment about how I cut you off and left you hanging."

"I am?"

"You are! You did exactly what you were admiring Diane for doing a moment ago."

Alison beamed right through her frown, as if a shaft of light had broken through the clouds of her confusion. "That was one of those Zen things, wasn't it?"

The whole room broke into laughter, and Alison joined in too, louder and louder, until she was laughing harder than anyone else.

AS THE GROUP FILED OUT of the room, David said to Rae, "I want to call Joann again. Can we debrief later?"

Rae peered over her half-frame glasses. "That's fine with me."

"Good." David turned to go.

"But you need to check with Gil."

David said over his shoulder on the way out, "Gil, is that okay with you?"

"What's that?"

"I need to make a call to Joann. Rae and I would like to meet after dinner."

Rae tilted her head quizzically at David, thinking, *That's an interesting representation.*

"That doesn't work for me," Gil replied.

"Well, how about if we meet at dinner and debrief?"

"No, I'd rather do it now."

"Listen, I'm late for my call home. You two figure out a time and Rae, you can fill me in at dinner. See you at 6:30," David said, walking out the door.

Gil looked at Rae. "What was that all about?"

"You need to ask David."

"I guess I will."

"So when do you want to meet?" asked Rae.

"I'd rather the two of us meet now. You can meet with David later. I've got other things to do tonight."

"I'm not going to do that. We all need to meet together. Besides, you and David have something to talk about."

Gil took that in. "We do, don't we? Okay, I'll meet you two in the lodge at 8 p.m."

"It will have to be brief. I'm really tired."

"Okay, I'll cut my hike short. Make it 7:30."

"Deal. Thank you." Rae picked up the readings and her notes and stood up. Gil walked over and held his arms wide. Rae joined him in a gentle embrace. "That was really good work today," she whispered in his ear.

"Thanks."

They separated. Gil looked into her eyes. "Where are you these days?"

"How do you mean?"

"I'm not sure. You've seemed withdrawn in group, and nowhere near as active as you usually are in setting the tone or leading the work."

"I don't feel the need to. You and David are doing a great job."

"No, we're not. We're stepping on each other's toes and tamping down our feelings. It's a distraction for the group. I miss the container you create for everything we're doing."

Rae was silent for a moment. "I need to think about that … maybe you're right." Rae sighed deeply as if she were releasing major tension. "I've been questioning my life with Alan lately. I'm wondering if I really want to continue in the marriage. I'm questioning if I'm in the right place anywhere in my life. I'm sorry if it's affecting my work."

"That's a lot. And it is affecting your participation, isn't it?"

Gil held Rae's shoulders and looked at her. It was as if he had never noticed that she was half a foot shorter. Suddenly, she seemed vulnerable and human. He wanted to protect her. For just a moment he was shocked at how capable and grown-up he felt.

RAE CARRIED her empty dinner dishes to the kitchen and walked out of the brightly lit lodge into the velvet black of a star-studded Big Sur night. Crossing the open grass, she looked up and caught her breath at the sheer scale of the vast sky. She teetered with vertigo for a second, closing her eyes to find her balance. Warmth inside her rose from the bottom of her abdomen to her chest, like a hot air balloon. *What was that?*

Taking a couple of deep breaths to clear her head, she began walking toward the phone booths. She noted how suddenly relaxed she felt about a call she'd been dreading to make all day.

All three phone booths were empty and dark. Rae opened the heavy wooden door of the center booth and sat down on the built-in bench. She always felt small in these booths, as if they were built for some larger species. She reached up to lift the receiver off its cradle.

Using her room-key flashlight to light up her calling card, she punched in the codes until she got a dial tone. When she reached home, Alan picked up right away.

"Hello, Alan Rabinowitz here."

Rae froze.

Alan repeated, "Hello?"

"Hi Alan, it's me. How are you?"

"Oh, it's you." Alan paused. "It's been a horrible day. My computer crashed. I missed an appointment. My stomach's killing me. My doctor's not returning my calls. I'm a wreck. And I'm dealing with this all by myself because you're away, teaching a workshop at some luxurious retreat center. When are you coming back?"

Rae's shoulders sagged as an overwhelming weariness swept over her. She suddenly felt twenty years older. "I'm sorry you're having such a hard time, Alan. I'll be back on Friday." *I'm not looking forward to coming back to you. Your life is absolutely joyless.*

"Three *more* days? Rae, I feel like I live alone. You've been gone twenty-three days in the last three months. I need you here! I feel abandoned, and I don't like you working so closely with those two men. You know that most affairs start with co-workers."

"Alan, David and Gil are good friends, not potential lovers. You know that. And I certainly can't, or at least I won't, leave in the middle of a workshop. Please get some rest. We'll talk more when I get home. I'm going to bed now. I'll see you on Friday."

"Rae, we need to talk about our relationship."

"Yes, Alan. But right now, I'm tired. And I'd rather not do this on the phone. Let's talk when I get home."

"I'm always last on your list."

"I'm sorry you feel that way, Alan. We'll talk when I get home. 'Night."

The connection had already gone dead. Alan had hung up on her.

Rae dragged herself up the hill to her room. The long tail of a shooting star blazed unacknowledged across the brilliant sky.

7

Wednesday Morning

RAE ENTERED THE LODGE FOR BREAKFAST, HER BODY tingling after a short, sweaty interlude with the thundering herd of dancers in the morning movement class. She filled her cereal bowl with granola and oats and turned around to see David hovering over the toaster.

Walking up behind him, Rae asked, "Afraid your toast is going to get away from you?"

David laughed. "A lot of suspicious characters are loitering around here. Someone stole my cinnamon toast yesterday while I was off getting orange juice. I'm not going to let that happen again. Why don't you grab us a table in the Solarium?"

Rae chose a table for two along the row of windows looking out on the deck and then made two trips back to the buffet. David was seated when she returned. As she sat down, he reached over, held her hands and offered the blessing in Hebrew. Rae closed her eyes and let the familiar sounds of the words wash over her, words that held no intelligible meaning, but like the deep tones of a Gregorian chant, put her in a meditative state. The sensation was pleasant at first, but started to become a little unnerving, as if the deep tones were echoing up through a bottomless space beneath her. She opened her eyes involuntarily.

David's eyes popped open. "What happened?"

"What do you mean?"

"Your hands were twitching, and you just looked startled."

"I don't know. I'm having an unusual morning." Rae sighed. "I talked to Alan last night."

"And?"

"Do you see me as cold and uncaring, David?"

"What?"

"Alan is so important to me, but when we have these run-ins, I just don't want to be around him. And then I feel like a hard-hearted bitch."

"Rae, you're not cold." David smiled. "And you're certainly not a bitch … at least most of the time."

Rae laughed.

"Listen, Alan's medical condition is difficult for both of you. He's probably really scared, and it sounds like you're trying to be present to him but it's not enough, he wants you there with him in person. Drop the guilt."

"So, I'm just a nice gal in a bad situation? It doesn't feel that way but I'll give it some thought. In the meantime, let's get to work. What are we going to have in our back pocket if no process work is up?"

"I'd like to do a new exercise," David replied. "It came to me in the tubs this morning. We'll have them write a letter from their child to their adult. Wouldn't that be the perfect follow-up to the Draw-A-Child exercise?"

"It would," Rae said with a wry look. "It worked well for us the last time we used it."

"I thought I just made it up."

"Nope. We used it last year." Rae looked at David with an appraising smile. "You're starting to lose it."

"Do you think so? I've been worried about words slipping my mind."

Her smile quickly faded when she saw the pain in his expression and remembered that his father had Alzheimer's. "It's a normal lapse," she said, quickly backpedaling. "My memory isn't as sharp as it used to be, and you're a lot older than me." She smiled.

David laughed. "Thanks a lot!"

"You know what I mean. Anyway, it's a good idea, and a great fit for this morning if no one has specific work. Afterwards, we could have them read their letter to one or two other group members."

David's eyes lit up. "I have an even better idea. We'll have them read their child's letter to their own reflection in a mirror. It'll be dynamite! The rest of the group can sit behind them, so that each person reading will see themselves in the mirror, surrounded by a whole group of loving people, a kind of Harry Potter effect."

Rae hesitated. "But we don't have a mirror."

Her lukewarm response was lost on David, who enthusiastically replied, "There's a mirror hanging in my room. I can bring it to the meeting."

Rae frowned. "I don't think that's a good idea. Anyway it won't be large enough to reflect much more than the person sitting in front of it."

"No problem, we can sit right behind him." He was beaming now, and Rae smiled at his excitement.

"Let's run it by Gil and see what he thinks," she said.

Five minutes later, Gil walked in and suggested they move to their usual corner in the main dining room, where they would have more privacy. No sooner had they gotten seated than David stood up again. "I'll be right back. I'm going to get another cinnamon toast. Does anyone need anything?"

"Yes, thank you." Rae handed David her empty mug. "I could use more hot water." Rae noticed Gil's wet hair and flushed face. "Were you swimming?"

"Yeah, I swam after my run."

Rae experienced a pang of guilt and admonished herself for sleeping in. *All I did this morning was a few minutes of movement.*

Reading Rae's expression, Gil smiled with feigned tolerance, and reached over to pat her shoulder, "Don't forget, Rae, I'm a lot younger than you."

She tickled him in the ribs and they both laughed.

David returned with the toast and water cup. He put on a stern face.

"Hey, don't be having fun without me." Then he broke into a smile. "What did I miss?"

"We just planned the rest of the workshop."

David sat down, grabbed Gil's plate and pulled it next to his own, smiling innocently.

"That's okay. I'll just spend my time in the hot tubs while you two do the work. That is, of course, after I eat your breakfast, Gil."

"That wasn't in our plan." Gil smiled.

Rae checked the clock on the wall. "Okay, guys, I want to leave for my room in fifteen minutes so I'll have time to brush my teeth. Let's get started."

David repeated his idea for the letter from the child. Gil didn't react or resist, but simply gave his support. Rae examined David's face to see if he showed any sign of the surprise she was feeling. Seeing none she wondered whether she had blown out of proportion Gil's insecurity about his role on the team and the tension between these two.

GIL SETTLED ON the pillow and looked around the familiar room. Everyone was present except Carmen and Diane. Just then they bounced across the deck, arm in arm, leaning their heads together conspiratorially and sharing a laugh as they took off their shoes at the sliding glass door. Carmen had been quiet all week, coming and going on her own. Gil was intrigued by the big change in her.

He watched as they arranged their cushions so they could sit together. Gil made a mental note to suggest a longer check-in. He was curious what had transpired, and hoped the two women would say something.

Gil picked up the Tibetan chimes.

"Let's start with our meditation." He took a slow, deep breath and brought the chimes together, allowing their pulsating ring to echo slowly until there was silence. He noted the time on his watch and closed his eyes.

"Just follow your breath in and out, in and out. When thoughts arise, return to your breath."

After eight minutes, Gil held the chimes up by their leather strap and brought them together. As everyone began to slowly open their eyes, Rae read the words of Alan Cohen.

When we are following our path, we are bound to rub some people the wrong way. Criticism and rejection are a healthy sign that you are doing something real and alive. If no one is upset with what you are doing, you are probably not expressing yourself fully. If you are not bumping up against some kind of reaction, reconsider your self-expression and find something to do that will bother someone. Then you will really be on your way!

If you would like a suggestion on how to start bothering people with your greatness, I would advise you to just start telling the truth more. The truth is the most threatening dynamic you could introduce into a world of guarded illusions. Many of our family interactions, careers and politics have been founded on protecting lies and keeping things appearing to be a way other than they are. Most people on the planet have a huge investment in keeping lies of some kind going, and anyone who jabs a hole in the wall of the castle of pretense makes the fortress of fear vulnerable. If you have been in a dysfunctional family, for example, you know that protection of the sickness was more important than bringing fear to the light. The truth scares the hell out of a dysfunctional relationship or family, and the first one to tell it is usually ostracized. But that's not a bad thing at all, when you consider that the alternative to telling the truth is to be alienated from yourself.

Do not be fooled by appearances. Behind our culture's obsession with fear and hiding there is a massive call for authentic self-expression. The most powerful gift of redemption you can offer a world that is sick with deception is to live in the dignity of your own truth.

Gil watched Carmen closely during the reading. Her eyes were slightly wider than usual and her posture more upright, yet there was still something of a deer in the headlights in her expression.

David looked around the circle.

"Let's check in. Please let us know if there's any unfinished business for you from last night, or anything you need to address."

Gil looked up.

"We want you to take a little more time this morning with your check-in. We're at the halfway point in our week together, and this would be a good time to look at where you are and what you need."

David cleared his throat and looked at Gil. "I'll start. I continue to be moved by your openness and deep level of work. I just can't stop smiling."

Rae carefully studied the room, as if taking the external temperature as well as her own before speaking. Her gaze lingered on Carmen. "When I look around this room, I feel bathed in love and so grateful to be here to do this work with you." She turned to her left. "Tex?"

"I'm feeling okay this morning. I had a talk with Sherri last night after group, and it went pretty well. Better than it's been in a long time. I'd say at this point, it's even money we make it down the home stretch."

Rae noticed several smiles around the room.

As Max started his check-in, Rae interrupted.

"Max, please wait just a minute. Tex, would you say a little bit about what you realized about your drinking after yesterday's session?"

"Well, I saw that I had broken my word. And that's not right. But I don't know what it means about my drinking. I know you three are all from AA, but I don't think it's for me."

Gil quickly said, "AA is not for everybody, Tex, and not all of us are members, but why don't you come to the meeting tonight and check it out?"

Tex didn't respond, and Rae signaled Max to continue.

"I want to applaud everyone who worked yesterday. Especially you, Diane. You showed great courage."

"Thanks, Max," Diane smiled. "I've felt so light since yesterday morning. I'm not sure how it happened, but I feel like I belong here now. Not just here at the workshop, but here on the planet."

Diane paused, as if considering whether to divulge more.

David did a quick assessment to make sure that Max was complete with his check-in, then gave Diane a nod.

"The best part of all is, I'm not judging myself all the time, like I usually do. I'm starting to see why I've been so depressed, and why it's been so difficult for me to be in a relationship."

Diane made eye contact with Carmen.

"Oh, and I made a new friend this morning."

Carmen blushed and looked down for a second, then back up at Diane and returned her smile.

After a long moment, Carmen turned back to the group and said, "I've been having a rough time, and feeling really bad about myself, but right now, I feel more a part of the group." Carmen smiled.

Rae noticed she looked more like her twenty-plus years just then and Rae wanted to hear more, but thought better of pushing Carmen so soon after she'd taken such a big step. Carmen was one of the last holdouts in the group and, although it was Wednesday, Rae felt sudden hope for Todd. She even imagined the group coalescing and soaring to new heights, once everyone had finally opened up. How was Todd taking this in? Rae couldn't read his enigmatic expression.

Then Carmen signaled Alison that she was done.

"Last night was a shocker for me. You telling me," Alison tilted her head toward Gil, "that I need Al-Anon took me by surprise. But the more I think about it, the more I can see how I need to fix everyone around me. I'm really uncomfortable if I'm with someone who's not happy. I called my AA sponsor and she thought Al-Anon would be a good idea. So I'll check it out."

"Good," said Gil. "The AA meeting tonight is an open meeting. You don't have to be an alcoholic to attend. Given the issues that are up for work in this group, I highly recommend it. Everyone is invited."

Alison sat very still, as if gathering herself. "I'm also a little tense and distracted. I'm holding onto an observation about a member of the group. I want some time later to bring it up because I want to be fully present for my own work."

David made a note on his yellow pad.

"Okay. We'll look at it with you."

Todd's check-in was brief.

"I'm here," he said. "Nothing else to say."

David and Rae exchanged a glance. Rae frowned. *What are we going to do with him?*

After the last check-ins, David said, "I'd like to touch base with Carmen and Alison. "When you checked in, Carmen, you said you were having a hard time, a 'rough time.' Would you be willing to say more about what's going on for you?"

Carmen gripped the side of her pillow.

"Um, I meant that I've been feeling bad about myself." She paused. "I haven't felt like I belong here, or that I have anything to add to the group. I guess I feel kind of useless, stupid even."

"Carmen, those are strong judgments and I imagine you must be uncomfortable." Carmen leaned forward to hear him as David continued in a low, gentle voice. "I know when I've felt that way, I've wanted to hide. I'm glad you told us."

Carmen's cheeks flushed as she averted her eyes.

David waited for her to say something more, but nothing came.

"Carmen, would you like to check out your inner reality with others' perspectives?"

"I guess so."

"All right. Would anyone like to tell Carmen what it's been like for you having her in the group?"

Diane put a hand on Carmen's arm. "You haven't said much but I'm glad you're here. I notice how you respond to what's going on in the group. Your face is so open, and your expression says a lot. I know we had some similar experiences growing up and I'd like to hear more about it."

"Thanks, Diane, but ..."

David interrupted her. "Carmen, just listen for now."

Diane continued. "That's it, really. I'm glad you're in this group."

Carmen blushed shyly.

"Anyone else have something to say to Carmen?"

Alison, Frank, Ronald and Max all spoke up. Each one had a slightly different appreciation, and as the feedback continued, tears moistened Carmen's eyes.

When Max was done and it was clear that neither Tex nor Todd had anything to add, David asked Carmen, "Is there anything you would like to say?"

Carmen sat still with a strained expression, as if David had put her on the spot.

"I don't know what to say. I don't understand this."

Then Carmen was crying. Not just sniffling, but full-on bawling. Through her mucous-choked convulsions came a strangled voice, younger, more desperate.

"My mom always said … that I wasn't worth the food I ate." Her tears gushed and she hung her head.

Rae quickly moved across the floor to sit by Carmen. Diane kept her hand on Carmen's arm, while Alison scooted over and made room. Rae kneeled, sitting back on her haunches, put an arm around Carmen's shoulder, and leaned in to whisper.

"Carmen, think about that little girl. Think about the picture you drew of yourself as a child." Rae waited a moment for her words to sink in. "Notice where you feel her in your body, and where you feel this sadness." Rae sped up her breath until she was matching Carmen. "Place your hand where you feel these feelings."

Carmen's left hand crept to her belly.

"That's right," Rae continued, "right there." She breathed quietly for a minute while Carmen held that spot. Rae leaned in, and her whisper softened. "Now listen to these words, and let yourself take them deep within this place your hand is covering."

Rae waited a few breaths, then continued.

"You have always been precious. You have always been valuable. Even when your mother couldn't see it, you were worthwhile and special. You are a precious little girl. Remember how little five is? Not even in school yet. So small."

Carmen bent over; her entire body shook as she sobbed.

Rae wrapped both arms around her and allowed Carmen to collapse sideways into her lap, then gently began to rock her, while Carmen cried herself out. The rest of the room was silent, except for the occasional sound of someone blowing their nose into a Kleenex.

Rae glanced around the room. She noticed the wet streaks on Ronald's face, and the brimming tears in Frank's eyes. Only Tex, who had a severe expression, and Todd remained dry-eyed.

As Carmen's tears slowed to a stop, Rae looked over at David.

"While Carmen and I sit here, let's have a go-round so each person can say how they're feeling and what came up for them during this work."

By the time they had gone halfway around the room, Carmen was sitting up and listening, her cheeks and forehead were smooth and her eyes bright. Rae sat next to her, gradually turning her attention back to the group. Her gaze settled on Tex, who looked stirred-up.

Tex's expression was something between annoyance and agitation, as if he couldn't get a grip on exactly how this was affecting him, but was pretty sure he didn't like it. When it was his turn to speak, he was typically short-winded.

"Your mother has no horse sense."

David tilted his head slightly, as if hoping Tex would elaborate. When nothing more came, David asked, "Tex, would you say a little more about what that phrase means to you and how you feel about it?"

"No, I'll stick with that."

David decided to move on. When the last person had spoken, David returned to Carmen. "Is there anything you want to say right now, Carmen?"

"No. I don't feel the need to say anything else."

"Okay, then, maybe this would be a good time to take a break."

Max and Alison immediately stood up and started towards the bathroom.

Carmen shot her hand into the air with a surprised look. "Oh, oh, I forgot to say thank you." She broke into a heart-melting smile.

Rae laughed and several others joined her. Carmen looked surprised, then shook her head with a wry grin.

When David stopped laughing, he stood up and raised his arms high.

"It's time for a stretch break." Rae and Gil stood up and soon, everyone had joined in. David invited everyone to share a different short stretch with the group. By the time they had gone around the circle, Max and Alison were back.

DAVID SAT DOWN and glanced at his yellow pad.

"Alison, you mentioned wanting to talk about something. This would be a good time."

Alison sat erect, her legs folded underneath her, and addressed David.

"I'm not sure where to begin. And as I said, I don't know how this fits with what Gil told me earlier about taking care of others."

"You said you wanted to say something to someone else in group. Why don't you start there?"

Gil held up his hand. "I'd like to take a minute with Alison first."

"Go ahead."

Gil leaned forward. "Alison, who does this issue involve?"

"It's about Tex."

"The thing to look at regarding codependency is whether this is really your issue, or whether you're trying to take care of or control someone else."

"Hmmm ... thanks, Gil. I think ... I think this is my issue, because I'm worried. I'm concerned about Tex."

"Well, go ahead and say what you need to say. I'll help you keep track of which side of the fence you're on."

"Thanks."

David asked, "Tex, are you willing to hear from Alison?"

"Yeah." Tex straightened slightly from his half-recumbent posture. "I owe her one."

"Alison," David continued, "just look over at Tex and see what comes up."

Alison watched Tex for what seemed like a long time and then said with a husky voice, "I'm worried about you, Tex."

"No need to worry about me, little miss, I can ..."

"Tex, just listen." David said, talking right over Tex's response. "Remember the work we've been doing with active listening. We'll have you paraphrase before you respond."

Alison cleared her throat and continued.

"Ever since you walked in the room the first night, I knew. I don't know how I knew, but I did. It was a hundred different things, probably—the way you walked in, stiff-legged and defiant, the way you held yourself erect, chin out, like you were daring someone to differ with you, the ruddy hue of your nose and cheeks, that slight odor of booze on your skin, or maybe simply because you remind me of the drinkers in my family. I don't know, really. All I know is I knew intuitively what I've come to know from your story. It takes one to know one, and I've sat where you're sitting."

Tex looked perplexed. Alison paused for several seconds.

"Tex, you're an alcoholic."

Tex bolted upright, turning red in the face. "That's bull-shit!"

David jerked up from his backrest, hands held up in front of him as if to physically restrain Tex.

"Hold on, Tex! You'll have a chance to respond. We need to slow it down. This is Alison's work, and right now she's speaking. Please finish, Alison."

"That's it, really. I've just been concerned and needed to say something."

"Okay, Tex, you know the drill. Just repeat back to Alison what you heard her say. It doesn't mean you agree, only that you heard her."

Tex's face became redder. "You have no right saying that to me, Alison. You don't even know me. And it's none of your business anyway. Plus, your own life's a mess…"

Rae reached over and placed her hand on Tex's knee. "Tex, take a breath!"

Tex was breathing rapidly, his chest visibly rising and falling. His eyes bored into Rae, and then into Alison.

Gil was sitting up straight, looking intently at Tex. David crawled over to Alison and was saying something quietly to her. She leaned into him as if grateful for the shelter from Tex's storm, but kept her eyes on Tex.

David scanned the room to see how others were responding. He noticed Carmen's wide eyes, her arms across her abdomen. He caught Gil's eye and signaled him to pay attention to Carmen.

Rae was staring intently at Tex. "Are you willing to try a simple technique to calm yourself down, Tex?"

Tex turned back to Rae and continued to glare, short breaths shooting out of his nostrils.

"I imagine you've felt this way before, probably with Sherri, and the result hasn't been what you really wanted. Would you like to learn a new way to control your reaction?"

Tex's eyebrows were raised and his breathing slowed down slightly as he continued to fix his eyes on Rae. She held his gaze.

"Okay."

"Fine. What I want you to do is close your eyes and picture in your mind the interaction you just had with Alison. Notice the sensation in your body. Use a feeling word or words to describe the sensation."

Tex closed his eyes for a few seconds, then opened them.

"I feel burned-up. I'm pissed."

"Good. Now I want you to close your eyes and picture something that represents being pissed."

"What do you mean?"

"Close your eyes... when you're feeling burned up, look and see what animal or object represents that feeling. Don't try to force it. Just let it come of its own accord."

Tex closed his eyes. Several moments passed, then he opened them.

"Got one?"

"Yeah, a polecat."

"Good. Now close your eyes and imagine the polecat growing bigger and bigger. Don't make it grow, just allow it to grow on its own. Let me know when it stops growing."

Tex closed his eyes again. After a long minute, he said, "It stopped."

"Okay. Now allow the animal to shrink smaller and smaller. Don't make it shrink; just allow it to shrink. When it stops shrinking, let me know."

Tex sat quietly with his eyes closed for a couple of minutes, then said in a quiet voice, "It's gone."

"How do you feel now?"

Tex opened his eyes, thought for a moment, then responded with a questioning look. "I don't feel so worked up anymore."

"And what about feeling pissed?"

"Gone. But I could get pissed real easy, just remembering."

"Fine. If you get angry, you know what you can do." Rae paused. "Notice no one had to do anything for you to calm down. Alison didn't have to apologize or take back her words. You did it on your own. And you can use this technique yourself anytime, anywhere. Once you start using this, it will help you in your marriage." She let that sink in. "Now are you available to hear from Alison?"

Tex looked over at Alison. As Alison met his gaze, Rae could see the glow in her eyes.

"Yeah."

"Okay, Alison, I want you to tell Tex what it was like for you to say what you said, hear Tex's reaction, and then watch him do that guided imagery."

"It was amazing. I was really scared when Tex..." Alison looked at Tex. "...when you started yelling. I might as well have been six years old. But I knew Rae and David were here and I felt protected."

Gil noticed that Tex had watched Alison intently. But he had a hard time reading Tex's expression. *Was it shock, dismay, sadness?*

"Would you like to say anything else to Tex?" Gil asked Alison.

"I don't know." Alison replied.

"He doesn't look so scary to me right now," Gil observed.

"No, he doesn't."

Rae saw that Tex's expression had changed from anger to concern. He looked much younger now.

Alison smiled at him.

He smiled back.

Alison let out a shriek. "His tooth is chipped."

Tex and the rest of the room burst into laughter. Alison and Rae joined in. A tear rolled down Tex's cheek as he laughed.

When the laughter subsided, Alison looked at Rae. "I'm finished."

"Okay. Take a look around the room. Just look into each person's eyes and then tell me what you see."

Alison moved apart from David and faced into the circle. She turned her head slowly as she gazed from person to person. When she got to Tex, she smiled again, her face open.

"What are you experiencing?" asked Rae.

"Love. Everyone cares about me, especially Tex."

"Take that into your heart," said Rae. "Anything else?"

"I like Tex. He's not scary now."

"Tell him that."

Alison looked over at Tex. "I'm not afraid of you now. I like you."

Tex blushed.

Alison smiled.

Rae asked, "Are you willing to hear from Tex what that was like for him?"

Alison nodded.

"Tell Alison what that was like for you, Tex, from your heart," Rae instructed.

"I'm not sure what to say."

"Start with what you're feeling right now as you look at Alison."

"I feel like Alison is ..."

"Keep the focus on yourself."

"I don't know what to say. You looked just like a little girl for a moment." Tex paused. "I felt bad that you were frightened of me. I guess I came on a little strong. Maybe that's what happens with Sherri when I lose my temper."

Rae held her breath.

Tex's back stiffened. "But I still don't like being called an alcoholic."

Rae turned to Alison. "Your six-year-old self is in good hands. I can see your dedication to your recovery and your fearlessness in confronting alcoholism wherever you think you find it. You walked your boundaries with Tex, and kept to your side of the fence."

Rae said, "Tex, I'm proud of the work you did. I can see it was a big stretch for you." Rae let that sink in. "And I'd be remiss if I didn't point out you have a ways to go with your denial around alcohol."

Tex's eyes narrowed, but he didn't say anything.

"Is there anything else you'd like to say?"

Tex shook his head.

Rae scanned the group, and then said to David, "I'm thinking that this would be a good time to introduce the letter-from-the-child exercise."

"Tex." Gil's voice rang out from the far side of the room. "It doesn't matter whether Alison, or anyone else in this room, thinks you're an alcoholic. When it comes to the question of you and alcoholism, there is only one person whose opinion really matters." Gil waited a beat. "That's you."

A look of surprise appeared on Tex's face.

"I'm an alcoholic and a lot of your behavior reminds me of myself." Gil's voice lowered to a conversational level but kept its intensity. "You are certainly at risk for alcoholism but I have to tell you straight up, I really can't know the answer for you, and even if I did, it wouldn't matter. My opinion, Alison's opinion or anyone else's, right or wrong, is of no consequence. You have to decide for yourself."

Tex remained quiet and listened.

"The question is: are you satisfied with how drinking affects your life? If you are, then it doesn't matter what we think. There is a solution for alcoholism, but it isn't for those who *need* it, it's for those who *want* it."

Tex appeared to take this in but his jaw was still tight. "I'll think about what you said."

Laying back on his pillow next to Gil, Todd started talking as if addressing no one in particular. "I didn't expect to spend so much time on addiction. The workshop description barely mentioned it. I'm wondering when we're going to get to the other stuff. You know, what we came here for."

Todd turned to look out the windows at the ocean. As an afterthought, he turned back towards the group. "I'm sure it was useful for Tex anyway."

A chill settled over the room. Gil looked at Rae, whose face was blank. He thought he saw a twinge of annoyance before she looked at her watch.

"We have an hour and fifteen minutes left." She turned to David. "Do you want to introduce the exercise?"

Gil couldn't believe it. *She was ignoring Todd's bombshell of a comment.* Todd's words had landed like a slap in the face, and Gil imagined they sent a chill through the group. *We can't let something like that slide.* He looked to David for some sort of response.

Appearing to follow Rae's lead, David picked up his notes and started on the instructions. "You are going to write a letter from your child-self to your adult-self. Write with your non-dominant hand, and say whatever comes to mind. You'll have fifteen minutes to write, then I'll call time and ask you to pair up."

Rae went over to the bookshelf, got a pile of drawing paper and a bucket of crayons and markers, and placed them in the middle of the room. "Before you get started, find your drawing of your child and lay it out in front of you."

Rae paused until the papers stopped rustling and everyone was back on their cushions. "Reconnect with your child. Close your eyes … that's good. Imagine yourself in the special place where you met your child in the guided imagery. Get in touch with your tender, younger self."

"When you're ready, take a crayon or magic marker in your non-dominant hand, that is, your left hand if you're right-handed and vice versa. Write to your adult self about your feelings and what you need from him or her. Write whatever your child needs to say, and trust that the adult will hear and pay attention."

Gil, who wondered if he was the only one concerned about Todd's outburst, caught Rae's eye, frowned and tilted his head questioningly. She shook her head and turned away.

As several people began writing, Gil noticed that Todd, Tex and Carmen hadn't started.

Finally, Tex leaned forward, got his paper and pulled a short, stubby pencil from his pocket. He licked the tip and began to make small awkward strokes on the page. Todd sighed heavily, opened his notebook and pulled a pen from his belt pouch.

Carmen sat silent, almost frozen. Gil walked over to her and sat down. "Carmen, you seem stuck. What's going on?"

Carmen didn't look at him. She opened her mouth, then closed it and opened it again. "It … it was Tex and Alison. When the yelling started, it was just like being back home with my mother and father. I got scared. I'm still shaking."

Gil saw the slight tremor as she held out her right hand.

"I forgot how scary it was for me when Mom got mean and called Dad names."

"Thanks for telling me. I want you to bring it up in group. You need to talk about this."

Carmen nodded. Gil reached behind him and handed her a sheet of paper and a crayon.

"Maybe there's something your younger self wants to say."

Still looking dazed, Carmen put the paper in front of her. Leaning forward on her right elbow, she held the crayon in her left hand, hovering above the page. By the time Gil was back on his pillow, she was frowning with concentration, scrawling away.

David kept one eye on the clock. When time was up, he looked up from his notes.

"All right, everyone. Please wrap up and sign your letter with the name you were called as a child."

Rae put her reading glasses down and looked around the circle. "Next, we're going to read the letters out loud, one at a time, in front of a mirror. Imagine being the child and reading it to your adult self in the mirror. We may not get to everyone in this session, and if we don't, we'll finish this afternoon. Any questions?"

The group was silent.

"Okay, who wants to go first?"

Max responded, "I will."

David said, "Great. Please come to the pillow in the center of the room. Gil, will you get the mirror and hold it up for Max?"

Gil resisted the urge to say no and pushed down his annoyance as he fetched the mirror and put it in front of Max.

"That's good Gil, just hold it right there. Max, I want you to be the child who wrote the letter and I want you to read it to the adult Max you see reflected in the mirror."

Gil didn't like David giving him orders but going along with it in the first place made it awkward to address now. He would not only be interrupting David, but he would also be cutting Max off. And he knew from experience that anything he said would likely reveal his resentment.

Ronald and Frank were still writing and Todd was thumbing through a notebook on his lap. Diane and Carmen were whispering to each other. Diane gently touched Carmen on the shoulder.

"Thanks for giving Max your full attention," said David. "Max, are you ready?"

Max settled himself, and then began reading.

> Dear Big Max,
> I'm afraid to talk to Mom. I hear her talk
> about all the dead people. I'm trying to be
> good, but I'm scared. Maybe I'll die too.
> I have to be grown up. I'm sad. I need you to
> play with me. I never get to play. Everything
> is so serious. Mom is sad. Dad works all the
> time. I'm lonely. Spend time with me. Please.
> Maxie

When Max finished, Rae handed him a tissue. He blew his nose. Then there was silence.

"Max, would you like to say what that was like for you?"

He was quiet for a few seconds. "I'm grateful for what the child has told me. All my fears of aging and deteriorating ... well, I think it's because I never got to have a childhood ... all the losses. I really want to find a way to be there for him ... for me."

Max blew his nose again.

"I'm finished. I don't need to keep talking so that I feel heard. I've said what I feel, and that's plenty. Thank you all."

Rae was startled by Max's insightful connection between his childhood losses and his adult anxieties. *Bright man.*

"Would you be open to hearing what it was like for others to listen to your letter?"

"Yes."

Everyone chimed in except Todd and Tex.

The usual suspects. Gil watched as Max looked at them expectantly. Tex held Max's gaze, softening his expression and giving a small nod of the head, while Todd looked away.

"Is there any other feedback?" Rae waited for a few more moments, then thanked Max.

Max was back on his cushion but before Rae could invite the next person, Diane raised her hand and said, "Can I go now?" She seemed to be trembling.

David held out a hand towards the center of the room. "Yes, of course, Diane."

Diane scooted across the floor, dragging her letter with her and settled onto the pillow. She faced the mirror, sat for a moment looking at herself, then reached for a tissue and wiped her eyes.

"Okay." She began to read.

Dear Diane,
I'm scared a lot. When I do something
wrong, I don't want anyone to know. I'm afraid
someone is going to get mad at me and hurt me,
like Daddy. Please don't leave me anymore.
Tell me you'll stay with me. It helps a lot when
you talk to me and tell me no one is going to
hurt me. I want you to protect me.
Dee Dee

Diane seemed oblivious to the tears coursing down her face and the mucous running from her nose.

Looking around the room, Rae observed tears in others' eyes, including David's and Gil's. Rae also found the little girl's pleas plaintive and compelling, and felt annoyed when she caught Todd looking at his watch. Rae was aware of heat rising in her cheeks. She gathered herself together before speaking.

"Diane, is it all right if I come sit next to you?" Rae asked.

Diane nodded, focused on the floor in front of her. Rae slid off the cushion and rested her hand on Diane's shoulder. "How are you doing?" Diane dropped her head onto Rae's shoulder and Rae's arms encircled her.

Gil watched as David put on a sad face and placed his hand on his chest before shuffling over to put his arms around both Rae and Diane. *What is he doing?*

David looked up at the others in the circle and vigorously waved them over with his right hand before dropping his head onto Diane's back and resuming his expression of empathetic sadness. Everyone looked at each other, but no one moved. Gil expected Rae to speak up at any moment and tell David to go back to his cushion.

Carmen looked at Alison, who shrugged her shoulders, then over at Max, who nodded encouragingly and rolled off his pillow to crawl towards Diane, David and Rae. Max threw his arms around David and Diane, and was quickly joined by Carmen. Then Alison and Ronald rose as one and became part of the growing pile of people in the middle of the room. Frank and Tex were the last to join, leaving only Gil and Todd.

Gil surrendered. Much against his better judgment, he joined the group hug, praying it would be short-lived.

Rae lifted her head. "This is the time to offer Dee Dee words of love and encouragement. No feedback, just the simple messages a caring parent would send a small child. When you're moved to speak, speak softly."

Rae spoke next to Diane's ear.

"You're safe now. You've been very brave."

David closed his eyes as he squeezed Rae and Diane.

"You're precious. So important to me. I'll protect you."

Carmen spoke in a whisper.

"I feel so much for you. I feel really sad right now."

"Diane, I mean Dee Dee," Frank added, "I'm really impressed with what you wrote."

Gil winced again. This whole piece was really off-target. He blamed David for starting it. He knew he should say something, but he was afraid that would just make matters worse.

From the center of the crush of people, Rae's voice broke out softly and firmly. "Just tell Dee Dee what your own child would want to hear."

The deep resonance of Max's baritone rode over Rae's last words. "You are my special little girl. I'll always be here for you. You're perfect just the way you are. I'm so glad you're here." Diane broke into a fresh cascade of sobs.

Gil looked up and saw tears on Carmen's cheeks. It seemed like everyone was crying now. Rae slowly began to softly hum a nursery rhyme and the others joined in.

Gil was bewildered. *What's going on here?*

After the nursery rhyme was over, the group was quiet for a minute; then people started returning to their cushions. When only Rae was left, she asked Diane if she was open to feedback.

Diane nodded, and Rae sat up, looking around the circle.

Almost everyone had something to say. The feedback was emotional, yet no one offered advice. Rae watched the lone holdout, Todd. He had moved further back into the corner. Rae tried to catch Todd's attention but he kept staring at the ceiling.

"What about you, Todd? Do you have anything to say?"

Todd leveled his gaze at Rae and re-crossed his outstretched legs. "No, I don't."

Noting Todd's lack of expression and nonchalant tone, Rae gave an involuntary shake of her head, then took in a slow breath and released it.

"Who would like to read next?" David asked.

Ronald raised his hand. "I'll go." He got up and walked to the center of the room and sat on the pillow in front of the mirror holding his letter. "Dear Ronald..."

Rae looked at her watch. "Ronald, sorry, I see it's 12:20. Rather than start your letter, I'd like to allow a little more time for one go-round before we break for lunch."

Ronald looked surprised. "What?"

"Don't you think we should discuss this?" David gave Rae a look over his wire-rimmed glasses.

"No." Rae kept a straight face.

"Oh, foolish me, I must have been thinking of that other workshop, where there were three co-leaders." David matched Rae's serious look for a moment, then broke into a chuckle. Rae laughed out loud and Gil joined in. Soon all three were beside themselves with laughter. The group exchanged glances but remained silent. Ronald was still sitting in the center of the circle.

Then as quickly as the hilarity began, it passed.

Gil let out a long sigh and wiped his eyes. "I think I needed that." He chuckled and looked over at Rae, who was wiping her eyes as well.

David had already regained his composure and was beaming at others around the room. As Gil followed David's example, and looked at the faces around them he quickly stopped smiling. Frank looked anxious. Diane and Carmen seemed puzzled. Max was smiling indulgently, and Todd looked bored. Others were inscrutable.

Rae was still grinning. "I love that you two make it possible for me to laugh like that. We have something really special."

Gil noted that Rae was unaffected by the blank stares around her. He wasn't sure what to do about it. He carried the mirror to the side of the room and leaned it against a wall. Ronald went back to his seat.

David glanced at his timer. "We only have a few minutes left, and we'd like to hear a brief word from everyone before we break. He turned to Ronald, who was now on

David's left. "Ronald, sorry for the false start. Why don't you begin and then we'll go around the room."

Ronald's face revealed a mix of hurt and annoyance.

"I'll pass," he said as he looked over at Frank, on his right.

Frank said, "I feel uncomfortable and confused."

Gil said, "Uncertain."

Todd spoke up, not looking at anyone in particular. "I can see that at least the leaders are getting something out of this workshop." He left his words hanging above the group like a ton of bricks on a trip wire. Then, with a bored expression, he turned to Alison. "Your turn."

Alison took a breath. "I'm concerned about Ronald. You cut him off, then ignored him. If there was some lesson for me in what just happened, I'm not sure what it is. I feel a little left out."

Carmen looked at Alison twice to make sure she was finished. "That made me nervous. I was really glad I had Diane sitting next to me."

"I'd like to be able to laugh like that." Diane smiled and looked at Max.

Max was grinning broadly. "That was fantastic. The real thing. Isn't that the point of life anyway: to find humor and joy where you can? I feel alive."

Tex was quiet for several seconds before looking directly at David. "You put Rae in her place with humor and without getting angry. Gives me something to think about."

Rae sat back against her backrest. "I feel blessed."

She paused for a moment, then picked up a sheet of paper and read her favorite quote out loud to the group. It's counterintuitive message led them from fear of not being enough to fear of being too much. From purposefully concealing our gifts so as not to offend others to giving all of who we are so that others might feel free to do the same. She finished and put down the sheet of paper. Looking confidently around the circle she said, "By Nelson Mandela."

"Marianne Williamson actually, and aren't you forgetting something?" David raised his eyebrows and looked at Rae expectantly.

Rae frowned. "It's definitely Nelson Mandela, and what is it you think I've forgotten?"

Diane interjected, "David hasn't checked in yet."

"Oh," Rae smiled apologetically, "David, please go ahead."

David nodded an acknowledgement to Rae. "It's a common mistake. Nelson Mandela quoted Marianne Williamson and it's been misattributed ever since." He paused. "And as for my check-in, I'm really enjoying myself." He looked around the room, smiling at everyone. "Ronald, you'll be first up in the afternoon session. Everyone please take special care of yourselves until then."

Ronald joined hands with him, and soon the entire circle was holding hands.

Gil suspected a lack of enthusiasm in the group's response. Tex seemed uncomfortable and disgruntled. Todd rolled his eyes.

Gil looked back with concern at Rae and David. Rae's eyes were closed and her face was slightly upturned, as if she were swept up in some kind of spiritual bliss. David was still beaming around the room, as if basking in everyone's good will.

For a horrifying moment, Gil had the impression David was about to raise his arms in exaltation. Gil knew from experience this could easily lead to David standing, arms raised, charging into the center of the room, expecting everyone to meet him there.

Thankfully the moment passed. David stayed seated, ending with a simple squeeze with both hands. Gil watched as the squeezes passed halfway around the circle and then died.

David released his grip. "We'll see you at four."

Gil thought David looked extremely satisfied with himself as the group broke up. People gathered their things and wordlessly walked towards the door.

On a sudden impulse, Gil found himself announcing in a loud voice, "I'm going for a hike this afternoon if anyone wants to join me."

He felt a twinge of anxiety. *I didn't check it out with Rae and David first.*

Alison and Frank turned around at the door and both said, "I'll go."

Ronald looked up from where he sat talking to Diane. "I'd like to go too." He turned to Diane. "Why don't you come along?"

"Thanks, Ronald. I'll pass. I'm going to take some time for myself."

Gil felt a stutter in his excitement. He was concerned Ronald wouldn't be up to the pace he planned to set. The last thing Gil wanted was to be babysitting someone on a truncated version of the hike he had in mind, while the siren song of the high ridge went unanswered.

Gil decided to warn him. "The topography around here is steep, so no matter which trail we take, it will be straight up followed by straight down."

Ronald looked worried.

Gil imagined Ronald might feel embarrassed to admit he couldn't do it, with Diane listening.

"If you want to come, we'll go out and back on the same trail. You can go at your own pace and if we get ahead of you, we'll just pick you up on the return."

Ronald smiled in relief. "I'm in." He stood up and joined Frank and Alison, as Gil told them where to meet and what to bring.

"We won't have time to eat, so put something in your pocket to eat on the trail. Bring water, sunscreen and a hat, and I'll pick you up in front of the lodge at one o'clock."

GIL STOOD at the foot of the bed, bouncing on the balls of his feet.

"What's with the bouncing?" asked David.

"Do you need to use the bathroom?" Rae asked, keeping a straight face.

Gil smiled. "I'm in a hurry. I'm picking up the hikers shortly."

David frowned. "What were you thinking, organizing an activity outside of group without us talking about it first? It's not appropriate. We never meet with group members outside of session."

"I've done it before and you never objected."

"You were a participant then, and what you did was your own business. It's different now."

David turned to Rae. "I think he should call it off."

Rae took in David's concern.

"I don't know. You played tennis with a group member a few years back. That didn't bother me, and this doesn't either."

"That was different. I arranged it on the side and didn't announce it in group or make it available to anyone who wanted to join, as if it were a group activity."

"No, but you did spend an hour driving to Monterey, an hour on the courts and another hour driving back with her. I would say that raises the same issue." Rae paused. "Anyway, I didn't object then, and I don't object now. As far as I'm concerned, we can meet outside of the sessions as long as we let the group know what we're doing."

"What happened to role clarity and group cohesion?"

Rae smiled. "I'm more relaxed about all that than I used to be."

David gave one laughing snort he couldn't hold back, despite his serious expression. The boldness of Rae's inconsistency was irresistible.

"I love that you don't feel held back by either ethics or precedent." His smile broke through and broadened.

"Well, now that we have that settled, I'll be on my way," said Gil.

"Whoa, hold your horses." David looked serious again.

"Yeah," Rae added. "Before you go, let's set a time to meet before the afternoon session."

"I may not be back in time, so let's decide right now who's doing what." Gil added, "I'll do the meditation."

Rae said, "I'll do the poem, and David, how about if you do the check-in?" She waited for David's nod, then continued. "We'll finish the letters from the child. Several people still need to go."

Gil was ready to spin on his heels and march out when Rae stopped him. "By the way, did either of you notice Todd's disengagement?"

"I'd have to be seriously checked-out," David chuckled, "to miss that elephant in the room."

"What's he doing here, anyway?" There was a sharp edge to Gil's tone. "He floats on some personal cloud a thousand feet above the group, dropping explosive comments at random intervals. His comments this last session were typical. And frankly, I was shocked that you completely ignored him."

Rae's face pinched as if she'd just bitten into something bitter.

"I'm irritated with his judgments and complaints, and I'm having a hard time engaging with him. I don't want to keep inviting him to work, only to be reminded one more time that we aren't doing it right. Unfortunately, he reminds me of Alan." She looked at both of them. "I need you two to step in."

"Why hide your feelings? It might be good for him to know." The corners of David's mouth started upwards toward a grin. "Weren't you the one who said she wanted to be her true, authentic self all week?"

"You're right. I'll look for a way to address his comments. And let's all look for ways to connect with him."

They broke up the meeting. Gil walked to the bedroom door. But he stopped, his hand on the doorknob.

"We need to talk about what happened at the end of the session."

"Talk about what?" asked David.

"You couldn't have missed the fact that the group didn't relate to our hysterics."

"You mean they couldn't grasp our subtle wit and crazy wisdom?" David grinned playfully.

"All I know is, something happened in the room that I haven't sensed before."

David kept a wry look.

Rae dropped her smile. "I'm sure they'll bring it up if it's important."

"I'm not so sure," Gil responded. "They may think it's crossing the line to comment on the behavior of the workshop leaders."

"Don't worry about it, Gil," David said. "Everything gets processed eventually."

Gil wasn't reassured, but he was running out of time.

"I'll see you in group." Without waiting for a response, he stepped out and closed the door behind him, crossed the meeting room to the stone hallway and pulled on his running shoes. As he laced them up, he felt a small elation rising through the cold mist of his concerns. He was really looking forward to the hike.

8

Wednesday Midday

T EN MINUTES LATER, GIL WAS PULLING HIS SUV UP to the front of the lodge, a sandwich in his pocket and a full water bottle on the passenger seat. Alison was already waiting, sitting on the low stone wall at the edge of the drive. Gil took in her bright turquoise-and-blue Lycra pants, the tight-fitting halter-top, a dark blue windbreaker and her water bottle on the wall beside her. He couldn't help but notice how the running gear accentuated the smooth lines of her well-toned body. He felt an involuntary stirring in his loins as he set the brake and moved his water bottle to the floor. Alison opened the door and dropped into the front seat next to him.

"Frank just went to his room to get his hat, so he should be back in a minute." Alison was all business. Gil liked that about her.

Gil glanced at his watch, ignoring his impulse to say something playful or provocative, then looked up to see Frank crossing the oval lawn, carrying a daypack. Gil hopped out to open up the back. Frank threw his pack in just as Ronald walked up, slurping a bowl of soup.

Gil raised his eyebrows as the soup slopped over the side of Ronald's bowl. Gil held back from saying something, then turned and slammed down the hatchback with a little more force than he intended. "We're all here. Let's go."

Behind the wheel and heading north on Highway One, Gil relaxed.

"Put something under that bowl, Ronald, or you're going to be wearing that soup, and who knows what predators you may attract," Gil said with a straight face, keeping his eyes on the road. Ronald laughed uncertainly, but quickly unfolded his napkin onto his lap.

Now the only thing left to do was pick the trail. Gil had one in mind, but he wanted everyone to share in the choice, so he started laying out the options. "There are really only three good trails that are close enough." As they drove by Pfeiffer Burns State Park, Gil pointed out the closure sign. "That's a really nice loop, but it's been closed since the fire. So our choice is down to Tin House Road or Separation Ridge. Both are steep up-and-back climbs. Both offer views. Tin House is shorter and partially wooded. But today I'm drawn to Separation Ridge. It's open, sunny and a longer climb. What do you say?"

He turned to Alison and then glanced at Ronald and Frank in the rearview mirror. No one said anything.

Ronald asked, "Are they both the same difficulty? I'd really like an easier trail."

"Yeah, they're basically the same. Separation Ridge is longer, but either way, you can go at your own pace and we'll pick you up on the way down. What do you think?"

Again there was an awkward silence. Gil realized they had no way of knowing and they'd probably rather have him decide.

Finally Frank spoke up.

"Why don't we do Separation Ridge?"

"Great." Gil broke into a grin.

They drove by the Tin House Road on the right and Vista Point on the left. In another five minutes, they were at the old sheep loader that marked the beginning of the route up Separation Ridge. Gil pulled over and parked.

Gil scanned the signs posted on the old wooden fence. They warned of ticks and mountain lions, but the closure signs were gone. Gil's tension dropped a notch. The group walked around the closed gate through an opening in the fence where the weathered planks had come loose. Once on the other side, Gil led them up the dirt road.

Frank moved up beside Gil. "I've been wondering about your choice to stop drinking. You seem pretty normal to me, and I'm curious why you did that."

"I hear you, Frank," Gil responded. "But I need to watch out for something before I can give that question the attention it deserves."

Gil surveyed the road ahead. It had been graded since his last walk here, and the thick Kikuyu grass and poison oak that had choked the trail were gone. But he wondered about last year's bee's nest just beyond the first bend, fifty yards ahead.

Maybe they've moved on. He hoped so.

Gil turned around to Alison and Ronald. "When we get around this bend, walk quietly along the outside edge of the road. There used to be an active bee colony halfway up the side of that road cut." Gil pointed to the sheer face on the uphill side of the road.

Then he saw it, a large crack in the rock with a constant stream of bees shooting in and out. He fixed his gaze straight ahead and pushed on through them, wondering whether his EpiPen was still buried somewhere in the back of the SUV. His reactions to stings were getting worse, but he had never had to use it.

Everyone passed by the hive safely. The grade ahead got steeper, and they all started digging into the climb. Ronald quickly fell behind. Frank and Alison matched pace with Gil, and the three of them moved in a tight pack through several turns as the dirt road snaked up the open grass slopes of the lower ridge. Gil's long legs outpaced his breath and he sucked in and blew out deep draughts of air as they pushed up the hill. The strong urge for more oxygen didn't ease up. Gil knew from experience that his breath would catch up eventually as his heart and lungs settled into a strong, easy rhythm. He gave some thought to Frank's question.

Gil picked his words carefully. The demand for oxygen limited him to five- and ten-word bursts between breaths.

"I stopped drinking in this same workshop almost four years ago." Gil let that sink in as he inhaled three quick breaths. "I found something I'd lost long ago, drowned in an ocean of drugs and alcohol. I found who I really was."

Gil knew his sentences were being clipped by deep gulps of air, but did his best to make his speech sound effortless.

"My whole emotional and spiritual experience shifted ... and I knew that drinking again would undo it."

They topped the first buttress of the ridge and the grade eased. At the end of a short straight stretch, they came to a hairpin turn and a second road veering off to the right. It was less traveled and had a cable across it. "Let's wait here." Gil didn't want to take any chances with Ronald. If Ronald took the wrong fork, who knew when or if they would find him again.

Even though they had only been walking for twenty minutes, it took Ronald ten more minutes to catch up. Gil saw that waiting for Ronald at each fork would reduce their speed and steal most of the walk's aerobic benefit. They'd never make the summit.

As Ronald puffed his way up to them, Gil decided to cut him loose.

"Just stay on this main road all the way. There's only one more juncture you're likely to reach. It's in a stand of oaks and bears off downhill to the left. If you stay right and keep climbing you'll be fine. If you're ever in doubt about which way to go, just stop where you are and wait for us to pick you up on the way back down."

Ronald nodded as he leaned on the gatepost and caught his breath.

Gil could see Ronald was a little uncomfortable being left on his own.

"Don't worry. We'll be back down in an hour or so."

Then Gil turned and started up the road. Alison and Frank followed him and Gil took up his story where he'd left off. "I had a hard time re-entering my old life after that workshop," he told Frank. "I still went out with my drinking buddies, frequented old haunts, and ordered beer just to avoid raising any eyebrows, even though I had no intention of drinking it. I didn't know how to explain my sudden sobriety, nor did I really want to talk about it."

The road got steeper still. Gil found himself speaking in shorter sentences as his breathing became labored. "I started going to AA meetings and making friends with the people I met there." Gil paused. "We shared something that was important to me … I felt free and hopeful … everything else in my life took a back seat."

Gil looked over to see how his words were landing. Alison was a couple of paces back and gave him a smile of recognition. Frank was behind her, breathing hard and staring at the back of her heels as if concentrating on keeping up.

Within another fifteen minutes of climbing, all conversation had ceased. The effort was taking its toll. Still, Gil was impressed with both of them. It takes a certain competitive spirit and level of fitness to maintain a fast pace up this slope. Anyone with a strong body could put out the effort for a quarter-mile, but to keep it up for an hour required fitness.

Gil expected that Alison would be fit, but Frank surprised him. He was seeing a side of Frank he hadn't appreciated before. He was much tougher than he let on. To stay ahead of them, Gil would need to concentrate on his push, bringing it right up to that fine line between a sustainable effort and oxygen debt.

He felt the impact of his sedentary lifestyle. Too many hours sitting in class, in meetings, in clubs, and at his desk. As a grad student in Forestry Summer Camp, he'd have left both of them far behind, with strength and oxygen to spare. Today he had to rely instead on his familiarity with discomfort and his knowledge of what lay ahead. The other two had to labor on, not knowing how long this climb would go on or how much energy to save for later.

He smiled at his competitiveness.

They passed briefly under the eaves of the oak woodland that spilled up and over the edge of the ridge from the north-facing slope on their left. Directly ahead, an old ranch road veered off and dropped down into the woods. Gil stopped momentarily in the shade of the last oak and looked up at their trail on the sun-bleached slopes above it. The grass was tall and the road overgrown. All he could make out was a narrow single-file path.

As Alison and Frank joined him, Gil thought out loud, "I wonder if Ronald will miss this turn."

Frank was breathing hard. "Let's wait for him."

Gil thought about it for a moment. Then he turned back upslope and continued the climb. "Ronald will figure it out."

But after a half-mile and a gain of 500 feet in elevation, Gil started considering the chance he was taking. A wrong turn by Ronald would mean a search, a lot of running in steep terrain, being late to group, and a host of other troubling possibilities. It wasn't like Gil to leave that door open, especially with a novice. He registered a twinge of anxiety, but noticed that it didn't stick, not out here, not on these hills, not in this wild landscape at once so strange and yet so familiar. He felt at home here. Not safe, but rather, alive and engaged. If only he could feel this way in the room, then he'd know he was in the right place.

Gil looked back down the ridge, hoping to see Ronald, but all he saw was an empty trail all the way back down until it disappeared under the oaks. He glanced at his steel wristwatch and allowing for a faster pace downhill calculated that he had seven minutes left before they needed to turn back.

Gil picked up the pace. Not because he had any illusion of reaching the crest, but rather due to the natural exuberance that arose as he wrung the last half mile out of this climb.

Frank fell back, but Alison matched his new pace and remained just two strides behind him.

Ten minutes later, the trail dipped into a headwater gully. Gil recognized the place and he knew that they were still a mile from the top. He surrendered. It was three minutes past the turnaround time and, even if everything went smoothly on the way down, there was already a risk of returning late for the afternoon group.

He led Alison a little further up the trail until they were out of the gully and onto an open ridge. Gil pointed out the view of the summit to Alison and then to Frank, when he caught up with them.

Gil took a long drink from his water bottle. "This is as far as we're going today."

"I wish we could get to the top." Alison gave Gil a wistful look.

"Not today."

Frank had his hands on his knees and was taking deep breaths. "I'd like to get a swim in before group," he gasped.

Alison lit up. "That's a great idea."

"Time may be a little tight," said Gil. *We'll be lucky not to be late as it is.*

Gil turned around and took off back down the road, pushing hard and lengthening his stride. Relieved of the conflict between wanting to reach the summit and needing to be back in time for group, he felt happy with the climb and grateful for Alison and Frank's efforts. It was something they'd done together.

Having fought gravity all the way up, Gil was now working with it like a kayaker riding the downstream flow. Gone was the racing heart and heavy breathing of the uphill push. Now it was all leg muscle absorbing the impact of each footfall. He was moving fast and effortlessly; the steeper stretches, like rapids, left him airborne on every stride as the land fell away beneath him, each foot suspended, lingering above the ground for a moment, then falling. Repeated over and over again, the sensation blended into one long effortless glide downhill. It was the closest thing Gil knew to weightlessness. Riding the mountain like the face of a wave, Gil let his mind clear and his thoughts run free. It was then that he saw the flaw in his plan.

Ronald.

Gil had counted on making better time on the descent, but the timing was based on the pace he was setting. Theoretically, if Ronald had turned around when they did, everyone would get back to the car at about the same time. But Ronald had no way of knowing when to turn around. In fact, he had specifically told Ronald to keep walking until they picked him up on the way back.

It meant that from the time they met up with him, it would no longer matter how fast Alison, Frank and he were walking. Ronald's slower pace would determine how long it would take to get everyone back to the car. Being late for group was something Gil didn't want to contemplate. The leaders always honored the rules they set for the participants.

He pushed the pace up a notch.

A short while later they came to the bare ridge above the oak trees. No sign of Ronald. Now Gil felt another foreshadow of doom. Ronald should have been here by now. He didn't even want to think about Ronald taking the wrong road. *It's too soon to worry about that.*

Gil cupped his hands to his mouth and gave a sharp "Whoop" that echoed down the canyon. Ronald answered with a shout and stepped out from the shade of the oaks a quarter-mile below. Gil sighed. All was well.

They picked Ronald up on the move as they slipped under the overhanging branches of the oaks and their feet began to crunch on the dry, brown carpet of leaves.

Ronald hopped up and swung into their wake, making a short series of shuffling skips to get into step with the others.

"I overheated so I sat in the shade," Ronald said as if an explanation were required.

Gil didn't respond but he noticed with relief that Ronald was staying right with them. Now that they were on the easy downhill, Ronald's fitness didn't matter. With all three of his charges in tow and everyone keeping up, Gil relaxed once again into the pounding rhythm as the trail unwound beneath his feet.

Gil's knees and legs felt the impact of every step, the dull ache of well-used muscles, but no pain. Everything was working just as it should. He noticed the spirits of the others picking up as they experienced the ease of descent and the abundance of oxygen afforded by their reduced aerobic output. Conversation was sure to follow.

Frank shot out ahead, slaloming back and forth down a steep stretch of loose dirt. He stopped at the edge of the road and looked back at them. "Just like skiing."

As they caught up with him, he fell into step and Alison asked, "Are you a skier?"

"Kind of. I started in college at McGill but nowadays, I probably wouldn't ski at all if it weren't for my college chums' annual stag ski weekend."

"Stag?" Alison wrinkled her nose. "It makes it sound like a bachelor party."

"That's the deal. The amazing thing is, I don't mind."

Gil raised his eyebrows.

Alison gave Frank a quizzical look. "Why should you mind?"

"I don't ... but it's one of the only times during the year when I'm not looking."

"Looking for what?" Gil asked.

"Women."

Frank looked at Gil as if he expected confirmation but Gil was waiting to see if there was anything else Frank wanted to say. Gil knew the exhilaration of an expansive ocean view, and the camaraderie of a hard climb could have a truth serum effect on some people.

Frank went back to staring at the path ahead as the three of them hustled down the road. "It's not just women; it's the whole process..." Frank seemed to be talking to himself. "... the flirtation, the body language, the possibilities that flow from an accidental bump or an exchanged glance ... it's a little like dropping a silver dollar in the slots. Every time I get that tingle it could be the jackpot."

Frank paused as his feet stutter-stepped to avoid a deep rut in the road. "Maybe I lose a lot more than I win. Nothing happens most of the time, but when it does ..."

Frank became more animated and Gil wondered if Frank was enjoying the abandonment of political correctness or just the relief of being honest.

Frank's words started tumbling out. "The anticipation is beyond description, just the possibility that she might give in freely and passionately ... that this girl, this night, this wild craziness might really mean something. She just might be as wonderful as I have always imagined her to be." Frank had finally run out of steam and gave Alison and Gil a look, eyes alight and eyebrows raised as if anticipating their enthusiastic agreement.

Instead Gil shook his head. "Wow, that's a heady brew you've got going there."

Frank returned his attention to the placement of his feet and after a few strides said quietly, almost to himself, "Yeah, I guess it is." He turned back to Gil.

"To tell you the truth it's really what gets me up in the morning. I mean, I like what I do, my friends, eating out, going to movies, reading books, getting exercise, but somehow it's all quite dull compared to the possibility that around the next corner there might be a girl with all the mysterious and magical possibilities she holds. It's all there, the great expectations of life—marriage, children, fulfillment, happiness ... don't get me wrong, everything is fine for now but I expect to start the other part of my life any day now."

"So what's stopping you?" There was an edge to Alison's question. Gil smiled, but kept his eyes on the ground ahead as they turned onto a side trail down the steep, dusty slope where the huge fallen oak blocked the road.

"Nothing's stopping me." Frank's voice rose in volume and pitch. "I'm available and looking all the time. I just haven't met the right girl."

"Oh?"

"I know it sounds lame, but it's true. I read an article recently about a study of attraction between men and women. I answered a series of questions about my personality and preferences, and it turns out I'm a relatively rare type. My type tends to be attractive to a large percentage of women but finds only a small fraction of them interesting. That makes it easy to find someone who wants to be with me, but hard to find someone I want to be with."

Alison looked skeptical.

Frank gave a sheepish grin. "The odds are against me. It's going to take time and luck."

"Luck's got nothing to do with it. When you're ready, there are all kinds of partners out there." Alison paused before continuing. "I think you should ask yourself what role sex is playing in your life."

"What do you mean?"

"I mean what you just described sounded a lot like my drinking problem."

"What are you talking about?"

"You said life is dull and tasteless without the chase. That's exactly how I felt about my life without alcohol. I remember my nephew asking me to chaperone his sixth-grade class outing. I was pleased he wanted me to go but unsure what I was getting myself into. Spending the night on an old sailing ship tied up to the Maritime Museum pier sounded like fun but I wouldn't know any of the other adults or kids.

"I didn't want to disappoint my nephew, so I went. I drove into San Francisco, parked at Fisherman's Wharf, and arrived on board just in time for dinner. I was glad to see a big table full of food: spaghetti and meatballs, tossed salad, French bread and sodas but where was the booze? I looked around for the bar, but there was none—no beer, no wine, nothing. I panicked. I could see no one else was drinking. What little hope I had for the evening drained away. I was miserable.

"I was going to have to get by somehow, get it over with as painlessly as possible and get back to a life where I could get my needs met, where people were more thoughtful, where an adult could get a drink at the end of the day…"

"Wow, that's exactly how I felt at my boss's wedding." Frank cut right over Alison's words. "I was the only bachelor and there were no available women. I looked around at the crowd and immediately wished I was somewhere else. I ended up chatting up the young woman serving drinks. When that didn't work, I called up an old girlfriend and dropped by late for some maybe-we-should-get-back-together sex. I knew it was a bad idea but I wanted something and I didn't know where else to get it."

Alison said, "Well, there you go, Frank."

"But what could be more natural?"

"Sure. What I did was natural too—natural for an alcoholic."

"I'm not an alcoholic."

Alison stepped ahead of Frank and turned to face him, putting her hands on his shoulders to slow him down. He stopped. Ronald and Gil stood off to either side and watched. Alison spent a moment looking up into his eyes.

"Frank, I don't know what your relationship to alcohol is. What I do know is that everything you've told me about your love life rings alarm bells in my recovering addict brain. You're an addict."

Frank stared at her for a second, his eyes clouded and his expression blank. "I don't understand. I mean, I hear your words, but they don't make any sense to me."

"You're a sex and love addict."

"Don't be ridiculous; I'm just romantic by nature. If I have a fault, it's my optimism about relationships."

Gil heard the doubt creeping into Frank's voice, but he also knew they couldn't stand there any longer.

"Keep moving." He started off down the road and called back over his shoulder, "Walk and talk, walk and talk."

Alison stared at Frank a moment longer. He looked away. Then she dropped her hands and turned to follow Gil and Ronald. Frank stood alone for 30 seconds, then started down the trail after them.

9

Wednesday Afternoon

THE DECK WAS IN THE SHADOW OF THE BUILDING and the room's subtle hues of wood and stone were muted in the indirect light. As the group got settled, Rae noted Gil's wet hair and beaming smile as he walked in the door at one minute after four. The last three missing group members quickly followed. Alison and Ronald were smiling, Frank looked pensive. All three had wet hair.

There's a story here. But Rae put her curiosity aside and said, "We were just about to start without you."

As soon as he was settled, Gil began the meditation. Rae followed with a short poem and David led the round of one-word check-ins. Next Rae took up where they had left off with the letter from the child exercise, starting with Ronald and continuing until everyone had a chance to sit in front of the mirror and read what they had written. When they all were done, David asked, "Would anyone like some time?"

No one spoke. David was about to move on when Tex leaned forward and pointed his finger at him.

"I've been thinking about what you said to me last night." Then Tex turned and looked across the room at Alison. "Your comment too, Alison." He looked back at David.

"I don't know about the drinking, but I'm beginning to see that my 'going-it-alone' has caused me problems.

"My wife isn't the first person to try to get inside my head. I've always kept to myself and thought that was the best way. Now I'm not so sure." Tex stopped and folded his arms as if the conversation were over.

"That's really important, Tex. Would you like to explore that with us?" David waited but Tex didn't say anything.

"I mean explore that with us now."

"I need to think about this some more on my own."

"Tex, is this just one more case of 'going-it-alone'?"

Tex sniffed at David as if he scented the trap. "I don't know about that."

"Are you willing to look at it?"

"I'd rather turn it around in my head first."

"Let's keep this simple. How do you feel right now about Alison calling you an alcoholic this morning?"

David saw Tex raise his eyebrows, as if implying David should think twice before asking. David took it as a warning that he might not like the answer. David felt his heat rising and flashed on the Detroit asphalt of his Junior High pick-up basketball games. Being one of only a few Jewish kids in his neighborhood, he'd been a target for anti-Semitic taunts and bullying. Basketball was where he learned to physically assert himself. *Bring it on.*

David locked eyes with Tex, who blinked and turned to Alison. Before he could speak, David asked, "Alison, are you willing to hear from Tex?"

"Absolutely." Alison squared her shoulders.

Tex said, "What you said about me being alcoholic was none of your business. When I want your opinion, I'll ask for it." Tex waited, tight-jawed, for Alison's reaction. When nothing came, he seemed lost for a moment. Alison sat calmly, listening, showing no particular emotion other than attentive curiosity.

David watched Tex look around as if someone else might jump in and give him the fight he seemed to be expecting. No one spoke. Tex looked back at David, who kept his eyes on Tex and his expression neutral.

Tex furrowed his brow. "Okay, exactly what's going on here?"

"Nothing's going on, Tex. You gave Alison some feedback and she appears to be taking it in. If you want to check it out, you can ask her to repeat back what you've told her."

Tex looked at David, then at Alison. "I think she heard me." Tex seemed to be considering something for a moment. "Look Alison, I know what a drunk is. My old man was a drunk, and I'm nothing like him." Tex paused. "I don't fall down. I don't beat my family. I don't get fired. I don't wreck cars." Tex's voice rose and the veins bulged on his neck. "I know what a drunk is, I've got the scars to prove it, and I'm ... not ... him!"

The emphasis Tex placed on his last words seemed to indicate he was done, but David waited a few moments to make sure. "Okay, Alison, take a breath and then let Tex know what you heard him say."

David noticed Tex's breathing was rapid and shallow. "Tex, your job is to listen to Alison and let her know if she missed anything." Tex's breathing slowed slightly and he nodded.

Alison adjusted her posture and took a deep breath.

"Tex, I heard you say that you know what a drunk is and you aren't one. I also heard you say that a drunk crashes cars and gets fired."

"Did she get it?" asked David.

"Yeah, she got it."

"Is there anything she missed?"

"I don't beat my wife."

David looked at Alison.

Alison kept her eyes on Tex.

"You don't beat your wife."

"You're damn right I don't."

"Got it." Alison kept her gaze level.

"But the fact that I broke my word and had a drink bothers me."

They sat looking at each other.

Alison broke the silence.

"Tex, may I tell you about my alcoholism?"

"Sure," Tex shrugged.

"I never got angry or mean when I drank. In fact, I got happy. I was the life of the party. I also quickly forgot everything that I promised or needed to do. All my responsibilities took a backseat to my drinking. I didn't want to grow up or take responsibility for things. I didn't want to have to do anything I didn't want to do. I just wanted to continue partying. When I almost flunked out of college, I finally had to face the fact that alcohol had taken over my life."

Here Rae interrupted, "Alison, stop there and give Tex a chance to paraphrase."

Alison looked at Tex expectantly.

"You said you weren't like my dad, either. You were a happy drunk. But you didn't take responsibility for your life."

Alison's eyes widened in startled awareness and she clapped her hands together.

"Oh, my God! Wow. Thank you. Thank you, Tex. Just hearing you say back what I said makes it all come into focus. Nothing has changed. I'm still not taking responsibility for my life!"

David asked, "How do you feel hearing that, Tex?"

"I feel good. I guess I helped Alison a little there."

"Yes, you did," said Alison. "Can I give you a hug?" Alison reached towards Tex.

"Well…" Tex was cut short as Alison threw her arms around him and squeezed. He hesitantly raised his own arms and lightly returned the hug. David watched a big smile spread slowly across Tex's face.

Alison whispered, "Thanks again, Tex."

Alison broke off the hug and looked into his eyes. "Look, Tex, I don't really know if you're alcoholic. All I know is that you have all the signs. But you're a wonderful man and I really want you to figure out what's driving your unhappiness and the difficulties in your marriage. I care about you."

Tex stared soberly at Alison and gave a slight nod.

"Thanks, Alison."

Alison returned to her seat.

Gil turned to say something to her, but she held up her hand palm outward and exaggerated her resigned expression.

"I know, I know." Alison closed her eyes and said, "Al-Anon."

The room broke into laughter.

———

RAE LOOKED AROUND. The room was filled with energy and a sense of release. Everyone seemed refreshed and alive except Todd and Carmen. Todd seemed to find something particularly interesting on the ceiling. Carmen's face looked constricted, frozen in a blank stare at nothing in particular.

Rae took one deep breath and let it out slowly, counting ten heartbeats. "Is there anything anyone wants to say right now?"

Silence. Rae waited a full minute. David looked at her inquiringly. She gave him a slight shake of her head. Gil sat erect, eyes closed as if in meditation.

Gil opened his eyes and glanced over at Rae. The intensity in her eyes scared him. He remembered the warning he'd gotten years ago from a woman who had taken Rae's workshop: "She isn't safe."

Gil had responded back then by telling the woman that if she didn't feel safe, maybe she needed to speak up about it. Now, he wondered.

Rae turned to Tex on her left. "Let's go around and say one word that describes how you feel right now. You start."

Tex's expression went blank. "I don't know."

Alison said, "Excited." David followed with, "Engaged." Carmen still wore that weak smile. "Uncomfortable." And so, around the circle they went.

While Rae registered the answers, she focused intently on Todd, waiting to hear what he had to say. She wanted to get through to him but she needed a handle, something she could grab hold of. There had to be some way in. All week she'd been aware he had a problem, but now she could see he *was* a problem, and she was determined to deal with him.

When his turn came, he looked at Rae and casually said, "Frustrated."

Rae waited until Diane had spoken, then turned back to Todd. "Todd, would you like to say a little more about your feeling of frustration?"

"Nope. I just want to get on with what we all came for."

"And what exactly did you come for?"

"Just exactly what you wrote in the description of this workshop. I need to know what to do next. I want your help in overcoming the, you know, limitations in my life."

"Such as …?"

Todd's voice picked up momentum. "What I told you the very first night." He paused, as if for effect. "I want to work on relationships and my … my life as an artist. On our first night, everyone said what he or she wanted from this week. I'm just waiting for you three to get us there!"

Rae, wondering if the stutter indicated strong emotion or just confusion about his identity as an artist, said quietly, "You've been saying you would like us to do something for you. And yet, I've noticed that your attention is often elsewhere during other people's work. When you're invited to work, you pass. I've had a hard time taking your dissatisfaction seriously, seeing how disengaged you are. I suggest you be more specific and take time now to do your own work."

Todd broke in, "And I've been waiting for you to teach us. I'm sure several of us are frustrated. Not just me. So I'd like to get on with it. What's the plan for this session?"

Rae took a slow, deep breath.

Gil noticed the problem was now back in Rae's lap, and felt a twinge of anxiety, as if he were no longer certain of the outcome. *How did Todd do that?*

Rae's face remained calm, her gaze unbroken. "Todd, let me ask you again. Would you like to do some work now?"

Todd responded slowly, with exaggerated modulation.

"No, Rae. I would like the workshop to go ahead as you three have planned it. If you take us through some exercises that relate to our present obstacles, I'm sure I'll get what I came for."

Rae looked into Todd's eyes for a moment, then sighed.

"All right. You don't want to do your work right now." Without missing a beat, she turned to Carmen. "You also used a word that I'd like to ask about. You said you felt uncomfortable. What did you mean?"

Carmen jerked as if startled. Her eyes blinked and darted back and forth between Todd and Rae. "I ... I'm not sure what to say." Carmen fidgeted with the top button on her blouse and looked around the room as if there were an answer out there for her.

Rae waited.

Finally Carmen settled her attention on Rae. "Um, I meant that this morning was difficult for me."

Gil frowned. *What is going on here?* He looked at David, but he seemed fully engaged with Rae and Carmen's interaction. Gil tried unsuccessfully to catch Rae's eye. *No way she's going to leave Todd's challenge hanging out there.* Rae was watching Carmen.

Just then Carmen seemed to decide something. She said, "I felt like I disrespected my parents. I don't think I would have done that if you hadn't pushed me. I'm not sure it's right. I felt uncomfortable about saying some of the things I said."

"Would you be willing to take a few minutes and say more about that?"

"No. I know you have other things planned." Carmen shot a glance at Todd.

"What we have planned is to address any unfinished business people have. What you just said is unfinished business. That is the work." Rae also glanced at Todd.

"Well, I don't want to take up other people's time. I already had my turn. Others have things they want to talk about, I'm sure. And this isn't that important."

Rae decided to address Carmen's lack of entitlement later.

"Well, let's see. We'll check with everyone and see if anyone has something urgent."

Gil shook his head, more to himself than anybody else since neither David nor Rae were paying any attention to him. Convinced that trying to move forward without addressing Todd's challenge was useless, Gil was floored by how oblivious Rae and David seemed to be.

Rae asked, "Who else has something they would like to talk about right now?"

Gil almost raised his hand. He felt like a participant again, like the early workshops when it was so exciting just to say whatever came into his head. But he stopped himself. He didn't feel that freedom or permission now. His role had changed. He wanted to look like he knew what he was doing. He needed Rae and David to look like they were in charge. The truth seemed secondary to that.

Rae slowly looked at each person in turn, as if divining his or her unspoken issues, but no one spoke up. When she got to Diane, she paused.

Diane looked squarely at her.

"I don't know what's going on here with you and Todd, but I don't want it to interfere with what I've gotten here. And I want Carmen to have the same opportunity I had."

"Why don't you tell Carmen directly?"

Diane looked across the room and caught the eye of her new friend.

"Carmen, I'd like you to take some time right now."

Carmen blinked and looked down at her hands. After a moment, she slowly raised her head, met Diane's gaze and then turned to Rae. A blush rose from Carmen's neck and reached her cheeks.

"It just doesn't feel right to talk about my parents this way. They were good people and really tried to teach me right from wrong. They're gone now, but I know they loved me. And I loved them."

"Yes," Rae said softly.

"Doing that drawing and talking about my mother was just looking at the ugly stuff. It doesn't say who she really was and how much I loved her."

"How about telling us some of the good things you remember?"

Carmen gave Rae a blank look.

David lowered his head, looking at Carmen over his glasses. "Carmen, why don't you hold up your picture and tell us the good things you want to add."

Carmen gave her head a shake, as if breaking a trance, and reached behind her to pick up her drawing. It had dark splotches on the top and several figures spread out across the page, each distinctly separate from the others. She held it up and showed it around the circle.

"These were the bad times when I felt alone and things were scary. My father, he's the small figure here on the right, he worked very hard to take care of all of us. He was quiet most of the time and didn't say much. He only raised his voice when Mom pushed him too far but never said a mean word to us. And my mother, she's the big dark figure in the middle, she yelled a lot but also gave us big hugs and took care of us when we were sick. She had to leave to go to work every night and got mad if we made noise when she was resting during the day. But both of them insisted that we go to church every Sunday and take communion and go to confession. I know that's because they worried about us and wanted us to grow up right."

In the pause that followed, David pursed his lips and half-closed his eyes in an intense expression of compassion.

"What happens when you tell us about the good part of your experience while admitting the bad part?"

Carmen put the picture down in front of her and studied it, as if searching for an answer. After a long pause, without looking up, Carmen said softly, as if to herself, "I feel confused."

Rae said, "Carmen, would you do an experiment with me? Just close your eyes for a moment." Rae waited. "That's right. Now I'd like you to imagine holding all the wonderful things about your parents in your right hand. Just open your palm and imagine holding every loving experience in that hand: the times you were fed, the times you were hugged, going to church, everything that you remember fondly about them."

Carmen lifted her chin but kept her eyes closed.

"When you're done, just nod once to let me know."

Carmen sat with her eyes closed for two minutes then dipped her head slightly.

"Now, I want you to hold open the palm of your left hand. Imagine placing in it the scary and unpleasant experiences with your parents. Imagine all the sad and painful times piled up there, times when you were yelled at or left alone." Rae waited again until there was a slight nod of Carmen's head.

"Next I want you to allow both hands to slowly, very slowly, move together until they meet palm to palm. Don't force them, just let them move of their own accord. Allow them to rise from your lap when they're ready and slowly move toward each other until they touch." Rae modulated her voice, slowing down and speaking softly. "That's right. And when they touch, allow them to gently clasp one another. Take a deep breath and notice the feel of your hands together. Good. Now, when you're ready, open your eyes."

Rae waited until Carmen's eyes were open. "Look around." Rae paused. "Take another breath. What do you notice?"

Carmen turned toward Rae. Her brows were furrowed into a questioning look. "Well, nothing big, really. I feel calmer."

"Excellent. Would you look at your drawing now and really take it in?"

Carmen registered the simple lines beneath dark scribbled patches.

"What do you feel when you look at it?"

"It's funny," Carmen began, "I feel more matter-of-fact about the experiences I drew. They don't seem to affect me as much. They're true, but they aren't the whole truth. They don't ... *I* don't ... feel so heavy."

"Wonderful. Just pay very close attention to where and how you experience that matter-of-fact feeling in your body. Is it in your gut or your chest? Is it a soft or a firm feeling? All you need to do right now is notice. You can come back to this sensation anytime you want. From now on, you can talk about the bad without getting carried away with pain or guilt. This calmness is now part of your life, just like all your memories of your parents."

Rae kept her focus on Carmen as she took all this in.

David looked around the circle. All eyes were on Carmen. *She's changing right in front of us.*

Max shot Rae a look and when she didn't acknowledge him, he raised his hand and addressed David. "May I ask a question?"

"Yes, Max. Of course."

Keeping her eyes on Carmen, Rae quickly put her right hand out towards Max. "Not right now."

Gil glanced at David and smiled.

Rae gave Carmen another minute to let the work settle in before continuing.

"Carmen, are you open to feedback?"

Carmen looked wary. "Yes ..."

"Okay, Max, go ahead."

Max said, "I don't understand what you just did with Carmen, that thing with her hands."

"Max, what was your reaction to Carmen's experience?"

"Oh." Max turned to Carmen. "I was completely swept up in what you were doing."

Rae asked for any other feedback.

Several people added their feelings and support and when the group's feedback was complete, David glanced at his watch and picked up the poem he planned to read.

"'Howl,'" he said, "by Allen Ginsberg."

Gil jerked to attention. *What? My God, David, not "Howl."*

David held the sheet in front of him.

Gil gave Rae an incredulous look, but she showed no sign of recognition. Desperate to stop the blunder that was unfolding, Gil blurted out the first thing that came to his mind. "I thought Rae was supposed to do the reading."

David looked up.

Gil didn't miss a beat. "If you're not ready, Rae, I've got one. We'll save "Howl" for another session." Gil was talking fast, not leaving any room for discussion. David and Rae seemed momentarily stunned. Gil picked up his daily meditation book and read the first page he opened to.

It turns out that the way out of our troubles lies not along the path of thinking. Our best thoughts led us to the problem and will invariably lead us back there again and again. We are nothing if not predictable in this matter.

If we are to recover at all, it will be through the surrender of our thoughts to the practice of this simple program. We are encouraged by others who have taken these steps before us. We see in them the health and happiness we seek. We do what they do. We go to meetings, we read the literature, we find a sponsor, we work the steps and we share our experience with others. In the beginning we do this despite our doubts, because we are desperate. Over time, our misgivings give way to pragmatic results and we continue practicing simply because it works.

Gil closed his book. "Don't forget, tonight is the twelve-step meeting. It's attended by locals and open to everyone on the property. We recommend you attend, especially if you have any questions about your own or another's drinking or addiction."

David added, "We'll meet here tomorrow morning at 9:30. Be sure to take good care of yourselves tonight."

As people stood up and gathered their things, David waved Gil and Rae over for a word.

"Rae, let's meet in your room before we go to dinner."

Gil looked at his watch. "I don't have much time. The meeting starts at 7 p.m."

"That's fine. This will only take five minutes."

Rae's expression was worn. "Good, because I'm burned out and just want to eat and go to bed."

THEY SETTLED IN RAE'S ROOM. She propped herself up on the bed, stuffing the two pillows behind her. David flopped on the bed next to her and playfully grabbed one of the pillows she was leaning against. Rae scowled at him and he jerked his hand away and shook it, as if the pillow had been too hot to handle. She didn't smile.

Gil stood, glowering, at the foot of the bed. "Let's get this over with."

David became serious.

"Okay, I want to clear up what happened with the poem. Does anyone have anything else?"

"No."

"Nope."

"Then I'll go." David turned to Gil. "What was that switch on the reading all about?"

"That's simple. You were about to read something we've never read before, never discussed, and that seemed grossly inappropriate." Gil's tone and expression were neutral.

"Oh, that." David chuckled ironically. "That poem is a classic, and the stanza I picked expresses perfectly the kind of chaotic mix each of us faces in the difficult places in our lives. I thought it would resonate well with the group's struggle to come to grips with why they're here."

Gil retorted, "It's famous for its obscenities, its metaphors are disturbing, and its content is adult while we are mostly dealing with sensitive childhood trauma. To me it seemed more likely to re-traumatize than to heal."

David looked toward Rae. Exhausted, she shook her head. "Leave me out of this one."

He turned back to Gil. "All right, you didn't like the poem. So why didn't you just say so? It would have been an opportunity for the group to see how to work through disagreement and conflict."

"Time was up, and I didn't want to air our dirty laundry when the group was already reeling from Todd's attack on us early in the session. I don't happen to think we have a lot of credibility to spare right now." Gil shot a pleading glance at Rae. She didn't respond.

David raised his eyebrows. "Wow. You've got a lot of negative things to say about the group and our teaching."

"On the contrary, David, I'm missing a lot and I don't know how to address what I am seeing. I'm only bringing this up is because I'm worried you're not seeing what I'm seeing." Again Gil snuck a questioning glance at Rae.

David, feeling the need for reinforcement, also looked to Rae.

She sighed, "I'm not sure what I think. But I can tell you I won't have the bandwidth to even consider it until I've eaten and rested."

"And we don't want to be late for the meeting. Let's talk afterwards," said Gil.

"I'm not going," David said. "I'm going to the Wednesday night program, and after that, I have a phone date with Joann."

Rae smiled regretfully. "I'm sorry, but I just don't have the energy. If I'm going to be any good tomorrow, I need a soak in the tubs and early bedtime."

Gil, embarrassed by how hurt he felt, turned abruptly and started for the door.

David called after him, "Whoa, we need to set a time to meet."

Gil called as he went out the door, "Tomorrow morning, 7 a.m., in the lodge."

Before either of them could answer, Gil added, "And ask them to set a dinner aside for me."

David frowned.

Rae allowed the sadness of Gil's disappointment with the two of them to wash over the mix of shutdown and confusion she was already experiencing. *Oh, well,* she sighed. *We'll get this sorted out.*

———

ONCE HE WAS OUT in the complete dark and chilled by the bracing sea air, Gil revived quickly. He took the landscaped steps two at a time, flew downhill past the lodge, and sprinted effortlessly over the lawn towards the gardens. He felt excited again. Something about movement, the juxtaposition of land and sea, and having a meeting to go to, felt good.

Frank came out of the far side of the lodge and yelled to Gil, "Where's the meeting?"

Gil altered course to meet up with Frank and was breathing easily as he slowed down to match Frank's pace. "It's in the middle of the row of rooms above the garden, around the back. I'll show you."

The meeting was just starting as they arrived. A dozen people were sitting on large cushions around the small room. The secretary was following the usual meeting script, a twelve-step amalgam tailored to welcome visitors from a variety of programs.

Gil found an empty space in the corner, settled in on a pillow and listened to the familiar format, which described the conditions shared by the members of half a dozen different twelve-step programs.

He missed the spartan spirituality of AA and began critiquing the script's New-Age message of recovery. Gil caught himself. He thought of a line from the Big Book, "We realize we know only a little..." and laughed. He let go of his judgments and settled in to enjoy the rest of the meeting.

Looking around the circle, Gil was heartened to see five people from the workshop and realized it was the first time in a twelve-step meeting for four of them.

The secretary asked if there were any newcomers. Several hands went up. Gil smiled when Ronald introduced himself and launched right into a check-in, not knowing a raised hand and a first name was all he was expected to offer. The secretary waited patiently for a break in Ron's share to thank him and move on. After the introductions and readings she opened the meeting up for sharing.

Alison raised her hand. "Hi. My name is Alison, and I'm an alcoholic."

Several voices echoed back, "Hi, Alison."

Alison sat up straight. "I'm really grateful for this meeting. I'm here taking a workshop and it's been a great week. I'm getting a lot out of it, but I still need a place where I can talk to other alcoholics. I had 15 years last month."

There was enthusiastic applause from the regulars.

"But I have other behaviors that feel less than sober to me. For one, I've been eating too much since I got here. I try everything they serve … it's all so good, especially the desserts." Several people laughed. "I end up feeling bloated and a little disoriented afterwards. I haven't told anyone else about this."

"Another thing," she went on. "I've been spending too much time on other people's business. I went on a hike today and got so involved in someone else's problems that I completely forgot my own. That's the most comfortable I've been all week." She was interrupted by the hearty laughter of recognition all around the room.

Gil glanced at Frank, who was smiling, probably relieved that after all it hadn't been all about him.

"I was completely focused and felt an urgent need to fix him. The more I explained his denial and shortcomings to him, the more aware and virtuous I felt. He was the problem, and I was the solution."

More laughter.

"I always feel better by comparison but it never lasts. I end up feeling embarrassed, empty and off-balance. I need to be reassured that I was helpful. I want to hear how grateful they are. That's what it's like at home a lot of the time. My husband and my two children have lots of problems I could help them solve, if they would only listen to me and do as I say. But the more I try, the more resistant they become. I wonder why I keep doing it."

Allison stopped talking and looked around the room.

"I don't know where I'm going with this, but I'm really glad for this twelve step meeting. I'm being told that I need to go to Al-Anon with these issues so if there is anyone here from Al-Anon, I'd love to talk with you after the meeting."

The secretary, a nicely dressed woman with long auburn hair pulled back in a ponytail, said, "Keep coming back."

As the shares continued around the room, Gil kept an eye on the members of his group. They all seemed to be engaged, particularly Diane, who was sitting erect, leaning slightly forward. And though Tex was pressed back against the wall, arms folded, his eyes were focused on each person as they spoke.

Frank raised his hand. "I'll go next. This is my first meeting, and I'm not sure what I'm supposed to say, but I'm here to see what this is all about."

"What's your name?" the secretary interrupted.

"Oh, yeah. Hi, I'm Frank, and I don't know what I am."

"Hi, Frank," several voices echoed around the room.

"I know I have problems in my life. I'm almost 40 and I don't have a girlfriend or a career path. I have a hard time staying in relationships, and I was recently removed from a position I liked at my company. I was asked what I would like to do next, and I realized I didn't know. That scared me.

"I'm doing the same things I've always enjoyed—work, exercise, sex, alcohol—but they don't give me the lift they used to. I don't know how this fits in this meeting, but my group leaders suggested I come, so here I am.

"I don't think I have a drinking problem. I drink in moderation, usually a martini or a couple of beers with dinner. But for a long time now I've been drinking every night, and I'm less likely to stop at one drink.

"I really look forward to that drink. I work hard all day—nine, ten, eleven hours—and when I get home I take off my suit, pull on my swim trunks and head out to the neighborhood pool. It feels great to hit the water, rain or shine." Frank's excitement ebbed as he paused and looked around the room. He seemed lost for a moment, then slowly shook his head. "Anyway, after a swim I feel much better and I'm ready to relax for the evening, which almost always means a drink."

Frank's last words were barely audible. Again, he glanced around as if trying to gauge the reaction of his audience before continuing. His voice remained soft and low, almost confessional.

"The first thing I did when I arrived at Esalen was to order a beer at that little bar in the lodge."

Gil half-smiled. *That would be two beers.*

"Then in the opening session of my workshop I agreed to no alcohol for the rest of the week. I had to think about it. I know alcohol is something special to me and I don't want to limit my drinking. It made me a little anxious to think about it. My life already feels flat as it is. My friends are all married and moving on in their careers and I still don't know what I'm doing. Anyway, I don't know if this meeting has any answers, but I appreciate the chance to find out."

Several voices chanted in unison, "Welcome. Keep coming back." One lone voice carried on, "You're in the right place."

Smiling, Gil spied an AA old-timer looking intently at Frank. *Frank will be getting an earful after the meeting.*

Gil watched his own hand go up but had no idea what he wanted to say. "Hi, I'm Gil, I'm an alcoholic, addict, and a grateful member of Al-Anon."

"Hi, Gil," a chorus of voices responded.

"I'm happy to be here. I love being at Esalen. I got sober here four years ago, and Esalen has had an important place in my heart ever since. It's a privilege to be leading a workshop this week and continuing to do this work. But everything meaningful in my life I owe to this program, this room and you who make these meetings possible."

RAE WAS SOAKING in a dark corner of an outdoor tub. Her head rested against the low stone wall and her half-closed eyes gazed through the rising steam toward the shadows in the next pool. She could just make out the dark shapes of bathers.

For the last half-hour, she hadn't been able to keep from hearing Todd's disembodied voice as he spoke to every female bather stepping into the next pool. He was met with marked silence several times and when he did get a response, it was short and dismissive.

Rae was trying hard not to listen as Todd finally trapped someone into a conversation. His monologue about his life as a struggling artist was too annoying to ignore. Rae was angry that Todd was here at the tubs, disturbing her peace, and not at the twelve-step meeting where he belonged. She felt her resentment building, hijacking her thoughts and removing her from the sensations, sights and smells of the healing waters.

She tried counting her breaths, one to ten, once, twice, three times, but each time, Todd's irritating voice broke through her concentration. It was hopeless. She recoiled from his voice, his insincerity, and his impenetrable denial. He said he wanted help and that he had come to the workshop to get it. But every time help was offered, he rejected it.

If he had just come right out and said that he didn't care, he didn't want to be here and he had no intention of doing the work, she could deal with that. It was his obstinate, dissembling resistance that drove her crazy. There was nowhere to go, nothing to grab hold of, no way to move him off dead center. Talking to Todd was like wrestling a greased pig; she always ended up lying in the mud.

Then a blazing thought struck her like an extinction event meteor. *Alan.* This frustration was what it felt like living with Alan. He was never wrong, always offended, and forever the injured party. Nothing she could say or do ever trumped his impenetrable self-pity, his judgments, and his cancer. She couldn't win. The best she could hope for was to get used to the mud and the despair.

She still felt furious at Todd, but she started to see the first glimmer of light breaking through. It might not entirely be his fault. She realized that she couldn't work effectively with Todd because she couldn't disentangle him from the familiar pain of her marriage. Everything Alan had ever said or done that annoyed her came flooding back. She recalled all the moments of Alan's upsets, demands, criticism and neediness. His needs were more important than hers and when she tried to meet *his* needs, he judged her as inadequate.

She finally saw clearly and absolutely that her marriage would never work. She could prolong the suffering, or face the truth. In that way, she was like Todd, living in denial and forever blaming someone or something else for the misery she felt. As if it were Alan's fault she was stuck. As if it were her job to say or do just the right thing that would finally change him. Now she saw her marriage in bold relief, as if someone had turned up all the house lights over the darkened stage of her life. She was never going to change Alan. She could either take him as he was or continue to struggle and suffer. Only she could choose. To her chagrin, it struck her that both she and Todd should have been at the twelve-step meeting.

She had no idea what the answer was, but she finally knew what to do next. With that came a sense of buoyancy she hadn't felt in a long time, a lightness she'd all but lost.

Then Rae noticed that she could no longer hear Todd's voice. It must have been a while since anyone had added hot water from the trough behind her, because the water was tepid. She felt the swollen ridges of her waterlogged fingertips. *How long have I been sitting here?*

She stood up slowly, testing for the dizziness of a blood pressure drop, sat on the edge of the tub for a moment with her head down, then walked straight up to the showers, dressed and went up the hill to pick up her keys and find her car.

The Carmelite Monastery was thirty minutes south of Esalen, and she knew their chapel would be open for Compline. She hadn't been to a Christian church in a long, long time, but she had spent a week at the Monastery three years before on a personal retreat. And, although she had avoided the chapel during her stay, her days were punctuated by the muted chanting of monks every three hours. She knew they would be there at 9 o'clock sharp tonight. Now she had an urge, a powerful intuition, to go to the chapel and sit with the monks.

The tiredness left Rae's body. She had no doubt about her choice. Bypassing bed and rest, she drove her car down the coast, sailing along top-down, the wind in her face, the light of a half-moon reflecting off the black ocean and obscuring all but the brightest stars.

DAVID STEPPED CAREFULLY around the cushions and back supports, and over the legs of the audience crammed in wall-to-wall on the floor of the large hall. The room was full for the Wednesday Night Program and the lights were low as he made his way slowly and carefully toward the door. Stepping over people, he quietly repeated, "Excuse me, excuse me," like a liturgy of repentance as he interrupted their view of two Shamans doing a ritual dream induction dance in the front of the candle-lit room.

Normally he was less concerned about the reactions of others, but his exit was anything but inconspicuous. Grumbling and cries followed him as he accidently stepped on those he was trying to go over or around. He was glad for the anonymity of the low light.

Once out in the fresh night air under the cypress tree limbs arching over the back deck, he thought of the performance he had just left, shook his head and smiled. It was an ever-surprising and amusing world after all.

He hadn't made sense of anything the Shamans were saying or doing, but he loved the fact that they said and did them, that the world would forever hold surprises for him, that there was no end to the learning, the participating and the living. He stared up at the stars peeking through the branches overhead, then out to the great half-moon four fists above the horizon. He felt alive and at home. At home in his aging body, at home on this far left coast, at home with the dark, the crazy, the uncommon. He loved watching the Shamans work, but he loved his decision to leave the presentation even more. That they existed was plenty for him tonight. He felt connected to this planet, this work and this life.

Maybe death was no different. It might not be so bad. Who knows? He understood in a flash that it wasn't death that scared him. It was the thought of being incapacitated. Right now, however, that didn't concern him. Right now this life was enough, this openness and curiosity he felt about everything.

He thought of Joann. He wanted to talk to her. He missed her, and looked forward to their intimate, albeit long-distance, connection.

His watch read 8:35. He was twenty-five minutes early, but strode off for the phone booths anyway. He was sure that now was the time to call her.

10

Thursday Morning

G IL ARRIVED AT THE LODGE AT 6:55 A.M. LAST night's dirty dishes were still piled high on the sheet metal tray in front of the opening to the dishwashing station. Several workers in aprons were moving around the dining room, stacking the benches on top of tables and carrying yesterday's coffee urns into the kitchen to be recharged for the morning breakfast crowd.

Getting hot water and a leftover lemon slice from the coffee bar, he headed for the deck. An aproned young woman with shaved sidewalls and a pink-and-purple Mohawk unlocked the door for him. He heard the sliding of the bolt as the door closed behind him. He'd forgotten they locked up the lodge for cleaning at 7 a.m.

There will be more privacy outside on a chilly morning anyway.

Gil sat on the long bench at the edge of the deck and put his mug down beside him. Closing his eyes, he relaxed into his ritual prayer and meditation. *God, grant me the serenity to accept the things I cannot change, the courage to change the things I can and the wisdom to know the difference. I offer myself to you to build with me and do…*

"I thought we were going to meet inside." David flopped down, straddling the bench beside Gil.

Gil opened one eye towards David, then closed it again … *with me as you will, relieve me of the bondage of self that I might better do your will. Take away my difficulties that victory over them may…*

"It's cold out here!" Sitting in this position, David's mouth was eighteen inches away from Gil's left ear and so, even though David was speaking just a little above a normal conversational volume, it registered as a shout to Gil's quieted mind.

Gil turned his head and opened his eyes.

"Would you scoot back a little?"

David raised his eyebrows.

Gil turned back to the ocean and closed his eyes … *bear witness to those I would help of your power, your love and your way of life. May I do your will always. My Creator, I am now willing that you should have all of me, good and bad…*

"I'm going inside and get some tea. It's time to meet, so when you're ready, join me." David stood up and lifted his left leg over the bench.

"The lodge is closed for cleaning." Gil kept his posture erect and his eyes closed.

I pray that you now remove from me every single defect of character that stands in the way of my usefulness to you and to my fellows…

"Oh." David sat back down. He pulled his hood up and drew the string taut, leaving a narrow opening just big enough for his nose to poke through. He sat there silently like an eyeless, beaked creature from a Hieronymus Bosch painting.

...Grant me strength as I go out from here to do your bidding. Lord, make me a channel...

"Hi, guys!" Rae called out as she crossed the deck, a towel wrapped around her wet hair and her skin glowing from a long, hot soak and the walk up from the baths.

David's head tilted back as he sniffed loudly three times. "Is that you I smell?"

Rae stopped in her tracks and bent over laughing.

Gil lowered his head until his chin hit his chest and pretended to sob.

Laughing, David turned back towards Gil and opened his hood. Gil covered his face with both hands. David redoubled his loud barking laugh and Rae joined in.

Gil continued to shake his head with mock frustration until he couldn't contain the laughter any more. All three laughed deep and long.

Gil wiped the tears of mirth from his eyes.

"I never know when that's going to happen with you two. I can be furious with you one moment and laughing hysterically with you the next." He laughed again and then let out a deep sigh.

"Funny how that is." Rae sat down on a short bench in front of David and leaned back against the glass table behind her.

Gil swung around to face Rae, his knees brushing hers and his shoulder next to David's. Rae looked at them both, then closed her eyes and slowed her breath. Gil and David joined her. After four days of group, the meditation came reflexively, an obvious choice before starting to talk about the workshop.

Gil had counted five breaths when he felt David's hand taking his. "What..." Gil twisted his head sharply in David's direction. He saw David holding Rae's hand as well. Rae reached over with her free hand. With a flushed face, Gil took her hand and closed his eyes.

He counted eight breaths.

David's sonorous tones began a morning blessing in Hebrew, breaking Gil's concentration.

Gil ground his teeth and was just about to pointedly ask, 'Are you done?' when Rae's voice preempted him. "Our creator, who art in heaven, hallowed be thy name..."

He sighed and settled in for a recital of the Lord's Prayer. Gil had nothing against prayer, but this was an imposition, an unwanted interruption of his silent reflection. His mood, which had been simmering since their last meeting, took a dark turn.

Gil was thankful for the silence when it came. But as it lingered and David and Rae still held his hands tightly, he felt dread rising. They expected him to offer a prayer.

Should he drum up an insincere prayer, or remain silent and expose his petulance? Either way, he was one down.

God.

The energy flooded through him and, before he could think about it, the words emerged. "God grant me the serenity to accept the things I cannot change." He meant it. He could hear it: the frustration, anger, annoyance finding voice in the prayer, a prayer that rang true. "The courage to change the things I can, and the wisdom to know the difference."

When he opened his eyes, Rae was smiling, and David had on his serious, let's-get-down-to-business face.

Rae turned to Gil.

"How was the meeting last night?"

"Good."

Rae smiled.

David didn't look satisfied. "Who showed up from group?"

"I really couldn't say."

"You didn't go, or you didn't notice?"

"Neither. It's an anonymous meeting."

"And this is a confidential consultation."

"Sorry."

"Sorry, as in, you're sorry you forgot the privileged nature of this conversation and our work together, and you're happy to let us in on what happened last night?"

"No. Sorry, as in, I'm sorry to disappoint you, but you needed to attend if you wanted to know anything about the meeting."

David rolled his eyes up. "So that's what this is about. I thought we cleared that up yesterday. Rae was tired and I had another engagement."

Rae put her hand on Gil's forearm.

"Are you angry with us?"

Gil was about to say no, but he could already hear how angry it would sound. He paused and closed his eyes instead. She was still his teacher. After a moment, he said what he had been hoping not to say.

"Yes."

He paused allowing the answer to stand on its own for a moment.

"The twelve step programs are an important part of my contribution to the team and our work together. I feel hurt and undermined by your lack of support."

"You do, don't you?" Rae tilted her head sympathetically. "I hear that you feel hurt and unsupported by our not attending the meeting." She waited for that to sink in. "And I want you to know that I have the utmost respect for you and the program. I want you to hear that I value the contribution you make to the group and that your experience in twelve step programs, while important, is only a small part of what you bring to the room."

Gil did his best to let that sink in as well. He could feel the warm spot in the center of his chest growing. But he still had something to say, and that's where his attention kept turning. Looking at Rae, he said, "Thank you," then he turned to David. "Anonymity is the foundation of all twelve step meetings, and this isn't a context that gives me the right to breach that."

David thought for a moment, as if choosing his words carefully. "When we suggest that members attend the Wednesday night AA meeting, we're making a therapeutic intervention. We discuss it beforehand and we need to follow up and discuss it afterwards. If AA won't allow that, then maybe we shouldn't be recommending it, at least not within the context of this work."

Gil looked sharply at Rae. Her expression was noncommittal. He addressed David. "We have no choice but to recommend it. It's the most effective tool in the tool box, and the only tool with any consistent success treating addiction."

"You're wrong about that." David's voice started to rise. "There's lots of support groups and therapies out there for addiction, and many have the singular advantage of being secular. AA is an anachronism. Its Christian ideology, archaic language and gender bias are major stumbling blocks for most of the population."

"You're missing the point, David. The language is dated, but the ideas are current and universal." Gil's face was coloring. "They're based on experience, the experience of some hopeless drunks who found a way back, an experience they passed on and shared with others. At its core, AA is a pragmatic program that has changed and adjusted according to what works. And it's fundamentally a spiritual program, not a religious one."

"The prayers recited at every meeting are Christian prayers."

"That's an historical artifact. The program borrowed heavily from the Oxford Group, who were Christian."

"And that's my point." David leaned over the table. "The Christian religion is bankrupt. Six million Jews were killed by the Nazis, and the Pope never took a stand."

"Are we back to the Holocaust thing again?" Gil sat back and shook his head. "You and Woody Allen."

David's eyelids fell half a notch and his face became expressionless.

Gil knew that impenetrable look; he had hurt David's feelings. Gil knew he'd crossed the line, but he wasn't in the mood to make amends. He looked to Rae for help, but she seemed a million miles away. David's eyes began shifting back and forth between Gil and Rae. Gil couldn't tell if the look was beseeching or mistrustful. He looked to Rae again. *Come on, Rae, you need to help us out here.*

But a fog of silence settled in thick and heavy over the table.

———

WHEN RAE WALKED into the morning session, everyone was already sitting quietly, eyes closed. She sat down and stretched her legs out in front of her. Flipping through her daily reader, she found today's entry and waited for the group to finish their meditation.

When David hit the Tibetan chimes, Rae began reading aloud.

People seldom seek recovery in order to enrich their lives. They come through the doors of these rooms only as a last resort, when everything else has failed. Here at last is a place where they can unburden themselves of their confusion, their pain, their sorrow and their anger hoping at last to find an answer to their difficulties. Noticing the seemingly unselfconscious joy in others around them, they begin to hope that there is, after all, a way to set their world right. They continue to lament their situation week after week until one day they notice that others who have what they want aren't doing this. Instead, the message they hear over and over again is awareness, acceptance and action. The solution isn't changing the world to suit our needs, but rather taking responsibility for changing ourselves, our attitudes and our actions. Only then do we find the serenity that has previously eluded us.

Rae closed the book and placed it on the floor beside her, then folded her hands in her lap.

Irritated, Gil put the sheet of paper with his selected poem off to the side. *I was supposed to read a poem. Now who's doing the check-in?*

"Nice." Todd's head was tilted back over his pillow and he was staring at the ceiling, which gave his words the omniscient quality of narration. "I couldn't agree more. There's work to be done." He paused. "So when are you going to get around to it?"

Rae smiled with a shake of her head. Gil felt confused. The rest of the group seemed to hold their breath.

"Thanks for the check-in, Todd," David said, with a flat affect and a dry, disinterested voice. "Ronald, you're next."

Ronald looked to David, and then snuck a glance at Todd, as if Todd might jump up and object.

Ronald said, "Well, I... uh, I'm not sure what to say."

David looked up from the note he was making and stared over the rims of his glasses at Ronald. "Just tell us where you're at, and if there's any work you'd like to do today."

Gil felt a wave of anxiety. *Are we just ignoring Todd again? This is bizarre.* Gil was starting to feel unsettled and Rae seemed to be somewhere else.

Ronald said, "I went to the AA meeting last night. I think I'm getting used to all this sharing. I'm not sure I related to some of the readings, but it was nice to have a bonus session with Diane and the others. I had my first full night's sleep last night and I feel ready to go today." Ronald turned to Frank and nodded.

Frank looked around the room. "I also went to the meeting, and it made for a very full day for me on top of two group sessions and the hike with Gil. And if that weren't enough, this old AA guy grabbed me after the meeting and read me the riot act. He suggested I do an experiment and try to stop drinking on my own. Between him and Alison,

I've got a lot to think about and I'm not sure what to do with it all." Frank sighed and looked across at Gil.

"I'll pass." Gil turned to Diane.

"I'm all right this morning. Something happened last night, but I'm not ready to talk about it."

"Are you requesting time to work later this morning?" David asked.

"I don't know ... I don't think so."

Rae leaned forward and caught Diane's attention. "Look and see if you're willing. You only need to go as far as you choose."

"I don't feel comfortable right now. I don't feel safe."

Rae settled back on her cushion. "What would make it safe for you?"

"I'd feel better if you treated Todd like he was part of the group."

Rae started to open her mouth, but no sound came out.

Gil smiled, his eyes glinting as he looked from Rae to David and back again.

David finally broke the silence.

"Diane, is there something you want to say to Rae or Todd?"

Diane looked at Todd for a moment, then shifted her eyes to Rae. "Todd just said something explosive, and you ignored him. You act like he's not here. It's upsetting." Diane closed her mouth and stared at Rae.

David scooted off his pillow and onto the carpet so he could see Diane and Rae at the same time. "Rae, would you paraphrase what you heard Diane say?"

"Todd said something and we didn't address it."

David turned to Diane. "Did Rae get it?"

"No."

David looked confused for a moment, and then concerned. "Add the part she missed ..."

"What Todd said really bothered me. But you pretended like it didn't happen, and that bothered me more."

Rae folded her hands across her lap. "You're bothered by what Todd said and by the way I handled it."

"Yes."

David nodded. "Okay. Rae, it's your turn to respond."

"Todd has chosen to avoid the work, and he's been blaming us for it. He's made it clear he isn't interested in taking suggestions or feedback. As I told him yesterday, I respect his decision and will focus my attention on people who want to work."

"I still don't feel safe," Diane said.

"Hold on, hold on." David held up his hands. "First, tell Rae what you heard her say."

"Todd's been blaming the leaders and refusing to work. You respect that."

David shook his head slightly. "Rae?"

"She got it." Rae smiled.

David hesitated, then turned towards Diane. "Okay, your turn."

"I don't feel safe, and I don't want to work." Diane sat back and folded her arms over her chest.

"Would you like to say more about that?"

"No."

"Would you like Rae to paraphrase?"

"No."

David turned back to Rae. "Do you want to add anything?"

"No."

David looked bewildered. "Really?"

Rae fixed him with a stare. "Really."

Gil's stomach began to twist. *We're dangerously close to the edge.*

There was an uncomfortable silence. Max raised his hand. "Are you open to feedback?"

David grabbed onto Max's question like a life preserver and turned to Diane. "Are you available for feedback?"

Diane nodded, and David looked at Rae.

Rae said, "Yes."

"Go ahead, Max." David scooted back to his cushion.

Max turned to Diane on his left. "You inspire me. There's something of Joan of Arc in the way you keep coming forward when there's something difficult that needs to be said. If we were to take a poll right now, you'd get my vote for the one most changed over the last four days."

Diane smiled broadly and looked straight at Max as he continued.

"And if you change your mind and want to talk about what came up for you, I want you to know I'm here for you. I'll do everything in my power to help you feel safe. Consider me your own personal pit bull, and just point me at anything that threatens you."

A tear formed at the outer edge of Diane's eye. She wiped it with the back of her hand and laughed throatily. "Thanks, Max." Her laughter quickly morphed into tears and Max moved next to her and put his arm around her shoulder. She leaned her head into his chest and cried freely for a moment, then sat back up, tears streaking down both cheeks. Diane smiled. "I wish I'd had you back then."

"Me too. But you have me now, so if there's anything you want to say or do, you can count on me to be right by your side."

He held her gaze for a few more seconds, then turned to David. "That's it. I'm ready to check in now."

"Okay, Max, but first let's finish with the feedback." David looked around the room.

Carmen, Ronald and Alison all seconded what Max had said. When they were done and no one else spoke up, David turned back to Max. "Okay. Let's continue the go-round."

Max took a deep breath, reached down and picked up a notebook and began to read.

"I had a long sit on the beach yesterday. I decided to have it out with death once and for all. I railed like Demosthenes into the crashing surf for half an hour, but nothing I said changed anything. The roar of falling water on rocks went on unabated long after I stopped shouting. Death had me. There was no way around it. There was no way to put it in a better light. I'm powerless to change it. My father died of ALS when I was twenty. He was still a young man himself, not halfway through his fifties. I lived most of my teenage life watching his slow decline. I hated him for it, and I swore that I would never let that happen to me."

Max put the book down and paused. He looked around the circle, making eye contact wherever he could.

"But of course, that's exactly what's happening to me." Max paused as he took in the reactions around him. "No, I don't have ALS." Max kept his expression solemn but his eyes began to twinkle. "I have O … L … D.

"Max." Rae's voice was surprisingly sharp. "I'd like you to keep this check-in brief. You can ask for time if you want to work later."

Max recoiled slightly and blinked. "Oh … right." He took a couple of breaths. "I know why I'm here, and I'd like to talk about it." Max made a single nod, like a punctuation mark. He turned to Carmen.

"I'm still sitting with what Diane said." Carmen looked at Diane and lowered her eyes. "I feel confused." She turned to Alison.

Gil listened closely as they went around the circle. Alison and Max sounded engaged, but mostly Gil heard a tentative tone in the sharing and no one else offered to work. *We've got a problem.*

When the check-ins were done, David held his hand out to Max. "The floor is yours, Max."

"Where was I?"

"You said, 'I know why I'm here.'"

"Okay." Max crossed his legs, leaned forward and made eye contact around the room, as if he were relishing the beginning of a long fireside tale. "The one thing I never wanted to have happen is happening, whether I want it to or not. I'm losing it. Maybe not as suddenly or as unexpectedly as my father, but losing it all the same."

Max took a deep breath. "I didn't notice at first. The changes were subtle and intermittent. I wrote off bad days to the ups and downs of life. A minor injury here, a bad night's sleep there, an off day, surely I'd had them all my life. They seemed like temporary setbacks, especially on a good day, when I felt back at the top of my form. On a good day, my spirits were up, my body was strong and my mind was still quick and agile.

"Then I started noticing that the downs were deeper and the ups were less frequent, shorter-lived and never quite as high. Over time, my running slowed to a shuffling jog, and then was replaced by walking. It felt hard to break out of a walking stride. It was as if there were mental or physical barriers that I couldn't or wouldn't surmount. When I had my foot operation, I stopped exercise altogether."

Max sat back and was quiet for a moment. He took in several breaths and then leaned forward again.

"My mind no longer retains new facts without pronounced effort. I get lost in complex arguments and calculations. I get tired earlier in the day, and I sleep longer but less well at night."

Max made another visual sweep of the room; his shoulders slumped but his eyes were still shining.

"I considered a second career in retirement but I'm not sure I'm up to it. I always thought being old was a state of mind, something to rise above, to put off, to hold at bay. I imagined my older years as an heroic struggle where I would persevere through valiant efforts before going out in a blaze of glory. Now I'm not so sure. I'm losing the energy and stamina I need to resist."

Max paused, then finished with, "There are moments I feel hopeless. There's no solution, and like my dad, I'm not going to get better."

Gil crawled off his pillow and kneeled in front of Max.

"Do you want to do some work?"

"I thought I *was* working."

"No, Max, you were telling a story. Working looks a little different."

"Okay."

"Good." Gil reached over, grabbed his own pillow and dropped it in front of Max. "Let's put OLD on the pillow and see where it goes."

Max looked at the pillow, then back at Gil.

"I wouldn't know where to start."

"Start by closing your eyes and following your breath. Imagine your whole body frozen in ice. Now, starting at the tip of your head, I want you to imagine melting that ice from the top down. Take all the time you need. Let me know when you get to the tips of your toes."

David looked over at Rae, his face scrunched into a wince of discomfort. Rae caught his eye and gave a slight shake of her head, then turned her attention back to Gil and Max.

Max sat there for several minutes with his eyes closed and a look of intense concentration. Slowly his face relaxed until he looked completely at ease.

"The ice is gone."

"Good. Now, keeping your eyes closed, I want you to imagine OLD sitting on this pillow in front of you. When you have him there, open your eyes and tell him whatever is in your heart."

Max took a deep breath and let it out. Opening his eyes, he raised his voice.

"You robbed me. ALS took my dad before his time, and now you're coming for me. You've been stealthily eating away at me while I walk around thinking all is well. All isn't well! I'm not well and there isn't any cure. You've taken parts of my life that I loved and I can't bring them back." He took a breath.

"I loved what my body could do when I was young. The way it worked. How strong I felt. The way it healed. The way it took all the abuse I could throw at it and still came back for more."

Max's voice dropped and his eyes left the pillow. He looked around the room.

"My body was a reliable friend. Sports were a huge source of joy. Now, one by one, I can't do them anymore. I lost basketball to unstable ankles, running to a worn-out knee, tennis to a torn rotator cuff, and walking to plantar fasciitis. Finally, a leaky heart valve took away my spin class. All that's left is coaching kids at the Jewish Community Center.

"I took up reading with a passion, and now I use reading glasses or listen to books on tape. I get lost in conversations where I either don't know or can't remember the names, places and events people refer to."

He faced the pillow again.

"You've got me in a deep, black hole and there's no way out." Max darkened and seemed to fold in on himself. Contorted with anguish, his face suddenly appeared much older.

"Let your feelings come out." Rae was sitting on her haunches beside Gil and resting her right hand lightly on Gil's shoulder as she concentrated on Max. "They've been building up inside you for years."

Max's face sagged and he released a soft sob from the back of his throat. A trickle of tears flowed down his cheeks.

"That's right." Rae kept her focus on Max, even as she nodded to Gil to continue.

"I have … lost … so … much," sobbed Max.

"Let all that agony out." Gil rested his hand on Max's right foot. "You've been holding it in long enough."

Max's sobs reached a crescendo, then gradually trailed off. Gil sat there cross-legged, maintaining a light touch on Max's foot, and waited for the crying to stop. After a minute, Gil said, "Now, when you're ready, give your tears a voice and let them speak directly to OLD."

Max gathered himself a bit and then a twisted half-smile hitched up the left corner of his mouth.

"There's nothing to say. He's got me. It's pointless."

"Just let the tears speak."

"Okay." Max sat up. "You're destroying my life. I hate you for it. I was strong and capable until you started stealing from me."

"Take a breath." Gil waited. "Anything else?"

"Yes. I feel totally defeated. There's nothing I can do or say that will stop you. My life is on a miserable downhill course, and I'm a hopeless victim." Max stopped and held his breath, as if willfully holding back the tears.

A moment passed.

Gil removed his hand from Max's foot and sat up.

"If that's it for now, I invite you to switch over to the empty pillow and be OLD."

"No way," said Max with a shudder.

"You need to hear back from him, or you're going to stay stuck where you are." Gil paused. "You choose."

Max grimaced for a moment and then shifted over to the pillow. After he settled in, he looked over at Gil beside him.

"Now what?"

"Just be OLD and let the words come of their own accord."

Max closed his eyes, then quickly opened them again. His body appeared to swell, his face took on a menacing disdain and he rolled his shoulders forward as if ready to pounce at the least provocation. Max's voice strengthened as he spoke for OLD.

"You poor wretch. Look at you. You're pathetic. How can you live with yourself, with all that whining and sobbing?"

OLD stopped and shook his head slowly.

"I've brought you to your knees. I've destroyed you. You disgust me." OLD looked away with disdain.

Out of the corner of his eye Gil noticed David rising up off his backrest and kneeling on his pillow, but Gil kept his attention on Max. Gil smiled. "Good. Now go back over to the other cushion and be Max."

OLD stiffened. "No way. I like it over here. I'm not going back to that mewling, shriveled-up pile of nothingness. I refuse to be him. The conquering lord of life and death doesn't give up his throne to be a pathetic serf."

Gil felt the air thicken. An uneasy silence hung in the room. Gil tried to remember this was Max's nightmare, not his.

"If you want full satisfaction, you're going to have to let Max go back and respond."

OLD smiled a sly lopsided grin. "You're a more worthy opponent than I thought. But why should I give way to you?"

Gil shrugged. "Suit yourself."

OLD held himself back for a moment, then deflated noticeably and Max quietly crawled off the pillow and back onto his seat. Once there, he cast a glance at the empty cushion in front of him, then looked at Gil.

"What do I do now?" He sounded exhausted and lost.

Gil knew this was a plea for coaching. But he had no idea what to tell Max. He didn't have an answer, and that scared him. He looked at Rae but she shrugged her shoulders.

Shit.

Gil's mind was starting to make up answers, but he knew this wasn't the time or place for faking it. Nothing he thought of to tell Max felt right. He'd never encountered a situation like this before, and he didn't have an answer. He felt inadequate. It confirmed what he had always suspected, that he didn't belong here. The word *fraud* came to mind.

Breathe.

He took a breath and waited. Max was looking at him imploringly. He held Max's gaze and continued to breathe.

David knelt behind Gil and Rae and placed one hand on Gil's shoulder and the other on Rae's. They looked back at him. David looked straight ahead, holding Max's gaze. "Max, may I sit in for you?"

Max looked at Gil, who nodded, happy to be relieved.

"Please," answered Max.

Max crawled off the pillow and sat beside it.

Gil was having second thoughts, *What's he going to do?*

David was on the pillow and yelling. "You arrogant son-of-a-bitch! You will never destroy me! Never!" Spittle flew from his mouth. "I can't stop you from taking my body but you will never, ever touch my soul." David glared at the empty pillow. "I've allowed my fear of you to dominate me for far too long."

David stretched out his long arm and pointed a finger menacingly at OLD. "You can't touch the things that really matter. My mind and body may be yours soon enough, but you will never have my heart, my dreams, my spirit. Enough. You're finished. You're no longer in charge. Get out. I'm reclaiming my life. Right here. Right now."

David continued kneeling, glaring at OLD on the empty pillow. The room was absolutely still except for the hiss of the breaking surf on the rocky beach far below.

David sat back on his haunches and looked over at Gil, Rae and Max. "That felt great."

The room broke into thunderous applause. Max was crying and pounding David on the back. Gil was hugging him from the front as Rae wrapped herself around both of them. Gil whispered in David's ear, "I don't know where that came from, but you nailed it."

When the room settled down and Max was back on his pillow with the three workshop leaders sitting in front of him, Gil considered what to do next.

Max should have the experience of saying those words. That's the form. But intuition said otherwise. Despite his concerns about completion, Gil knew it was done. What had happened was enough.

"Max, is there anything you need to do or say to feel complete?"

Max smiled.

"Just to thank you and Rae, and particularly David, for a real gift. If nothing else happened this week, and already many other wonderful things have happened, then I would have gotten more from this workshop than I have gotten in a lifetime of workshops. Thanks so much."

"You're welcome. Are you open for feedback?"

"Yes." Max sat back, smiling.

The leaders returned to their seats. Gil opened up the floor for feedback. He was surprised to see Tex's hand shoot up.

"Go ahead, Tex."

"I liked what I saw, Max. You were scared, and you weren't afraid to admit it. To me, that's the real deal." Tex's chin trembled. "I watched you cry, and for the first time I wasn't embarrassed by it. I was right there with you, all the way."

Tex's eyes watered. "It was like I was seven again, watching the hands break horses, and thinking, that's what I want to do when I grow up." Tex held Max's attention. Max gave him a single nod.

The comments went all around the room. Everyone, even Todd, had something to say to Max, as he sat straighter and taller with each appreciation. Gil watched as Max's face took on color and his presence seemed to expand. The whole group was animated and emotional as they opened up to Max and shared their experience of him and his work. *What had happened to all their reticence and distrust?*

Rae calmly breathed it all in. She found no mystery here, just one more time where what needed to happen, happened. She looked over at David, who was lying against his backrest, notepad in hand, his eyes still burning with the immediacy of the moment.

He was on fire. Could I have underestimated him all these years? Rae wondered.

David waited as Gil and Rae gave Max their feedback. Having made such a powerful intervention on Max's behalf, David knew that the last spot in the feedback lineup was reserved for him. He had already hit the ball out of the park. Now all that was left was the ceremonial jog around the bases. *I love this work,* David thought.

When David finished and Max had thanked him, the room got quiet. The silence gathered, settling on the group like snowfall on trees, the stillness consecrating the moment.

DAVID LET OUT a contented sigh. "The floor is open."

Gil sat back and surveyed the room. The energy level was high. The feeling of openness and connection had come back into people's expressions and postures. Even Todd seemed to be more present.

Diane raised her hand. "I'd like to share a little about what happened to me last night."

Rae smiled.

Frank said, "I'd like time to say something as well."

Gil shook his head as he thought, *How quickly things change.*

David looked over at Frank and back at Diane. "We have 45 minutes left. You decide which one of you will go first."

"You go first, Frank. I've already had a lot of time to work," Diane remarked.

"Okay, thanks." Frank paused. "But I'm not sure where to begin."

"Take your time." David put down his notepad and gave Frank his full attention.

"I have to say I'm confused about it and hope you can help me."

"It?"

"Something Alison said to me on the hike yesterday." Frank took a deep breath.

David tilted his head and raised his eyebrows.

"She said my dating was like her drinking."

David had a neutral expression. "Would you like to explore that a little more?"

"Not really." Frank smiled. Tex let out a great guffaw, and there were several chuckles around the room.

David leaned forward and looked past Tex to Alison. "Are you willing to repeat what you told Frank yesterday, Alison?"

"Sure." Alison remained propped up against her back support. "I told him he was an addict."

Gil bristled. *This is all wrong. David needs to bring this conversation into the present moment. He needs to have Alison talk directly to Frank.*

David looked surprised. "An addict?"

"Yeah, a sex and love addict."

This is a nightmare. David's having a conversation with Alison, while Frank sits on the sidelines, Gil observed.

"Alison," Rae interrupted, "I want you to pause."

Both Alison and David turned to Rae with a start.

Rae sat up and looked at Frank. "Would you be willing to talk about this with Alison?"

Gil breathed a sigh of relief.

"Yes."

Rae turned to Alison. "Okay?"

Alison nodded.

"Okay, I want both of you to bring your pillows into the center of the room and sit facing one another."

Frank threw his pillow into the middle and sat down on it. Alison got up and moved her pillow two feet forward. She sat down, composed herself and looked directly at Frank.

"Alison, when you're ready, I want you to tell Frank what you've observed, how you feel and what you want. Frank, your job is to listen."

Alison squared her shoulders and looked into Frank's eyes.

"You told me how exciting the chase is for you, how important sex and romance are, how other aspects of your life pale by comparison, including family, friends and important occasions, and how you never get very far in a relationship before you're done and want to start the chase all over again." Alison stopped and looked at Rae.

"That's good, Rae said. Now tell Frank how you feel right now, having said that."

Alison turned back to Frank.

"Right now I feel sad."

Frank's eyes widened.

Rae slipped off her pillow and moved to the right and a little behind Alison. "And what I want from you is…"

Alison glanced nervously at Rae, and then at Frank.

"I want you to see what I see. I want you to get help."

"Great." Rae sat up and faced Frank. "Now it's your turn. Repeat back to Alison what you heard."

"You said I told you how important the chase is to me and how I repeat it over and over. You feel sad, and you want me to get help." Frank looked at Rae.

Rae said, "Ask Alison if you got it all."

Frank looked back at Alison. "Is that it?"

"Yes."

"Frank, now you can respond." Rae smiled.

Frank sat quietly for a moment, as if uncertain which tack to take. "I was going to correct this misimpression you have of me, but something happened when you said you were sad." Frank paused. "I felt sad, too."

"Stay with that feeling," Rae quietly interjected.

Frank looked at Rae. "Yeah, I feel heavy, and I don't know why."

"Look at Alison and tell her."

Frank looked at Alison.

"I feel heavy." He turned back to Rae. "I guess I don't know why she's sad. And I don't know what it has to do with me."

"Just stick with 'I feel heavy,' and see where that takes you. Look at Alison and check inside."

Frank sat quietly for a minute then looked at Rae again. "I don't know …"

"Tell Alison what it is you don't know."

"I don't know anything about being a sex addict. I don't know where you came up with something like that. I'm a normal guy. There's nothing I do that's any different from anybody I know, or any guy in any story I've ever read." The words poured out of Frank like he'd finally been given a task he knew how to do. "Of course I like women, of course I'm attracted, of course I'm turned on; that's how it's supposed to work. My problem isn't sex. My problem is finding the right woman. I can't help the way I feel. If I lose interest, there's nothing I can do about it, and pretending otherwise doesn't help. I've tried it."

He took a breath.

"Yeah, I'm sad. I'm sad that it's taken me this long and I still haven't found somebody. But I'm busy. My job takes up a lot of my time. I've got other interests. I read, I work out, I go out with friends. My life is pretty full."

Rae leaned forward.

"That's a lot. Stop there and check in with Alison to see if she got it all."

"Did you get it?"

"You feel sad and heavy. You don't know about being a sex addict. You're a normal guy. You haven't found the right woman. You have a full life."

"Wow. That's it. You got it!" Frank showed the beginnings of a grin, but seemed to be resisting it.

"Now respond to Frank."

Alison put her hands on her knees.

"Everything you said might well be true, but you left out the important part for me. Yesterday you told me that you felt stuck in a pattern of relationship that repeated itself over and over. You said that you loved the chase, but always ended up feeling dissatisfied with the person, and that your constant obsession with the chase and finding a lover interfered with other important relationships and events in your life. That's the part that reminded me of my disease."

Frank looked uncomfortable.

Rae put a hand on his knee.

"Breathe, Frank. Just take in what this thoughtful, loving woman is saying to you. Keep as much eye contact as you can right now. You don't need to say anything. Just notice your feelings. Notice where they are in your body."

Frank closed his eyes and his face relaxed a little. He took several deep breaths. Rae and Alison quietly watched him.

After a minute, Rae noticed a slight increase in Frank's rate of breath and tiny twitches at the corner of his left eye.

"Right there." Rae spoke softly, almost a whisper. "Yes, that's it."

Frank teared up. Rae placed her hand on his knee. "Just let the tears come … that's right."

Frank cried softly, his eyes shut.

Rae shifted closer to Frank while she continued to apply gentle pressure on his knee with her left hand. She let her right hand rest lightly in the middle of Frank's back. "You've held this sorrow back for a long time … so just keep letting it out."

Frank began to sob.

"Remember to breathe."

Frank gasped and cried harder. He gasped again and again, each time with a fresh cascade of tears. Finally after several minutes, he began to quiet down and his sobs were replaced by sniffling. He opened his eyes and looked at Alison, then searched the floor as he repeated his loud, wet sniffs. Rae reached behind him, took the Kleenex box from Ronald's outstretched hand and held it in front of Frank. He grabbed a handful of tissues and blew his nose loudly, followed by one coughing laugh before wiping his nose and eyes.

When he looked back at Rae, he was smiling, and his eyes sparkled.

Rae returned his smile.

"When you're ready, look and see what you'd like to share with us."

"I've felt so alone." The words came quickly. "Like I've been alone all my life." Tears overran his eyes. He dabbed his eyes with the tissues and laughed. "It's just so strange. I'm almost forty, and here I am blubbering…"

"Yes, you are, aren't you?" Rae said with a smile.

Frank smiled back. "Yes, I guess I am." He dropped the smile and sat there looking at Rae. It was the most eye contact she had experienced from him all week. She had a lot she wanted to ask him, a lot she wanted to say to him, but right now she knew eye contact was the best thing for Frank. He would have plenty of time to explore the new internal world that had just opened up to him. Right now, the most important thing was for her to receive him with an open heart.

After a long pause, Rae said, "You've taken a big step this morning, Frank. Look and see if you're open to taking another one."

"What kind of step?"

"Just make eye contact with Alison."

Frank turned and met Alison's soft eyes. Another tear rolled down his left cheek. After a moment he looked back at Rae. She said, "Now, if you're willing, make eye contact with each person."

A flush came to Frank's cheeks. He looked at Max, who grinned and nodded, then at Diane, who smiled warmly. Next was Ronald, and so on around the circle until he came back to Rae.

Frank was quiet; his face glistened with tears.

"I don't know how much of this I can take," Frank laughed.

Rae joined him and several others in laughter. Rae gave Frank a long deep hug, noticing how soft and pliant he felt in her arms. She leaned back, holding his shoulders with both hands. "I'm proud of you."

Frank laughed as more tears rolled down his cheeks.

Rae dropped her hands. "Is there anything else you need to say?"

Frank shook his head.

"Alison, how about you?"

Alison raised her right hand to her chest. "Frank..."

Her voice caught and she cleared her throat. "I'm so glad for you. Thank you for hearing me."

They both leaned forward and hugged from their seated positions.

After they separated, Rae paused and asked, "Frank, do you want to hear from the group?"

"Yes."

Rae turned and looked around the circle.

"Frank is open to feedback. Be sure you confine your comments to how you were affected by his work."

Tex barely waited for Rae to finish. "You really gave me something to think about, Frank. All the things you said about not having a problem rang like a bell for me. I'm starting to wonder if there isn't something to this addiction thing after all." Tex glanced at Alison. "And you've got a lot of gumption, little Missy."

Ronald let out a loud guffaw, but stopped when no one else joined in.

Carmen looked at Tex, who met her gaze with a slight inclination of his head. She turned toward Frank and said, "I felt protective toward you. You seemed so vulnerable and young." She paused. "I haven't felt comfortable around you all week, but right now I feel close to you."

Frank smiled. But before he could respond, Rae put a hand on his knee and said, "Just take it in. You don't need to say anything; they're sharing their experience with you."

In the end, everyone had something to say to Frank, mostly support and appreciation, with the exception of an admonition from Gil to go to at least six twelve-step meetings to explore this issue.

It was time to end the meeting. Past time, in fact. They were already five minutes over. Rae, Alison and Frank returned to their places.

Rae looked around the room after the closing poem had been read. No one moved. She saw the light in their faces and spontaneously reached to either side for David's and Todd's hands. Soon everyone was linked hand in hand around the circle. Rae felt the energy flowing through her, gratitude rising in her. The group was alive and well. They really were all heroes.

This was it. This was the real payoff for all the tears and hard work—a blissful connection, hearts open, eyes clear and hands joined.

She took in a deep breath and let it out slowly to mark the moment. Then she squeezed Todd's hand and waited for the squeeze to come full circle. When, seconds later, David squeezed hers, she smiled. "Take good care of yourselves over the break. We'll see you at four o'clock."

———

DAVID AND RAE were laughing when Gil opened the door to Rae's room. As he closed it behind him, there were still a couple of people talking in the adjacent meeting room.

Rae looked up, smiling. "We were just congratulating ourselves on a brilliant session."

How does she do that?

Gil was speechless for a second, marveling at Rae's ability to be self-congratulatory without seeming egotistical. Maybe it was her good humor or her ability to simply state something true without personalizing it. He shook his head.

"Yeah, maybe."

"Maybe, maybe?" David's voice gained in volume as his playful indignation swelled. "What do you mean 'maybe'? We were great. The best ever."

"Yeah, well I guess it turned out okay."

Rae looked at Gil with worry.

"What's wrong, Gil? It's not like you to miss a chance to celebrate."

"I think we came close to crashing in the first half of the session. Diane, for one, declined to work because of that weirdness with Todd."

"But that's just it," David said. "We turned it around, grabbing victory from the jaws of defeat. We're unbeatable."

"I don't feel unbeatable. I'm troubled by the group, and I'm not sure what all is going on. I do know I want some time alone to think it over. I'm going for a hike."

"Well, you have between now and 4 o'clock to figure it out," Rae said. "That will be our last working session. After that, it's Friday morning re-entry plans and we're done."

David studied Gil with a thoughtful expression. "You've been struggling all week. I'm concerned for you." David paused, thinking for a moment. "I'd offer to keep you company, but my ankle is still recovering."

"Thanks, that's okay. I want to get off on my own for a while."

"All right, let's set a time to meet before the next session." David looked at his watch. "It's 12:45 now. Let's say we meet back here at 3:45."

For once, Gil didn't argue. All he could think about was getting outside, up high on the ridge, where there was room to think and air to breathe.

11

Thursday Afternoon

RAE WENT THROUGH THE DOUBLE DOORS OF THE dining room, with David right behind her. It was almost 1:00, and a long line was moving slowly past the serving table. She loved the colors on the open salad bar: red beets, dark green kale and golden carrots. The rich sweet smell of cream of leek soup wafted from the five-gallon cauldron at the far end of the table.

Rae went straight for soup and salad, while David stood in line, waiting for a toasted cheese sandwich.

As Rae passed him, she said, "It's gotten colder. I'll look for a table in the Solarium."

"Okay." David picked up a plate and selected a fork, knife and napkin from the wall rack.

Rae found a table near the small wood stove next to the short bar. The room was small and cozy, and Rae was happy to see someone had lit a fire. She sat down facing the stove soaking up the radiated heat.

A few minutes later, David slid into the other seat with a pile of grilled cheese sandwiches and a bowl of potato chips.

Once again, Rae compared the colors and calories of their food choices. *How does he stay healthy?*

Just then a young man in overalls, holding a two-way radio in his hand, came through the glass door and walked up to their table.

"Are you Rae Milford?"

Rae hesitated, as if she didn't recognize the name. "Yes."

Something's happened. Someone has had an accident.

"Your husband is at the gate, and we don't have him on the guest list."

"Here? Now?"

"Yes."

"Is anything wrong?" she asked.

"Not that I know of," the young man said. "He simply asked to see you."

"I didn't know Alan was going to join us," David said.

"Neither did I." Rae kept staring at the messenger, looking for some sign of the disaster that brought him here. "What do I need to do?"

"If you want to come up to the gate, we can add him to the list for you."

"I'll come." Rae pushed back from the table, stood up and said to David, "Watch my lunch for me."

"Okay."

Rae followed the young man through the lodge. The clatter of dishes and the blended white noise of a hundred conversations receded as she noticed, for the first time, the crisscross pattern of wooden slats in the false ceiling. *How could I have missed that all these years?* They went out the front door, along the covered walkway in front of the office and across the oval lawn. The brisk air and sea view had no impact. Rae kept going over the list of those closest to her: her daughters, her mother, her brother? *Please, not one of them.*

As they started up the hill, she saw Alan standing by the wooden kiosk. She searched his face for some clue to the disaster, but he was smiling and waving at her. At first it didn't compute. Alan was smiling.

Then it struck her. There wasn't any bad news. Alan needed something.

"Hi, sweetheart." Alan reached out to embrace her.

She stepped back, frowning.

"What are you doing here?"

Alan shot a quick glance at the woman in the kiosk and the young man in overalls.

"I came to surprise you."

Rae registered his public face, his forced breeziness and unaccustomed jocularity. She replied flatly, "Well, I'm surprised."

"Yes. Good." The lilt was fading from his voice. "It would be nice to see a little more spontaneous joy."

"What I feel right now is anger. Did you ever think about how I might react to being told that you were here unexpectedly?"

"I did. And in my mind, the scene involved shrieks of delight, which appear to be absent at the present."

"I was terrified that something had happened to someone close to me, and you had come to tell me."

"Oh, well, that. Yes. Of course." Alan paused. "But let's get me checked in so we can get caught up at our leisure with a little more privacy."

Rae crossed her arms.

"Checked in? I don't know if you'll be staying that long."

"What do you mean?"

"This isn't a good time for you to be here." Rae wanted to leave it at that; a simple statement of fact, and listened with regret to her next words, which seemed to arise of their own accord. "I'm very busy wrapping up a difficult workshop and I don't have any free time right now."

"Oh, I see." Alan dropped his mask of good humor. "And I'm part of the problem rather than part of the solution."

Rae heard the strain in his voice. She looked at the two gatekeepers, then uncrossed her arms and took Alan by the elbow. "Let's walk up the hill."

"I don't want to walk up the hill," Alan complained as he allowed himself to be guided forward. "I want you to check me in so we can both go sit somewhere comfortable."

"There's no sense in doing anything until we've had a chance to talk." Rae continued to lead him up the asphalt drive.

"You know I'm not as strong as I was."

"We'll go slowly."

They continued up the steep driveway in silence. Rae was consciously holding back her stride and allowing him to set the pace. She was flooded with feelings. Resentment, disappointment, despair, anger.

Right now, I just want to be sitting next to the warm stove, enjoying my lunch with David.

When they got to the top, she steered them south along the shoulder of Highway One. Alan was panting heavily, so she stopped. The vista southeast took her breath away and she felt the adrenaline of fear receding from her bloodstream. It was a familiar sight but at the moment she felt an expansive openness in her chest as she gazed at the tall crumbling cliffs topped by brave patches of Monterey cypress and the singular homesteads of Big Sur. She felt an upwelling of joy she missed so terribly in this relationship.

"I needed to see you." Alan wheezed slightly as he tried to recover his wind.

"I see that."

"I'm lonely, and I need you at home."

"I know you do," Rae said softly. "Please understand that there's a lot going on in my career and I have commitments. I'll be home on Friday. That's tomorrow."

"I can't fight this cancer alone." Alan's voice was husky. "And I can't fight for your attention and get well at the same time. I don't have the energy."

"I see that." Rae put her hand on his elbow and turned to walk again.

"You know how I hate to give myself those injections. I want you to come home and help take care of me."

Rae grimaced at the mention of that witch doctor's brew from Mexico that Alan had been smuggling in every few months, the latest acquisition in his unending quest for alternate miracle treatments. She winced every time she thought of his falling for that hokum. It just didn't jibe with the intelligent, capable man she had married. Recoiling at the thought of her life revolving around taking care of him, she let go of his elbow.

"Maybe it's time you stop taking those nostrums and place your faith in your doctor's recommendations." Rae tried to keep her voice free of judgment. But her opinions were never far from the surface, and Alan's criticism sensors were on full alert.

"When you get sick, you can make that choice," Alan barked back. "But as long as it's my body at risk, I'm going to keep doing everything I can to save it. I'm fighting for my life!"

"You're fighting for something, that's for sure." Rae regretted the irony in her tone, but was unable to curb it. "But one thing that's not on the table is your life."

Alan stopped walking and faced her, his eyes narrowing.

"And what the hell is that supposed to mean?"

With a tone of exhaustion, Rae continued, "You're sixty years old. Your doctor told us that this particular cancer will take decades to develop, if treated properly." Rae's voice quivered. "You have every likelihood of outliving most of your family and friends!"

"That's outrageous! You don't know what you're talking about. And neither does the doctor." Alan was shouting now, firing his words like bullets. "You are the most uncaring, unfeeling, unresponsive person I know."

Rae reeled backward. A tear came to her eye, then she remembered the chanting last night at Compline.

"You're right. I'm judging you and trying to change you; doing everything but accepting you just the way you are." Rae paused. "I'm so sorry."

Alan moved his head to the right and angled his eyes left, keeping Rae in his gaze as he furrowed his brow and said, "And ..." as if he were waiting for the other shoe to drop.

He's right. Rae decided to just say it. "And I need some time away, some distance from our chronic crisis, to sort out what it is *I* want."

"We could go to South America. There's a clinic there that's really more like a spa …"

"No, Alan, I need to take time off from our life together, from our marriage, from you." Rae couldn't believe she said that.

"What are you saying?" Alan's voice stalled. He stood there, staring at her. Alan, who always had a rejoinder, a quip, an argument, was speechless.

It broke her heart to see him this way, but she had to admit there was a rising buoyancy in the midst of her pain. It felt something like hope.

DAVID WALKED DOWN the steep dirt road towards the concrete bathhouse built into the cliff fifty feet above the pounding surf. He was anticipating a relaxing massage, but his thoughts kept coming back to Rae. *Why had Alan shown up so unexpectedly?* David waited for them as long as he could, then covered Rae's plate with plastic wrap, wrote her name on it and left it on the side counter, hoping she would find it if she came back.

He inventoried his aches and pains, starting with his right ankle, which still hurt every time he took an unexpected sideways step. Next, he noted the dull pressure in his knees, the soreness in his lower back, and his stiff neck. Sitting on the floor for five days wasn't helping and he was eager for relief.

But his thoughts kept coming back to the workshop. Gil was acting surly and resentful and Rae was distant. Pausing at the bottom of the hill, he took a deep breath, smelling the salty mist from the breaking waves below, and then watched his warm exhaled breath condense into clouds in the cold air.

I hope the room is heated, he thought.

David went down the narrow flight of stairs, taking two turns to end up in the small changing room. Two young women were getting dressed. He turned to the wall, found an empty hook and slowly started to remove his hoodie, hoping they would be gone by the time he dropped his pants. The small co-ed dressing room always unnerved him.

It was cold in the open-air shower room. David slid the glass panels shut to close off the open space looking out to sea, but the chilly breeze still found its way through the gaps. He shivered and got gooseflesh as he cranked the shower up, all the way to hot. The tepid temperature and low flow were no help, so he soaped and rinsed as quickly as he could, anticipating the warmth of the waiting tub.

He turned off the tap, walked quickly out onto the deck and slipped into the first tub, allowing the sulfurous hot springs bath to banish the chill.

The relief was short-lived; it was hard to stay in the 110-degree water. He got out and sat on the edge of the tub. Too hot, and too cold. *Like Gil and Rae.*

David felt unsettled and was no longer looking forward to the upcoming massage, or anything else.

GIL WANDERED ACROSS the lawn below the lodge and continued out towards the cliff. He didn't know what he was going to do right now, so he let his feet take the lead. For the moment they seemed to be a little lost.

The possibility of a hike had melted away in a series of small encounters; little chunks of time whittled away until there was no time for even a quick dash to the hills. Time was like that. Small segments could expand into just enough time, while larger chunks often fell to the tyranny of small distractions.

The next best thing for him right now would be a nap. He needed to get out of the cold and find a quiet spot where he wouldn't be bothered. He decided on the empty massage tables on the roof deck at the baths. As he strode off across the lawn, he spotted someone who looked a lot like Rae's husband turning a car around at the bottom of the hill and heading back up toward the highway.

That can't be right. Gil continued down toward the baths.

DAVID HAD JUST FINISHED reading The Goose Story to the group, an inspirational tale of the benefits geese derive from sticking together. The tale ended dramatically, with two geese falling out of formation to accompany an injured goose to the ground. They stay with him until he either recovers or dies. This part usually evoked a tearful response, but all eyes were dry and somewhat unfocused.

Gil took in the circle. The energy was very low. The afternoon session was often slow to start, but this seemed different. *Something's off.*

Gil shot a worried glance at Rae, but she merely shrugged her shoulders.

David was businesslike, picking up his yellow pad to check his notes. "Gil, why don't you lead the check-in?"

Gil closed his eyes and counted three breaths. Then he spoke slowly and quietly.

"This will be our last working session. Tomorrow morning is dedicated to developing your re-entry plans and to saying goodbye." Gil let that sink in. "For check-in, let us know where you are right now and if there's any unfinished work that you'd like to do. Let's start on my right and go around the room—Carmen?"

Carmen looked up, startled. "I'm not ready. I don't know what I want to say." She seemed embarrassed. "I wasn't expecting to be the first one."

Diane, seated to Carmen's right, said softly, "You can pass."

Carmen looked relieved. "I pass."

"Okay," Gil said, and looked at Diane.

Diane sat up straight. "I know I asked for time last session, but I talked it over with Alison during the break and I've decided to share briefly about my experience last night and stop there." Diane glanced at Alison, who nodded reassuringly.

"I've gotten a lot out of this week and I don't want to open up a whole new can of worms at the eleventh hour."

Diane hesitated, then continued.

"Sitting in the tubs late last night, I had a visceral memory of inappropriate touching from my childhood. I'd been avoiding the baths all week, but last night something shifted. I woke up at three in the morning and couldn't go back to sleep. I felt restless and a little anxious, and I thought the warm baths might help.

"So I got up and went down to the baths. It was dark and I couldn't see very well, but it didn't look like anyone was there. I was shocked when I slipped into the large round tub and heard Alison's voice from out of the shadows. We were the only ones there. The strange thing was that I felt safe there in that tub, in the dark, with Alison. And, when I was the most relaxed, it came back. That horrible, frozen, numb body feeling I felt as a child, being touched where I shouldn't have been touched."

Diane paused, looked up and made eye contact with Alison. Alison gently nodded, her cheeks wet with tears. A tear came to Diane's eye and she brushed it away. Then she turned to Rae and said, "I wanted you to know." Diane cried softly.

Rae began to rise off her cushion.

Diane wiped her face and held up her hand at arms' length, palm outward. "That's it. That's all I want to say about it right now."

Rae was caught off-guard and almost lost her balance. She sat back down with a flop and took a moment to regain her composure.

"Thank you, Diane. You're being very clear." Rae waited for that to sink in. When Diane returned her gaze, Rae added, "Are you open to feedback?"

"No."

While Rae struggled with how to respond to that, David interjected, "Thank you for your check-in, Diane. Ronald, you're up."

I'm leading this go-round. Gil flashed David a look but he didn't catch it.

Ronald said to Diane, "That was really powerful. You stuck to your guns. I'm so glad you're in this workshop." Ronald's voice was half an octave deeper than usual; his words came out in a slow, measured cadence.

Diane smiled and Ronald returned her smile. He took a deep breath and turned back to the group. "I feel really grateful to be here, and spend this week with you. I came more on a whim than anything else."

There was an accepting, confessional tone to Ronald's words. "Frankly, I didn't have much in the way of expectations beyond California sunshine, time away from work and the continuing education units. I don't even remember what I said the first night about my purpose for being here." Ronald smiled again. "I've definitely experienced more than I expected."

Max snorted a bark of laughter.

Ronald continued, "I never would have believed I could feel so comfortable in such an intense group. I'll be really sorry to leave you tomorrow." Ronald turned back to Diane. "Particularly you."

Ronald paused for a few moments. "You have a way of saying something difficult that makes it easy to hear." Ronald paused. "I would like to be in a relationship with a woman like you."

Diane's eyes reflected the light from the wall of windows as she looked at Ronald. He sat there for a moment, taking it in, then cleared his throat.

"I'm done."

David flipped through his yellow pad until he found what he wanted. He looked up at Ronald and read, "Your miracle from Sunday night was to meet the woman of your dreams here at Esalen and to live happily ever after."

"Well, it looks like I got the first part." Ronald smiled ruefully. Frank and Max laughed and several others chuckled.

"You met the woman of your dreams," Gil said, "and you're free to live happily ever after."

"But she's not available."

"Maybe living happily ever after isn't about whether she's available or not."

Ronald laughed.

"Is this some kind of Zen thing?"

"Maybe." Gil smiled. "A Buddhist might say if you want to find the woman of your dreams, find the woman of your dreams. If you want to be happy, be happy. Just don't confuse the two."

Rae laughed, and so did several others.

Ronald was at a loss for words.

David said, "Max, you're next."

Gil frowned at David before turning back to Max across the circle. "Go ahead."

Max smiled under his four-day growth of beard and his eyes danced with pleasure and anticipation.

"I don't know why, but I've been really excited today," he said to the room. "I woke up that way. My first thought on opening my eyes was, 'I'm ready.' I don't know what that means; I just know I woke up full of energy, like I was part of something grand and meaningful. I felt ten years younger. I couldn't wait to see what today had in store for me. It's like I knew that something was about to be revealed."

He stopped. "No, that's not quite right. It's more like I've always known the answer, and it's just now bubbling up to the surface. All I need to help make that happen is right here in this room. You are the key, and I'm about to unlock something I've spent my whole life looking for. I'm ready to work."

Max turned to Tex. "You're up."

Gil nodded to convey his confirmation, but Tex was looking straight at David.

"I'm a little out of sorts this morning, and I'm starting to think about what's going on back at the stables." He paused. "With horses I know who's in charge." Tex sat still as if he were done. The whole room seemed to be leaning in to hear the next thing.

"Just keep both those thoughts present as we go around the room," David said as he paused to make a note. "You feel a little out of sorts here this evening, and with horses you know who's in charge."

There was a vacuum-like silence after his paraphrase of Tex's words.

Tex showed no inclination to respond.

Gil said, "Do you want to work on something this session?"

"I don't know."

"You have an open invitation if you decide you want to."

Alison cleared her throat, then caught and held Tex's gaze.

"I desperately want you to see the truth about your drinking. I can't stand the thought of letting you leave here without that."

Before Tex could respond, she turned back to the group. "In fact, I see what each of you needs to do, what your problems are and exactly what it is you need to learn." Smiles broke out around the room. "But why is it that the more I think I know what's going on with each of you, the less I can see what's going on with me? I just know that somehow, when I think about Tex's problem, I lose myself."

Alison took a deep breath and let it out as if registering what she had just said. "Right now I'm able to hold on to that idea, but it won't last." She looked between Rae and David: "If one of you knows how to make this stick, I want to work on it."

David scribbled on his yellow pad and replied to Alison, "Gotcha." He then looked expectantly past Rae to Frank.

"Frank, you're up," Gil said.

"I don't know what to say. You haven't exactly solved my problem."

Todd snorted.

"I still don't know what I'm going to do about my job. If anything, I feel more unsettled about it. What's more, you've given me a whole new batch of problems to worry about."

Tex erupted in one loud guffaw and several others joined him, laughing in recognition of their shared experience.

"I really had no idea what was going on all this time," Frank continued, "and even though it isn't exactly good news..." More laughter. "... I've felt more alive this week than I ever have. It's hard to explain, but in the middle of all the discomfort, I feel solid and grounded. Go figure."

Frank sat silently for a moment, then said, "I'm done."

David turned to Todd.

Todd half-smiled and blinked twice at Rae.

"When I was a boy growing up in the Bronx, my mom and I lived with my aunt. She never spoke. I always thought that was strange, you know? I knew something was wrong, but I also sensed that asking about it wasn't allowed. So I ignored her. She was always in the house, never went out, no one ever visited her. Every meal, she sat in the same chair at the table, never saying a word. She had a little dog, a mutt, that she took care of but never allowed out of her room. I would sit in my room doing my homework before dinner, listening to that dog yap. Whenever my aunt left her room, the dog barked until she came back again."

Todd paused without looking directly at anyone in the room, and then went on.

"Barking dogs have always held a fascination for me. I mean, why do they bark on and on and on? What is it they want to say to us? When I finally left home and went to college, the city pound was right across from my dorm. All night long, they barked. My sleep was punctuated by dogs, dreams of dogs, with the silences between barks becoming just as annoying as the barks themselves.

"My roommate, Ward, was from an upper-middle-class family in suburban Connecticut. He put on earphones connected to his stereo every night and didn't take them off until he got up the next morning. He never mentioned the dogs. I knew there was no way I could ever talk to him about the barking or my aunt. I knew he came from a world where aunts talk and dogs wag their tails."

"Todd, I'd like you to come back to your check-in," Rae gently interjected. "Just a few sentences about where you are now, what the memory of your aunt and the dogs has to do with what's happening right now and whether you have anything you want to work on."

Todd's face tightened and his voice was sharp.

"So I finally try to tell you what's going on, and you interrupt me. It's so frustrating. I'm always either getting interrupted or being ignored. I never finish what I'm saying. Even back then, though my aunt didn't talk, didn't interrupt me or tell me what to do, I still wasn't allowed to say what was on my mind."

"I just want you to stay focused on what is on your heart right now," Rae added.

"If you people would just let me finish, you'd find out," barked Todd, brow furrowed and eyes narrowed. "Everyone else has had their turn. I'm just following your rules."

"Take a minute and finish your check-in," suggested David.

"I can't finish in a minute. Why should I finish in a minute when we wasted huge chunks of time on the paranoid reaction Ronald had about Frank not liking him and Max's bizarre fantasy about getting old. I waited through those boring ramblings and didn't complain, did I?"

Todd was looking directly at Rae. "No, I didn't. Now, when I have something to say, I'm harassed. What is it with you?"

Rae raised her head to watch him.

"So what is it you want to tell us?"

"I *was* telling you before I was so rudely interrupted."

"Continue, please."

"It's like I was telling Diane yesterday, about this friend who worked for the post office. You know, an underemployed artist type. I spent every Sunday rehearsing with him in a community theater company. We had bit parts, and afterwards we'd always stop by the neighborhood corner bar for a few beers and to critique the pitiful performances of the others. We had more experience than they did and should have been given better parts. But the director had it in for us. He didn't like the fact that we were theater majors and knew more than he did.

He seemed to take pleasure in shuffling us off into small parts. That's what…"

"All right, Todd," David said in a neutral tone. "Please let us know how this relates to your experience here and now. We are still on go-rounds."

Todd gave David a hard look. "My friend killed himself a year later."

David held Todd's eye contact, keeping his expression open and receptive.

After a moment, Todd continued. "He was sensitive and couldn't handle the disregard and inexplicable calamities that hit just when you're about to get somewhere. But that's the way it is. Everything falls apart in the end. Just like Tex was saying the other day about being a complete failure in his marriage. And look at Frank, still clueless after all the education and all the advantages he's had." Todd took a breath and raised his chin. "That's it."

"Todd, you've been asked several times to focus on your feelings, and that seems difficult for you. It seems to me you're frustrated, even angry. You've also said some things that may have affected other people's feelings, and I'd like to give them the chance to respond before we continue." Rae paused.

"What do you mean?"

"You said Tex was a failure, Frank was clueless, Ronald was paranoid and Max was bizarre."

"Oh, they know what I meant."

"Maybe so, but I see Frank looking like he's going to burst and Tex is glowering at you. Can you see that? Are you willing to hear from them?"

"Yeah, sure, but I don't think we have time for this."

"Tell me, Todd. What do you see when you look at them?"

"Just Tex and Frank."

"You don't notice anything unusual in their faces. Okay, so now I want you to pay close attention to what they have to say. Will you do that?"

"Sure," Todd said with an eye roll.

"Who wants to start?" asked Rae.

Frank immediately raised his hand. "Todd, I felt angry when you called me clueless. I want you to keep your opinions about me to yourself."

Rae said to Todd, "Just repeat back what you heard Frank say."

Todd glanced at Rae from under hooded eyes. "There's really nothing to say. Frank and I have talked about this. He knows all about his problems."

"Just say back to Frank what you heard him say," Rae repeated.

Todd squinted at Rae and tilted his head. Rae added, "If you don't remember, just ask Frank to repeat it."

Todd looked at Frank. "What did you say?"

"I said I didn't like you saying I was clueless. I want you to take it back."

Todd brightened.

"Oh, don't worry about that. It's just a turn of phrase. Don't get all twisted up about it."

Rae broke in again, saying, "Just tell Frank what you heard him say."

Todd's eyes rolled upwards. He said to Frank, "You're not completely clueless, really, it's just that you're a little out of touch. Nothing to get bent out of shape over."

"Ask Frank to say it again," Rae repeated.

Todd said nothing.

Frank waited, and then spoke in an even tone, "I don't like being called clueless, and I want you to apologize."

Todd turned to Rae and shook his head.

"This is ridiculous. Here we are, wasting time again, putting off the work you've been promising us. I feel like we've all been tricked. Time is going to run out, and we're never going to hear what it is you're holding back, assuming you have any answers at all. I want to know how to avoid limitations. That's why I took this course. It wasn't easy for me to get here, and I've waited patiently all week. Now time is running out, and you're having us do the same exercises we did yesterday and the day before. When are we going to get to the real, specific information?"

Rae crawled across the room while he was talking and sat right in front of Todd. He stopped talking and looked at her.

She put her hand on his foot, peered out at him through her bangs and spoke softly, with a measured cadence.

"This *is* the information. This is your self-limiting behavior. We have been working with it all week. You said you wanted to stop getting in your own way. You want to stop blowing up all your meaningful relationships. Well, this is how you learn to stop."

Rae paused to let that sink in. Todd's face remained blank. She saw no sign of recognition in Todd's eyes. Rae decided to continue in spite of her sense of futility.

"You just hurt Frank's feelings, and he's asked you to listen to him and to acknowledge what he's saying to you. Frank's tried three times and you've been unable to repeat back what he said. Frank needs to know that you heard him. The way to do that is to tell him what you heard him say. If you still don't know what he said, ask him to repeat it."

Todd stared at Rae for a moment.

"Repeating what Frank has to say is *not* what I came here for. But if it's so important to you…" He looked over Rae's shoulder to Frank. "Could you repeat it again?"

Frank, more relaxed now and with a softer expression, said, "When you said I was clueless, it pissed me off, and I want you to apologize to me."

"You want me to apologize for saying you were clueless."

Rae looked at Frank. "Did he get it?"

"Not quite. I also said I was pissed off."

She looked back at Todd, who said in a monotone, "And you're angry."

"Yes."

"Now you can respond to Frank," directed Rae.

"I like you, you know that. I was just repeating what we talked about at breakfast the other day."

Rae coached Frank, "Tell Todd what you heard."

"You think I'm great, and were just repeating something we already talked about."

Rae turned to Todd, "Did he get it?"

"It's okay, we have an understanding. I know what kind of guy Frank is. I don't have any problem with Frank. I had a cousin who used to get upset all the time, and he and I just came to an understanding. You don't need to take these things so seriously. You learn what's important and what isn't. You move on…"

Rae saw that Todd was digging himself in deeper, and interrupted again, "Todd, did Frank get what you said?"

"Well, yeah," Todd said, staring at Rae quizzically, as if wondering where she'd been for the last two minutes.

Rae continued, "So, Frank, where are you right now?"

"I'm okay. I'm fine with Todd."

Out of the corner of her eye, Rae saw Gil tilt forward. Without turning, she put her left hand out towards him. The last thing Rae wanted was any intervention from Gil that might start Todd up again.

Gil held his position for a few seconds, then slowly collapsed back on his pillow.

"This is the work that you need to do," Rae said holding eye contact with Todd, "what we just did right here. You need to start noticing when your words affect other people, then stop and take the time to really understand what it is that you said that impacted them, and clean it up. This is your self-limiting behavior."

Todd looked away, his face blank. She tried to catch Todd's averted eyes. "Todd."

"If you say so," Todd said gazing somewhere over Rae's shoulder.

Rae frowned.

"I know this is hard for you to see, but it's happening all around you all the time. When a girlfriend breaks up with you, or you get fired, you wonder what happened." Rae paused for effect. "You need to notice when others are affected by what you say and do. Then work to resolve the situation, like you just did with Frank."

Todd nodded solemnly.

"Good." Rae sighed. "Now, before we hear from Tex, are you open to hearing what it was like for the others to watch you during this interaction?"

"Whatever."

"Is that a yes?"

"Sure."

"What about you, Frank?" Rae asked.

"Sure."

"The floor is open for feedback." Rae returned to her pillow.

Several people offered their feelings and thoughts, and although somewhat subdued, they seemed to be making an effort to be supportive and a couple expressed appreciation for Frank's clarity. Alison, however, expressed frustration. "This took almost half the session, I don't think Todd got a damn thing out of it, and others want to work."

Rae turned to Tex. "Do you have anything you want to say to Todd?"

"Nope." Tex folded his arms across his chest.

Rae was about to move on when Gil said, "We still need to hear from Ronald and Max."

"You're right." Rae turned to Ronald. "Do you have anything to say?"

"I'm fine. I didn't take Todd seriously." Gil and Rae waited. "That's it?"

"Well, I know what a paranoid reaction is, and it doesn't apply to me," Ronald said.

Rae turned to Max.

Max looked bemused. "I'm more at peace with myself than I have been in a long time. I'm good."

With a sardonic smile, Todd said, "So this is the important information I'm missing? Not a big loss, if you ask me."

Rae replied curtly, "Take from it what you will." Turning to David, she asked, "What's next?"

Gil leaned forward to speak.

"All right, then," David said, "We have three people who've asked to work, Max, Alison and maybe Tex, and one hour remaining. So each person has twenty minutes."

"What about Carmen?" Diane blurted.

Carmen looked up, as surprise flashed across her face. "No, no, that's okay."

"Four people," David said, without missing a beat. "So each person has fifteen minutes."

Ignoring David, Rae looked across the room at Carmen.

"You haven't checked in yet. Would you like to go now?"

"I really don't have anything." Carmen looked at the carpet with an expression somewhere between calm and vacant. "I've listened to everyone, and I'm really impressed with their progress. This is an amazing group of people. I don't have anything to contribute."

Rae bit her tongue and waited. Carmen appeared to be looking for something else to say.

Finally Carmen looked up. "My life is pretty dull compared to everyone else's."

"That's a judgment," Rae interjected. "How about letting that go and focusing on how you feel right now?"

"What do you mean?"

"Just tell us, what are you feeling right now?"

"I feel fine."

"Say more about 'fine'."

"I feel like I don't have anything to say, and I'm taking up everyone's time. We should be working on more important things."

"Those are thoughts, not feelings. When was the last time you thought your needs were as important as everyone else's?"

Carmen stared blankly at Rae.

Rae met and held Carmen's gaze.

Carmen's eyes teared up, but her back remained straight and her expression neutral. She said nothing. The room dropped into a deep silence, as if holding its breath. Rae looked into Carmen's eyes for several moments, and then quietly asked, "May I come sit next to you?"

Carmen hesitated. Rae crawled across the circle and kneeled beside Carmen, placing her arm around Carmen's shoulder. Carmen began to lean into Rae, then her body stiffened and she pulled back.

"I'm not going there," she blurted out.

Rae leaned forward, tilting her head and giving Carmen a quizzical and appraising look.

Carmen crossed her arms and repeated, "I know where you want me to go, and I'm not going. Not for you. Not for them. Not for anyone."

Carmen sat up straight and turned her head toward Rae.

Rae took in her gaze.

"I get it," Rae repeated. "You're not going to let anyone take you where you don't want to go. You can take care of yourself. You're a strong and competent woman."

Carmen seemed to take this in. The tightness in her face eased a bit as she nodded in agreement.

"Now that we have established that, are you willing to take some time today for yourself?"

Carmen stared at Rae, but said nothing.

"Good. We'll put you on the list for work today."

Carmen said nothing in response, but Gil felt somehow Carmen had agreed. *How did Rae do that?*

Rae looked back at David. He glanced at his timer and said, "We have fifty minutes left, and four people want to work."

Diane looked upset.

"That's not enough time. I want to make more time for the rest of them."

"I agree," Gil said.

"That's not an option." Rae's voice had an edge Gil hadn't heard in a long time, not since the early days of their workshops, when she confronted alcoholics with denial-busting fervor.

David looked up. "We have a commitment to begin and end on time. Now there are forty-nine minutes left."

"Four of you have work to do. This is your time. So you decide how to use it," Rae looked at Alison, Tex, Max and Carmen in turn.

Gil felt his discomfort growing. "Is that okay with those who have asked for time?"

Max and Alison nodded. Todd's head slowly shook back and forth as if in disbelief.

"Who wants to go first?"

"I've had a chance to work already," said Alison. "So I'm willing to wait and see if there's time left."

"Me, too," Max piped up.

"I'm done," Tex said gruffly, almost drowning out Carmen's reedy, "I can wait."

Now Gil felt the fear about the group's functioning that he'd been skating over all week crack like spring ice over running water. He looked at Rae. Still at Carmen's side, she seemed removed from the group, as if she were on her own separate planet.

David's eyebrows shot up and he let out a loud guffaw.

"Don't everyone fight for a chance to work!" He laughed at his own joke. "All right, who's first?"

No one spoke.

The silence gathered itself like a dog circling for a place to lie down. Gil began to feel nauseous.

David looked at Carmen and brusquely said, "Okay, Carmen, you're up."

Carmen looked startled. Gil's nausea deepened. *You can't force this.*

"I'm not ready." Carmen's pitch went up on the last word, as if her statement were really a question.

David was about to respond when Rae said to Carmen, "You need to take this slow, don't you?"

When Carmen responded with a slight nod, Rae continued.

"I'd like you to look at each person in turn and ask yourself this question: 'Do I feel safe?' Are you willing to do that?"

"Yes," Carmen answered hesitantly.

"Good. Start with Diane. Look in her eyes. You don't need to say anything. Just ask yourself that question, and be aware of how you feel."

Carmen looked at Diane, who met her gaze. They sat perfectly still for thirty seconds. The room was silent.

"That's right," Rae smiled. "Trust what you're feeling right now as you look into Diane's eyes. And Diane, there's nothing you need to do or say. Just be present, exactly as you are."

After a few seconds, Diane broke into a smile and Carmen smiled back. Then slowly and deliberately, Carmen continued around the circle, lingering a little on Alison and Max, but brushing quickly past Todd. When she was done, she turned back to Rae, who asked, "How was that?"

"Okay, I guess."

"I guess?"

"Well, I'm not completely comfortable."

"And..."

"I don't want to share anymore."

Looking thoughtful, Rae paused. "You've already let me know you're strong, and that no one can make you do something you don't want to do. So you need to see if you want to do what I am about to ask you. Any answer is fine. You can say yes or no, whatever is true for you. Okay?"

Carmen looked skeptical.

"I'd like you to look at each person you feel safe with and say, 'I am important.'"

"I don't want to do that."

Rae moved directly in front of Carmen.

"Do you see that this is the same work Diane did? You have the same rights as Diane and everyone else."

Carmen looked straight at Rae and said nothing.

"Start with whoever is easiest to say that to."

Taking a breath, Carmen turned to Diane and said in a quiet voice, "I'm going to pass."

Diane smiled broadly, and nodded her support.

"Okay, that's good," said Rae. "You don't have to practice with anyone you don't want to. Pick the next person."

"I'm done."

"Don't stop now. You're never going to get a better place to practice this. You came all the way down here. You took time off from work. Give it a try."

Gil crawled over to whisper in David's ear. "You've got to stop Rae."

Carmen folded her arms across her chest. "I pass."

Rae stared intently into Carmen's eyes.

Just then David moved in behind Rae and put his arms around her in a loving embrace. "Let it go."

Rae resisted at first, then leaned back against David's chest. Gil was both relieved and embarrassed.

David continued to cradle her while speaking softly in her ear. "There is nothing you need to do or say right now."

David looked over Rae to Carmen.

"Carmen, while I hold Rae, I want you to close your eyes, and just be present to your own feelings and your own strength."

Gil crawled onto David's pillow and crossed his legs in a meditation pose. As he closed his eyes, words passed by his awareness as if on a huge banner pulled by a small plane: *Finally, something real.*

Rae stirred in David's arms, sat up, and looked at him. David crossed his eyes and soon both of them were laughing. Gil opened his eyes and smiled, then chuckled and finally laughed out loud. Pretty soon the whole room was laughing. Everyone except Todd, who sat in stony silence.

When the room had settled down, David sat in Gil's place and Rae crawled back to her pillow. Gil wiped his eyes.

David asked Carmen, "Is there anything you'd like to share with us about this experience?"

Carmen still was a little shell-shocked and shook her head.

"All right." He turned his head to Rae. "Is there anything you would like to say?"

"Thank you, David, I love the way you have my back. Carmen, I respect your right to pass, and I applaud you for standing up for yourself. Even against me."

Carmen seemed doubtful and said nothing.

Next, David turned his attention to Tex. "Tex, you mentioned feeling out of sorts. Do you want to talk about it?"

"I've already got plenty to chew on for now, thanks," said Tex.

"Okay." David glanced at his list. "Alison, you were frustrated with not having enough time; and Max, you said you might want to work again if there was time. Both of you decide what you'd like to do. We still have fifteen minutes remaining."

Alison spoke up.

"My request is pretty simple. Well, it may be simple. I want to know how to hold on to myself when I start getting wrapped up in other people's problems."

Rae immediately responded.

"The answer is simple, but not necessarily easy. You need to continue taking care of yourself as you have this week. As you do that, your focus on your own well-being will be strengthened, and you won't get so lost in your relationships."

Rae paused to let that sink in.

"And when you start to lose yourself—because it will happen again and again—stop and see what's coming up for you that you don't want to deal with. That's what really needs your attention."

David smiled at the irony of Rae's advice, coming right on the heels of her interaction with Carmen.

Gil looked over at Alison and said crisply, "Go to Al-Anon meetings, get a sponsor and work the steps. Al-Anon is the indicated program for you. Period."

"And that goes for everyone here who thinks others are more important than you are." Rae looked meaningfully at Carmen.

David checked the time.

"Alison, does that answer your question?"

"That helps." Then she gave Gil a smile and a slight nod.

"Great. Max, what about you?"

Max's eyes were bright as he leaned forward, arching his back.

"What you just said to Alison is very helpful for me. I'm going to keep that for myself. I don't need to work on anything else right now."

Gil looked at his watch. Five minutes to go. *We're actually going to make it.*

There was a moment of peace. Gil was cherishing the sense of completion when Rae's commanding voice broke through his reverie.

"Todd, you've said more than once that there hasn't been time for you to get what you came for. This is your last chance."

No, no, no. Gil stared at her in desperation willing her to take back those words.

Todd held up his right wrist and pointed at his watch. "Uh, five minutes?" He spoke slowly, emphasizing each word. "I don't think so." All week I've waited for you to teach us about self-limiting behaviors and obstacles, and all you've talked about is childhood stuff and alcohol. Now you give Alison one solid piece of advice and we're done. That doesn't cut it with me."

Rae imagined reaching out and throttling Todd. She took a slow, deep breath and held eye contact with him. *Where in the world is my compassion?*

David and Gil exchanged looks of disbelief. No one said anything. Gil felt the change, like a solar eclipse, the day darkened and a chill passed through the room.

After a short pause that seemed to last forever, Rae said, "I'm sorry you feel that way. You're right, there really isn't much time left today. However, there is time before our last meeting tomorrow morning for you to think about what you might have done differently this week to get your needs met. We won't be doing any new work tomorrow, but you can report back on what you discovered when we go around for check-ins."

Todd fumed. His voice dripped with sarcasm. "Oh, I see. *I* didn't do the workshop right. *I* need to look at how *I* could have done it differently. It was all up to *me*. Not the leaders, *certainly* not the leaders!"

Todd stood up.

"I don't need to wait for tomorrow. I know what I could have done differently, and now I'm going to do it." He snatched up his sweater and notebook and strode over to the entryway, stooped to grab his shoes and continued out the double doors into the hall. A couple of seconds later, the slam of a solid wooden door echoed back down the corridor.

DAVID WAS THE LAST of the three workshop leaders through the door to Rae's room. He closed it behind him and leaned back against it, his hand still on the doorknob as if securing it against the avenging hordes.

"Wow! That's the first time in the twenty-plus years someone's walked out on our workshop, and the first time I can see us getting negative reviews." David held up his blank yellow pad as if reading a review. "Started strong, ended badly." He flipped the page, as if leafing through a sheaf of evaluations. "They never got to the topic in the catalogue, leaders seemed to have it together until their incompetence and conflicts were revealed."

David kept dramatically flipping pages as his words tumbled out. "Leaders tricked and manipulated us to do what they wanted us to do, rather than what we needed to do ... Leaders were more interested in themselves and in their own power struggle than in our well-being ... Worst workshop, bar none, in my thirty-five years of coming to Esalen ... And so on and so forth."

Rae lay back against the headboard with her legs stretched out.

"And your point is?"

"My point? My point?" David was starting to yell again until Gil shushed him back into a conversational volume. "We were so smug, so self-congratulatory ... what a wonderful team we were; how smoothly we worked together; how our strengths made our whole so much greater than the sum of our parts; how fortunate these participants were to be in our workshop. Past reviews were incredible. 'Changed my life … best leaders I have ever had' … 'most amazing experience in my life.' And now, this!"

"So what are you saying?" Rae asked.

"Maybe we should sneak out under the cloak of darkness. Steal off into the black Big Sur night and disappear entirely." Gil was glad to see David was lightening up now. "Let those ingrates run their own closing session. See what it's like to be trapped in a room together without our wise and competent leadership."

David ran out of steam. He sank heavily into the nearest chair.

Rae was thinking about a small chapel on an open ridge high above Pacific waters.

Gil felt helpless and abandoned. "I feel frustrated." *How could you not have seen this coming?* he asked himself.

David said, "So ends our twenty-year run at Esalen: workshop leaders forced to leave by damning reviews and dwindling numbers!"

Gil's face dropped. He had hoped David would offer some reassurance.

But David was already up and moving. He had his hand on the doorknob, about to leave. "I've got a dinner date with an old friend, so what time do you want to meet tomorrow?"

"What?"

"My friend Peter drove down from Santa Cruz. I have to go now."

"This is too important to put off!" Gil looked intently at David. "Can't your friend wait?"

"No. He's driven a long way, and has to return tonight. How about after dinner?"

"I'm not available after dinner," Rae said.

Gil looked at her, then back at David. "You were the guy who came in shouting 'Fire!' and now you're picking up the fiddle?"

David gave Gil a quizzical look.

"Roman history." Gil saw no recognition in David's expression. "Never mind."

David opened the door. "So we'll meet tomorrow morning at 8:30 for breakfast. I'll see you there."

"Okay," Rae said.

"No!" Gil's voice rang out.

David stopped and looked over his shoulder.

Rae's eyes widened.

"I want your undivided attention." Gil waited until he had it. "At breakfast, there are always interruptions. You get up to make toast. Rae wants more tea. We end up eating for an hour and talking for five minutes."

David took it in and thought for a moment.

"Okay, let's meet at the lodge at 7:45 for half an hour, and then have breakfast together.

Gil didn't like that, but realized he had boxed himself in. All he could do at this point was agree and take his lumps. "Good."

Rae agreed. And with that, David slipped out, shutting the door behind him.

Rae gave Gil an appraising look. "You're pretty upset."

She was propped up against the headboard, her half-moon reading glasses pushed down her nose, her robin's-egg blue eyes at once receptive and uncompromising.

"I felt like a spectator." Gil's voice was low and intense. "David has been way more assertive lately. Also, you waved me off from getting involved with Todd, when I thought I needed to intervene. I've been struggling with whether I really belong on the team. In fact, I think this mess has happened because we aren't a team."

Rae wanted to comfort him, but thought better of it. She waited.

"Todd went on and on, and we didn't stop him. He skated through every session and when he spoke up, he did nothing but complain. He violated the guidelines and we let it ride. Now he's walked out and left us, with no time to process his desertion and no way to undo the damage. And the worst part is, I knew what was happening and did nothing to stop it."

"So you think it was your job to stop him?"

Gil looked blank, then laughed. "Of course it's my job."

"Yes, I see that." Rae reached out and held his forearm as they laughed together.

"Oh, that." Gil wiped away a tear as he stopped laughing.

"Yes, that."

"Al-Anon," smiled Gil. "Just like I've been recommending all week."

"Yes, Al-Anon." Rae looked at him and said, "Alison, Todd and everyone else in the room are just finding their way. We're no different." She thought for a moment. "You could have ignored me. Your anger might have gotten through to Todd. Things might have gone differently. There's no way to know. At the time I wanted to keep it dirt-simple for him since he's such a moving target.

"But that's not as important as your feelings of not being part of this team. We need to talk about that. Right now I'm feeling drained and hungry and unable to take in anymore. Walk down to dinner with me."

"Sure," Gil said, realizing it was getting late. Rae needed to eat. He felt the familiar, warm feeling for her in his chest. "Let's go."

Rae went to the bathroom and came out combed and fresh, ready to put her shoes on. Gil slipped on flip-flops and waited for her outside. They went off, arm-in-arm, under a gray sky. Without discussing it, they took the longer path, down the driveway and around the garden towards the lodge. The strengthening south wind drove the salt spray up the cliff and made the Monterey cypresses dance. Gil and Rae leaned into the wind as they crossed the lawn. The storm was coming.

12

Friday Morning

GIL WOKE AT FOUR IN THE MORNING TO THE SUDDEN silence. The rain had ceased and the clouds had parted. It had rained all night, pounding on the rooftops and lulling Gil into a deep and restorative sleep. All of the confusion and worry of the day before was gone. His body was relaxed and his mind was fresh as he unzipped his sleeping bag and got dressed.

He knew exactly what he wanted to do.

Gil was out of the car by 4:15, using his headlamp to navigate the line of trees leading from the pullout on Highway One to the gate. The starlight reflecting off the frozen puddles gave Gil scattered clues to the line of the dirt road ahead. He felt claustrophobic, walking in a thirty-foot tunnel of light, and at the second bend in the open road above the gate, he switched his headlamp off. With a sense of relief as the darkness opened up around him, he followed the deeper shade of the roadbed through a sea of starlit grass.

Now he was more than halfway up Separation Ridge, with some of the steepest slopes behind him. The synthetic turtleneck next to his skin was soaked through, and he was taking in deep draughts of freezing air. The temperature had plummeted during the night and was cooling further with the higher altitude and the coming dawn. The grass on the hills high above shone preternaturally bright. As he worked his way up the ridge, it slowly dawned on him that it wasn't grass that was reflecting starlight, it was snow.

By the time he reached the first break in the relentless climb, the snow was several inches deep under his feet. As the road leveled out, he saw the darker shadow of trees before him. They were the oaks Ronald had waited under two days ago. The headwater gully and the ridge where he had stopped to show Alison and Frank a view of the summit was still above him but he was making good time. Already the sky to the east was turning a lighter shade of blue-black. He pressed onward and upward. After a steep mile the road flattened and he got a whiff of bay laurel as he passed under the small grove nestled around the seep.

Now the road turned right and started climbing again. The sky above the ridgeline was turning deep blue; he could just make out the silhouettes of individual trees on the skyline. By the time he stood under those trees, there was enough light to make out the branches. Gil was at the highest point on the coastal ridge, but the trees still blocked his view of the jumble of mountain ranges beyond. He continued down off the hilltop along a spur ridge to the north. After a quarter-mile, he was clear of the trees and standing above the old Coast Ridge Road, looking east over a shadowy white confusion of ridges and drainages.

His feet were soaked through and cold. The snow was half a foot thick, and he cooled off quickly as he stood there transfixed by the expanse of wilderness. He began to jog in place to keep warm, knowing he would need to start walking soon. Just then, the first rays of sunlight flooded across the peaks and ridgelines, lighting off the snow-covered trees in a shower of refracted sparkles.

Gil's mind went blank and for a moment he had no thoughts at all, just the experience of expansive presence. When his thoughts returned, he felt a kind of lonely ecstasy realizing he was the only person witnessing this magic. Then he realized he wasn't alone. He was surrounded by the living land, and woven into it every bit as much as the Santa Lucia fir and the mountain lion.

He thought of Rae and David, snug in their warm beds 3,000 feet below and seven miles south. With a shiver and a slow *gassho* to the rising sun, he spun on his heels and loped off back down the snow-clad trail, following his own footprints in reverse.

Though his limbs were stiff and his fingers hardly able to move, he felt a flicker of warmth kindling in his core as he pushed hard downhill. In fifteen minutes he was warm inside and already turning to cross the headwater gully. Suddenly he stopped short.

There were two sets of tracks ahead. He knelt down and looked at them. A large coyote had followed him up the road and diverged just here at the seep. He got up and tracked the interlacing footprints back down the road for a quarter-mile, to where the coyote had come down from the slope above.

He turned around, his eye tracing the tracks back upslope. The light was good, low-angled and bright, and the new snow was still firm in the cold morning air. If he followed the tracks, who knows what they might reveal. But he had other things to attend to. The shared paths of those in the workshop would wind together one more morning before splitting off on their separate ways. Like this quarter-mile of overlapping imprints in the snow his time with them was short, its meaning unrevealed.

He turned down the slope and lengthened his strides.

DAVID'S OATMEAL sat cooling in front of him at the table, untouched, as he watched Rae peel a soft boiled egg, then slice it up carefully on a piece of toast. She methodically diced it, letting the yolk run, and added salt, pepper and a dash of Tabasco. He was deeply concerned about what she had just told him, but he didn't know where to start.

As she cut a small piece of toast with her knife and pushed it through the puddle of yolk, she observed, "You're not eating."

David frowned. "I'm thinking about what you said." He paused. "I don't think Alan is going to agree to a year's separation so that you can go off on some kind of spiritual quest."

Rae steered the toast and runny egg into her mouth and chewed while looking at David. *He really looks worried.* Rae picked up her cup of hot tea and blew across the rising vapor, took a small sip, then put the cup down, picked up her napkin and slowly dabbed along the edge of her lower lip.

"It's a Buddhist retreat center and I'm needing time off from my marriage, not a religious conversion." She resumed eating.

"I don't think you've thought this through. You're going to lose your marriage. It's in trouble and needs your attention." David paused. "I also think you haven't thought about your daughters and your mom. She isn't out of the woods yet with chemo, and your daughters haven't launched yet. I don't think you realize how much they depend on you."

"I do. They all think they need me, especially Alan. But I can't be there for them if I don't have a better grip on myself. When the air pressure drops in an airplane, you put your oxygen mask on first."

Rae put down her fork. "I felt something utterly true the other night at the baths, and later at the monastery. I found a piece of myself I've been missing for a long time."

"So get help. You're a professional. You have resources."

"That's exactly what I plan to do."

"You know what I mean."

"I do, David. I've been looking better and doing worse for a long time now."

"What do you mean?"

"You've heard me say many times that in recovery, people often find they're doing better and looking worse as they start to get real. I'm experiencing the opposite. My private practice has never been better, I'm receiving recognition from my colleagues, I live in a beautiful house near the beach and my daughters are both in college and doing well. My life looks great from the outside, but I feel completely drained and defeated on the inside.

"I had a moment of clarity Wednesday night. If I turn away from that insight now, I may never climb out of this stuck and painful place. What they say about drunks is true of Al-Anons as well: when you have a slip, you don't know when, if ever, you'll be willing or able to come back. This is my chance, and I'm taking it."

GIL DROVE DOWN the steep driveway, the windshield wipers throwing aside the downpour of a sudden cloudburst. After reintroducing himself to yet another new face at the guard shack, he parked and looked at his watch. 8:15. He was a half-hour late for his meeting with David and Rae, and for the first time in memory, it didn't bother him.

Inside the lodge, he hung up his coat and went into the dining hall. He passed through the hot cereal line and filled his bowl with steaming quinoa. After sprinkling on raisins, coconut, and granola, he made a quick stop at the milk bar to pour in a lake of whole milk before walking through the main room and into the Solarium. Rae and David were deep in conversation at a table for two by the windows. He registered their intensity and paused until Rae noticed him and waved him over.

"Sorry I'm late," he said, pulling up a chair.

Rae took in his ruddy complexion, matted hair and the energy radiating off him. "You've been out already."

"That I have."

David frowned. Gil's whirlwind arrival and small talk were threatening to minimize the importance of his conversation with Rae. "Rae has announced that she intends to take a sabbatical."

Gil froze, a spoonful of quinoa and milk halfway to his mouth. He put the spoon back in the bowl and looked at Rae.

"What does that mean?"

"I'm not sure." Rae took a breath. "But I've already started by gradually turning this workshop over to you two. My next step will be a retreat at Plum Village."

"A Retreat? How long? And what is Plum Village?"

"It's a Buddhist retreat center in France—for at least a year. After that, we'll see."

"What about our summer workshops?"

"You and David can do them."

Gil's jaw dropped. "What?"

David looked at Rae with an exasperated shake of his head. "You know it's not the workshops you should be worried about."

"My family will do just fine without me for a year. My daughters will both be away again at college next year. My mother has caretakers and my sister to look after her. And my marriage will surely go down the tubes if I don't go."

Rae's expression softened.

"I appreciate how concerned you are, but this has been coming for a long time. It took you two, this workshop, Alan's anger, and most importantly, my acceptance of Alan as he is to finally bring me to this decision. I need to take a year to get to know myself and, in the process, make a decision about the future of my marriage."

Rae reached out and took hold of David's right hand and Gil's left hand.

"I'm so grateful for you two and for this work that we do together, but I need to practice what we teach. This decision is right for me. And if that's true, it's certainly the right thing for my family as well."

Gil felt tears welling up. He had been all geared up to deal with this workshop crisis, which now paled in comparison to

Rae's announcement. It wasn't just *this* workshop on the line; it was *all* their workshops. He looked at David.

David and I working together? I don't think so.

David looked at his watch.

"It's 8:30. Let's continue this conversation after the session. Right now, we need to talk about our game plan for this morning. If we don't get on top of this, we may not have any summer workshops to worry about."

Gil was still holding Rae's hand, looking into her eyes. His words came with firmness and clarity.

"I know what I need to say this morning. There's been an elephant in the room all week, and I'm going to talk about it."

David tilted his head and furrowed his brow. Rae smiled. She had no idea what Gil was going to say, but could tell that he was in his truth-telling mode and that thrilled her.

Gil looked back and forth between Rae and David. "We've focused a lot on drinking, but missed the dry drunks sitting right in front of our faces. It's not all about alcohol, it's about denial, delusion and blame. And that goes for everyone affected by someone else's drinking or behavior as well, including Todd."

Rae felt her shoulders slowly relax. There really wasn't anything she needed to do about the workshop and, by extension, Alan, her children or her mother. As Gil was demonstrating right now, if she did what was right in front of her, her family, indeed the world, would unfold as it should.

Rae said, "I have absolute faith that what you say will be just what someone needs to hear."

As David watched Rae and Gil smiling at each other, he felt anything but happy. The last session was looming, the group was in disarray and he was worried about the consequences. Gil's messianic diatribe and Rae's New-Age spirituality were anything but reassuring. This wasn't going to go well.

Gil, taking note of David's facial expression, reached over and grabbed David's free hand.

"I want you to imagine that your worst fears about this workshop have already happened."

David laughed nervously.

"Imagine we've received the worst possible evaluations, the institute has canceled all our workshops and we've been blackballed from the entire retreat community. We've been publicly humiliated, are being sued by several workshop participants and you've both lost your licenses."

Rae's eyes shone. "I love it!"

David moaned.

Gil's face reddened as his voice built to a crescendo.

"Now, let's go lead the session!"

He squeezed their hands and raised their arms high. Rae returned the squeeze, then they all released their hands.

An imaginary *Ready ... break!* echoed in David's head. He made a mental note to never again, under any circumstances, take up with a former football player turned mystic.

They ran through the details of what they would do this morning and agreed on their agenda and assignments. Gil would lead the meditation, Rae the reading and David the check-ins. Finally, Gil would talk about self-responsibility and recovery. Then all three would help the participants to formulate their re-entry plans.

David was more worried about *his* exit plan.

———

RAE'S VOICE BROKE the silence of the meditation.

> Live the questions now. Perhaps then, someday
> far in the future, you will gradually, without
> even noticing it, live your way into the answer.

The last words of the Rilke quote faded slowly away, as Rae made a silent appraisal of each person in the circle. The room was quiet, and no one was looking at Todd's empty pillow. They were hard to read this morning, as if uncertain themselves about what to make of Todd's leaving. She was glad for Gil's decision to lead a long meditation.

When you're in a hurry, go slow.

"I spoke with the office this morning," Rae announced. "Todd checked out last night and left."

The silence deepened, and the whole room seemed to be waiting for something. Max nodded as if to himself, jumped up and walked across to Todd's empty pillow. Picking it up, he turned to carry it off.

"Leave it there, Max," said Gil.

Max looked perplexed for a moment, then put the pillow back and sat down.

Gil looked around the circle.

"Todd has been part of this group all week and whether he chooses to be here or not, I'm holding him to his commitment."

Rae smiled broadly at Gil. She turned to the group.

"We have a very structured process to lead you through, and it will take most of our remaining time. But before we start, we'd like you to tell us where you are this morning, and how that relates to your goals and miracle outcomes for the week. And if there is anything you need to say about how you were affected by Todd's leaving, or anything you need to say to him, now is the time."

"I'll start." Gil folded his legs under him and arched his back forward before settling into an erect posture. "I want to clear something up." Gil settled his gaze on the empty pillow.

"Todd, I've held back this week when speaking up might have served you and me better. I held back because I was uncertain, afraid of your response and forgetting that the results weren't up to me. For that, I owe you an amends. You deserved better from me. Not that you wanted to hear it, but rather that I owed it to you to say it."

The room was still as everyone focused on Gil as he spoke to the empty pillow.

"You have the 'ism.' I can't tell you what your relationship is to drugs, alcohol or those who use them, but I can tell you from personal experience, you display all the characteristics of the disease. You blame everyone and everything for your experience, and that keeps you from changing the only thing you can change, yourself.

"If you were happy with your life, there would be nothing for me to say to you. But since you showed up here for a reason, I'll tell you plainly. You're a drunk. You may be dry, but you're still a drunk. You're like me and every other drunk—selfish, self-centered and deluded. The only difference is you don't drink."

Gil turned back to the circle and said in a lighter tone, "I'm having a really good day. I'm clear on my path ahead for the first time in years and I'm scared and excited about it.

"I'm dedicating myself to experiencing and understanding this world. I'm going back to my first love, biology."

David's anxiety bumped up a notch. *Biology?*

Rae's eyes went wide with surprise and she glanced at David to see how he was responding, but he seemed to be more concerned with how others were reacting. She waited. When their eyes met, Rae held her hands palms up slightly as she shrugged.

David's eyelids drooped and he let out a long exhale. *What next?*

Meanwhile, Gil had given Carmen a nod.

Carmen seemed stunned.

"I'm not sure what just happened." She looked at Rae to get an answer, but Rae calmly waited for Carmen to continue.

Carmen seemed to shift gears and looked around the circle.

"I want to thank all of you. I've gotten so much from you this week." She paused at Diane. "Especially you, Diane. Your friendship and example meant more to me than all our group work combined. Thank you."

Diane smiled and her eyes teared up, but she said nothing.

Carmen continued, "I don't remember what my miracle was."

David looked down at his yellow pad.

"You wanted to know what was bugging you."

"Oh, that." Carmen gave a rueful smile. "That's easy. I didn't know what was wrong, and whether I had a right to do anything about it. In here, I learned to pay attention to my feelings when something bothers me, and by watching others, I learned that I could speak up about it." Carmen scanned the circle of people sitting against the glass wall until she came to Rae. "I see how simple it is, but that hasn't made it any easier."

Rae laughed, and several others joined in.

Carmen seemed bewildered by the laughter and then smiled. "Again, thank you, everyone, for all you've done for me this week." She paused and turned to the empty pillow. "Even you, Todd." Then she frowned. "Although I never really understood what you were doing here."

Carmen sighed and sat back.

Diane looked over at Carmen. When there was no response, Diane turned back to the circle.

"I feel really full right now, but still a little shaky from yesterday. I'm not sure what I want to say."

Rae offered, "You might want to see if there's anything you need to say to the empty pillow, or to anyone else."

Diane turned to Todd's pillow.

"You really pissed me off. You sat there all week like you were auditing the class and judging the rest of us for participating. Well, screw you! I know why I was here, and I got what I came for. What about you?"

Todd's pillow remained silent.

"I thought so." Diane nodded affirmatively. "You've run out of smart-aleck things to say, haven't you? Well, that's fine by me."

When she was finished, Diane glanced at Gil, then David, and then Rae.

"And as for our leaders, I would have liked to see you deal with Todd. You pretty much ignored him right from the start. Whatever your reasons were, I don't think that worked out well."

David's eyes were hooded as he lowered his head. Gil was sitting up straight and listening intently. Rae's head was cocked just slightly to the right. No one responded.

After a minute, David looked up.

"Are you done with your check-in?"

"No." Diane adjusted her posture, folding her legs under her.

Gil noted the shift. It wasn't just that she was challenging them; it was the ease with which she was doing it. *At least someone's gotten something out of this week.*

"I had no idea what I was getting into when I arrived on Sunday night. I thought maybe I'd just come, sit quietly in the back and see what it was all about. You can't imagine my dismay when I walked in and saw the circle of pillows on the floor. There was no back of the room to sit quietly in." There were some smiles and chuckles. "Five days later, I feel different about everything: my life, my relationships ... but most of all, myself."

Diane looked at Rae and smiled. "This workshop should come with a warning label."

David's loud barking bray drowned out Rae's laughter and all the laughs around the room.

Laughing along with everyone else, Diane turned to Ronald and tagged him on the shoulder with a playful shove.

"You're up."

Gil felt a release, though he couldn't explain it. It was as if Diane's simple words and laughter had lifted the pall that had sat over the room since the end of the last session.

Ronald made no mention of Todd. He talked instead about his excitement about going home and looking for his dream woman, now that he knew what to look for. He definitely wanted to stay in touch with Diane and Max, and was eager to share what he had learned with his own clients.

Max was next, and he was beaming, as usual. His enthusiasm was unquenchable. Max counted this week among the most impactful he'd ever had, and announced that he was actually looking forward to the next phase of his life.

With a twinkle in his eye, Max said, "Thanks to you, I'm reluctantly and fearfully embracing the inevitability of my decline."

David barked out another laugh, and several others joined in.

Max laughed along with them till it played out. Then he turned serious. "I cherish the loving awareness you taught me, and I look forward to the wisdom aging offers." Max smiled. "Not that there is much in the way of an alternative."

After more laughter, Max gave a nod to Tex.

Tex sat silently for a moment before turning to Rae.

"I think that Sherri and I have a better chance of ending up in the winner's circle. It's not a sure thing, but our odds are a hell of a lot better than before I came here."

Then he looked over at Alison. "And you, young lady, are quite a handful." He smiled and said, "Drinking may never be the same."

Alison laughed and gave Tex a sweet smile. "I hope not."

Tex chuckled as he looked down the row to Diane. "You've got a lot of spirit, gal." His words trailed away as if he were done; then, almost as an afterthought, he said to her, "I imagine things are going to get a lot better for you." Tex's voice got a little husky. "I'm placing a bet on you." He winked and sat back, folding his muscled arms and resting his chin on his chest.

Alison smiled and her eyes shone with emotion as she caught her breath. "Tex, you were a bright spot in my week. When I was talking to you, I knew just what to say." She paused. "The contrast with my experience of myself was striking. When I arrived Sunday night, I pretty much dreaded everything and I didn't know why. I wanted my old self back." She laughed. "I guess I didn't think it was very likely, or I wouldn't have called it a miracle. Now I'm starting over in a new program. I feel humbled but I'm back on track."

Alison turned to her right and made eye contact with Rae, who turned to Frank and nodded.

Frank looked blank.

"I'm not sure what I need to say. It's been an amazing week." He shook his head. "I can't believe it's almost over. I don't know how this is going to fit into my life back home. I'm different, though I'm not sure I could tell you how. I have the feeling I got the answer to a lot more than just what to do with my job." Several people laughed.

Frank sat there for a moment, staring at the floor in front of him. When he looked up, his eyes locked onto the empty pillow. "There's something I need to say to Todd."

Frank glanced at Rae. She smiled and gave him an encouraging nod. He turned back to Todd's pillow and took a breath. "I've been afraid of you all week. I've avoided you and made sure I never sat next to you." Frank let out a long exhale, then sat up a little straighter.

Rae was watching closely and said, "Notice how you feel inside right now, Frank. Take a snapshot. This is what it's like to know who you are and know what you need to say and do. It's that simple. When your insides match your outsides, the confusion is gone."

Frank was grinning and a new light shone from his eyes as he looked at Rae. "I feel solid."

Rae smiled and nodded emphatically.

Frank looked back at the empty pillow.

"I regret not telling you sooner, and I apologize for holding myself back." Then he scanned the faces in the circle around him. Frank concluded with, "I don't want to go home." He smiled as tears ran down his cheeks.

"I don't think they're going to be ready for you back at the office," Rae said, and she and several others laughed out loud. Frank joined them laughing for a moment and when he was done he sat back on his pillow.

David watched Frank and, when he saw nothing more was coming, he said, "Okay. Now I want you to break up into two groups, three in one group and four in the other."

Diane, Carmen and Ronald were sitting in a row to Gil's right. They simply pulled into a group and Gil joined them.

That left Frank, Alison, Max and Tex. Alison scooted her cushion near Tex and Max. Frank got up and sat on the floor in front of Max.

Rae walked over to the easel and flipped over the welcome page, revealing an outline for their re-entry plans.

"If you are willing to commit to a plan and be accountable, you will keep what you have found this week. Continue telling your support team the truth about yourself and the way you are living and your life will never be the same.

"There are three steps:

"First, name the behavior or situation you want to change.

"Second, list the concrete steps you're committing to take and when you'll take them.

"Third, name the resources you'll turn to for support, and a person who will hold you accountable. It could be someone from here or someone you trust at home."

Frank half-raised his hand. "What if we have more than one issue?"

"Just repeat the steps for each one. But I suggest you focus on no more than three." Rae paused. "You have fifteen minutes to write out your plans. Then you'll each have time to present them and get feedback and suggestions from your small group."

David opened the cupboard and took out a stack of notebooks and a plastic cup full of pens. He handed them out and then sat down with Alison's group.

Rae said, "Start working on your plan. I'll let you know when the fifteen minutes are up."

The room grew quiet. Rain pattered on the deck and splashed back up onto the bottoms of the sliding glass doors and row of tall windows. Rae looked around at the earnest faces bending to their task.

She stared at Todd's empty pillow and felt sad.

Not everyone made it.

Rae comforted herself by thinking of the lives that would change. The group would return home and send a flurry of texts and emails relying on each other to stay accountable. As time goes on that reliance would need to expand to existing friends and family to ensure ongoing support.

Alison would get her butt into Al-Anon. Tex would tell Sherri something like, "I may have a drinking problem and I need your support." Even if they slipped back into some of their old patterns, they would now be conscious of their peril. Like they say in AA: You might drink again after finding AA, but your drinking will never be the same. Tex got that right.

Rae sighed. She felt the weight of their work, the hope and the tears. She looked around at the plank walls and masonry hearth that stood witness to this week and all the weeks and groups in the decades before. The wood and stone held it all. She imagined the accumulative effect of so many open hearts and revealed truths on an energetic level she had no words for.

The sun came out from behind a small cloud and the room flooded with light. In an instant the weight she felt was replaced by joy. This was it. This was all there was: light or its absence. Life isn't a plan, an outcome or a better way. Life is lived only as it comes. And in that flow lies the potential for moments, like the moments that came and went all week, for Diane, for Max, for Frank, for all of them in their own ways, moments of pure experience without promise of a particular future.

Then she understood. What happened after they went home wasn't the point. This work, this living closer to their own source, this illumination, was all the purpose and meaning there was. A deep sense of peace and gratitude welled up within her. She thought of the participants. The memory of this week, whether they recognized it or not, would always be there. When the next crisis hit, they would remember the light.

She looked over at Gil and David sitting with their groups. Rae smiled. They were both so committed. Realizing this would probably be their last session together, Rae felt a melting warmth in her chest, and her eyes teared up. She was so blessed to have these faithful colleagues.

David looked over at her and pointed to his timer. Twenty minutes had passed. Rae felt a pang of guilt and spoke up to be heard above the soft conversations that had started up while she was lost in her thoughts.

"Finish up your writing if you haven't already. Take ten minutes each to share your plans and get feedback from your group."

David turned back to Tex, Max, Alison and Frank. "Okay, who wants to go first?"

Alison shifted her posture as if intending to speak, but Frank raised his hand and said, "I'll go."

Frank stared at his piece of paper for a moment.

"I had a really hard time narrowing it down. My job choices got me here, but so much has come up, I didn't know where to stop. Something happened this week. I experienced feelings I didn't know I had. I don't know if it was the no coffee and no alcohol, or the group, or the leaders, or this incredible place, but whatever it was, I don't want to lose it."

Frank paused for a moment. Hearing no comments, he went on. "So my plan is to keep doing the things I've done here. I'm giving up coffee and booze. I'm going to go to some meetings. I'm going to stay in touch with Rae and find a therapist in my area. I'm going to work less and do more with friends." He paused. "That's it."

David asked, "Any feedback for Frank?"

Alison leaned forward and looked directly into Frank's eyes.

"I think not drinking is a good idea, but I also suggest you go to a meeting for sex and love addiction."

Frank flushed.

"I don't have a problem with sex." He seemed surprised by his own vehemence and he softly added, "It's relationships that throw me."

He paused.

"I'm not an alcoholic either. I'm just not going to drink."

As if it were an afterthought, Frank repeated, "Something happened to me and I don't want to lose it. I don't want to go right back to living the way I used to."

Alison said, "Frank, that's up to you. Like they say, Twelve Step programs are not for those who need them, they're for those who want it. Still, I think you need to check in with someone about sex and alcohol in a month and in three months, just so you don't go unconscious about it."

"Okay. Would you be willing to take those calls?"

Looking surprised, Alison smiled and said, "Sure."

Max piped up.

"Can you be more specific about work and friends? What are you going to do differently at work? Who will you check in with? What are you going to do, and when are you going to do it?"

Frank, surprised and overwhelmed by Max's barrage of questions, paused for a moment.

"First, I'm going to limit my work hours to 8-to-5. Second, I'm going to take time off for lunch every day and get out of the office. And I'm going to do something fun on my time off.

"Friends are trickier. I don't know how they'll respond to what I've been doing here. A lot of them are drinking buddies. I'm not sure they'll understand."

David interrupted him.

"You might want to look for new friends in the meetings you're planning to go to."

"That's a good idea."

"Who will you check in with, besides Alison?" Max asked.

"Time to switch to the second person," Rae called out from across the room.

Frank looked over his shoulder at Rae.

"I'm going to ask Rae if I can call her next week, and Alison has agreed to check in with me on my relationships."

"Sex," Alison corrected him with a smile.

"Oh yeah, that." Frank blushed and looked around the small circle. He stopped at Tex.

Tex gave him a curt nod.

Frank smiled.

"I guess I'm done."

"Good work," David said. "Who's next?" As he looked expectantly at Alison, he heard Gil's voice and raucous laughter coming from the other group. *What does he have to be so happy about?*

David found it hard to be completely present. He envisioned a batch of bad reviews ending his chances of teaching here again. He knew the thin thread on which their relationship with the institute hung. They used more resources than other groups, as the only workshop with three leaders, and they had consistently low atten-dance. The workshop provided intense facilitation for each participant and garnered excellent reviews, but it was only marginally profitable.

It was now clear that he would be the only one still around to take care of the fallout from this workshop. Despite all his advice to Rae about staying the course with her marriage and her work, part of him envied her and Gil too, for that matter. It would be nice to be able to just walk away from everything.

His marriage to Joann had brought him some of those moments: moments when he guiltily imagined what it would be like to leave. But persevering was in his nature and had served him well all his life. Everything he valued depended on it—Joann, his children, grandchildren, his profession and his long-standing friendships. He wasn't going to change now.

Everybody had his or her own way of being in the world. Rae was an enthusiast who did everything in bold gestures. Gil was a romantic, always yearning for some missing connection. David thought of himself as a tree and more firmly attached with every passing year, a neurotic tree maybe, certainly a tree with a wacky sense of humor and some fears, but rooted nonetheless, and not likely to get up and walk away anytime soon.

Max's voice cut through David's reverie.

"Good plan, Alison. I'd like to be part of your support system, if that's okay with you. I'll remind you to connect with your old self, speak up at home and go to your meetings."

Alison's eyes lit up as she reached out and held Max's hand.

"I'd like that very much. It means a lot to me."

When no one spoke after an extended silence, David decided it was safe to step in. "Who's next?"

Tex, then Max, laid out their plans and got comments and suggestions from David and the others. Rae had already called time when David thanked them and suggested they get back into the larger circle. Everyone else was already waiting quietly on their pillows.

After everyone was seated, Rae asked, "Does anyone have something they want to share with the larger group?"

Diane raised her hand, but before she was acknowledged, Carmen, her eyes wide and bright, looked at Rae and quickly said, "I'll go." Ronald, Diane and Gil were smiling. Gil thought of the item he had added to Carmen's plan about speaking up assertively in the larger group and sharing her plan.

Carmen looked around the room.

"I've just accomplished the first item on my list by speaking up." She gave Rae a triumphant look. "I thought about how uncomfortable I've been this week, sitting here afraid to speak, upset when I did speak and worried about not doing what I was supposed to do. I'm still uncomfortable speaking, but it's more than that this morning. When I think about going home, leaving all of you and facing things by myself, I'm terrified.

"I'm not afraid of what's back there waiting for me, I'm afraid of losing what I've found here. And I don't know how to keep it, except to do what I've seen everyone else doing all week—speak up, tell the truth and get support."

Carmen took a breath.

"So here's item number two. I'm going to get into therapy." The room erupted into applause.

"Yes!" Frank exclaimed. Max shouted over the tumult, "Go, Carmen!" Everyone was smiling.

Carmen's smile broke through and tears ran down her cheeks.

She looked at Rae again, and said, with a serious expression, "If you're available, I'd like to continue working with you, if I can afford it. If not, would you suggest someone I can afford?"

"That's wonderful, Carmen," Rae said. "After group we'll set up a time to talk."

Alison beamed across the room at Carmen. "Go for it, girl."

When the room quieted down, Carmen looked around the circle. "Thank you all so much for being patient and not pushing me! This may not be much for someone else, but it's huge for me!"

"Yes, it is," Rae smiled.

No one else spoke up. David noticed that his breakfast knot had begun dissolving in his stomach.

This is a whole different group today.

He looked over at Diane. "You had your hand up earlier."

Diane looked at Carmen. Their eyes met and Carmen nodded. Diane turned back to David and Rae.

"I just wanted to tell you that this workshop has changed me, and I intend to come back."

Rae thought back to how hesitant Diane had been on the first night.

A warm smile spread across David's face. Diane had just given them the best possible compliment. Maybe this workshop wasn't a disaster after all.

Gil noticed that Diane had spoken directly to David and Rae and yet he felt none of the hurt or jealousy of earlier sessions. He was glad it was going well this morning. He felt part of it. Bigger than that, bigger than this morning, this group, this work, he felt part of a larger world, a world he belonged in where this work, his plans and everything else he did had a place.

THEY ALL HUGGED and cried and said their goodbyes before leaving the meeting room to go to lunch. Rae knew that, for the participants, this was a joyous and terrifying transition. They had done their work and felt the relief of coming to the end, but they also were losing the safe container and close-knit community of the group.

Gil, David and Rae stayed behind to clean up the room, throw away the leftover notes, drawings and wadded tissues of six days of intensive living in this small, semi-rounded room, with the glass wall facing the Pacific Ocean.

For Rae, this cleaning up was like a long, contented sigh. She had finished her work and all the uncertainty about how it would turn out was gone. It was done. The evaluations were filled out, the group had gone off together in a bunch, talking loudly and laughing, and she and her partners were looking forward to a quick debrief and a bite to eat, unhurried by having to plan an upcoming session. The workshop was whatever it was going to be, and by the smiles on the faces, Rae knew it was good. Now she could look forward to reading the evaluations without worrying about what she would discover.

David picked up his notepad. "I'm going back to my room to pack up. I'll meet you both on the deck for lunch. I'm still a little shocked, Gil. I want to hear more about your plans."

Gil said, "Okay." Rae stuffed a folded pile of paper into the trash can. "I want to load the car and leave as soon as we're done eating."

David exaggerated a deep salaam. "Your wish is my command." He smiled broadly and walked out.

Gil shook his head. *What a change one session can make!*

Rae continued picking up the room. "That was quite a bombshell you dropped this morning. I felt guilty that my choice might have influenced yours."

"Not at all. If anything, you simply opened up the possibilities for me. Once again you're a source of inspiration." Gil had stopped moving cushions to the center of the room and stood there watching Rae. "You were the reason I did this work."

Rae paused and looked up. She walked over to Gil and placed her hands on his shoulders as she stared intently into his eyes. "You're a natural for this work. You intuitively know what to do and say. And more than anyone I know, you lead by example." Rae took a deep breath and let it out slowly as she continued to look into Gil's eyes. "Whatever you choose to do next, I'll support you. And you need to know that you have a calling here if you choose it."

Gil blushed and smiled. "Thanks. It's good to hear that, especially from you." Gil closed his eyes and took a long breath. "And there's something about my choice today that isn't subject to reason or persuasion."

Rae nodded and dropped her arms. "I can see that. You look different to me this morning, less quicksilver and more bedrock. I like the change."

"So do I."

"I'll get my bags out of my room and then I'll be ready for lunch with you."

Gil turned, picked up a pillow and threw it onto the center pile.

Five minutes later, they finished packing Rae's car and struck out down the path, arm in arm, smiling with the brightness of the sunlight and the brilliance of the blue water and sky. The uncertainties of what lay ahead were banished for the moment by the excitement of new beginnings, the warmth of old friendship and the sensuality of the beauty around them. Something about this place demanded their attention. It wasn't the first time that Rae thought it. *There's something about this land. It's no accident that the institute is located here.*

On the last flight of steps down to the lodge, Rae noticed the long table assembled in the center of the deck. The group had lined up two glass tables so they could all eat together. Max and Carmen waved at them and pointed to some empty seats at the head of the table, which was adorned with two water glasses full of flowers. David and another glass of flowers were halfway down the left side, squeezed in between Alison and Ronald.

Everyone looked up as Rae and Gil approached. Diane jumped up and gave Rae a hug. Gil waved at the others. "We'll sit with you for a minute."

Gil and Rae shared the short bench at the far end. Rae studied the contents of the plates around her, and made a note of what looked good. Then she listened in on Max and Gil as they talked about the trip home.

Max waved a forkful of salad. "I fly out Sunday morning from San Francisco. I'm ready to go now, but when I planned this trip, I thought it would be a waste not to take in Monterey before going back, so I'm booked for one night in a bed and breakfast in Pacific Grove. I'll sleep at the airport Saturday night."

"Don't miss the aquarium," suggested Gil, "and there's a path along the water in Pacific Grove that takes you all the way to Monterey if you're up for a hike."

"How far is it?"

"Depends where you are in Pacific Grove, but probably about 45 minutes."

Max nodded twice. "I can do that."

Rae turned her attention to the conversation Ronald was having with David and Alison. Ronald was describing a woman he had met before coming out to the workshop. He was saying that he was thinking of asking her out on a date.

"The thing is, she has a child by a previous marriage." Ronald paused. "I don't know if I'm ready to take that on."

"Are you going to ask her to marry you?" asked David.

"Of course not," Ronald smiled. "At least, not on the first date."

David laughed. "Good, then let's focus on the first date. Do you want to go out with her?"

"She's a little abrupt, but I find her attractive, and it turns out we both read James Lee Burke novels. I'd probably ask her out, but I'm not sure what to think about her daughter."

Alison looked up from her soup. "Don't get ahead of yourself. Just take it one step at a time."

Ronald smiled. "Maybe you're right..."

Rae and Gil signaled David that it was time to go. David wrapped up his conversation then stood up, wishing everyone a safe journey.

Max jumped up and embraced David, then went around the table to hug Gil and Rae. Pretty soon everyone was up, and a new round of hugs and goodbyes ensued.

A few minutes later Rae, David and Gil were walking into the lodge and shopping the salad bar and entree table.

They found a spot inside at the window end of a long table. Rae held out her hands for a shared blessing. Gil winced, then smiled and offered his hands to Rae and David. Gil said, "Thank you for the work, and the company along the way." He looked at David and Rae. "We've been through a lot together, and my life is better for it." His eyes shone even in the filtered light of the lodge.

David's prayer was in Hebrew. Gil bowed his head. Rae said a blessing over the meal and their friendship, then all three squeezed hands and picked up their forks and knives to dig into the colorful food on their plates.

Rae noted that even David had broken the monotony of his bland lunches, adding green beans, carrots and beets beside his white-bread sandwiches. "Careful, David, there's unprocessed food on your plate."

"Don't worry; they're just garnish," David smiled drolly through a bite of peanut butter and jelly on toast. Rae laughed and David joined her, spewing crumbs. Gil shook his head resignedly at their small humor, but in the end couldn't resist their infectious merriment and finally joined in.

They discussed the details still to be handled before they left the property and then made light conversation until nothing remained on their plates or in their glasses. Still they sat there looking at each other in silence. The dining room was thinning out. The hubbub had reduced to a background hum. There didn't seem to be anything else to do but talk about what they had put off talking about since the group ended an hour and a half ago.

By some unspoken acknowledgement, Rae took the lead. She cleared her throat.

"I don't know when I'll be coming back here again." She looked at Gil. "What about you?"

"I'm done leading workshops for now." Gil smiled. "I may come back and take one sometime."

They both looked at David. He said, "I've thought about it, and though I'll miss you both, I'll continue leading this workshop at least through our commitments this year. For now, I'm planning on doing it alone, but I've already thought of some colleagues I might ask to join me. I know it won't ever be the same," he added, "but I'm eager to find out what it will be like."

"So this is it." Rae reached out and the three of them held hands once more. "I love you both."

Gil, despite all his newfound clarity, was at a loss for words. He had words, actually, but they wouldn't come out. It was like there were too many of them, or the emotion attached to them was too much for him. All he could do was squeeze Rae and David's hands.

"Ouch." David pulled his hand back.

Gil let go of both their hands and blushed. "Sorry."

Rae rubbed her hand and smiled. "Having trouble letting go?"

They all laughed together, louder and longer than the small joke warranted.

Gil's eyes watered and his vocal cords loosened up. "I'm going to miss you both terribly." Rae and David sobered up and looked at him solemnly. Gil added, with a smile, "But not enough to do *this* again."

They laughed all the harder. It seemed to Gil that they'd begun this way, they'd worked this way and it was only fitting that they would end this way … in laughter.

Acknowledgements

I am deeply indebted to all those who have shaped and inspired me along the way. I am particularly grateful for the gift of my father's imagination, the inspiration of my brother's poetic heart and the example and friendship of my coauthors Julie Bowden and Richard Balaban.

My wife, Julie, is my constant source of joy and my greatest teacher. Finally, this book would not have been possible without the founders, staff, teachers, community members and seminarians who have made being at Esalen Institute such a magical, transformative experience.

—CHRIS CHOUTEAU

My gratitude begins with the love of my parents Pearl and Sol Balaban, my brother Robert Balaban and Grandma Rose Finkman. My family is a constant source of wonder and growth. My mentors Max Hutt and Murray Levine were my guiding lights. My dear friends provide humor, care, warmth and perspective.

The Quarry Writers inspire openness and creativity: Mark Albrecht, Vic Gregor, Dianne Haaga, Mary Anne Herrick, Clement Soffer, Marylyn Tymon, June Utecht and Judy Warren. I want to thank Steve Arnold, Julie Bloom, Matt Bloom, Douglas Eck, Lois Klein, Ron Lustig and Amie Neff for their contributions to the manuscript.

Special thanks goes out to my life partner Julie Bloom for love, intimacy, fun and always keeping it real.

—RICHARD M. BALABAN

To all the precious souls who shared their deepest selves with us. To my children, Dondra, Anthony and Danae, and my grandchildren, KC, Marcus and Julianna who continue to be my greatest teachers.

To all the extraordinary mentors I have had along The Way: Mr. Irvin who gave me hope in my dark childhood; Kate Reiss whose attention helped me feel valued as a teen; Sam Gadol and Stan Sherman who led me into psychology and group work; Mike Kelley who taught me the basics of addictions treatment; Maria Nemeth, group facilitator extraordinaire; Julie Bloom for generously sharing my struggle; and Herb Gravitz and my fellow founders of the National Association for Children of Alcoholics who inspired me to be more than I thought I could be.

To Armando, week after week cheering us on. And to Esalen Institute, the container for this tender, profound work. Thank you all so much. I am grateful; I am blessed.

—JULIE D. BOWDEN

Our thanks go out to all the people who made this book possible. We particularly want to thank our developmental editor, Alan Rinzler, for encouraging us to turn our non-fiction manuscript into a novel, giving us the title and connecting us to several invaluable resources including Leslie Tilley, who gave us developmental advice; Laura Duffy, who created the cover design; and Karen Minster, who patiently guided us through the process of designing the layout. Linda Jay did a thorough line edit. Amie Neff, Mel Sellick, Candace Johnson, Marcia Cebulska, and Karen LaPuma reviewed early drafts of our manuscript and provided helpful comments. Mark Burstein rapidly and ably proofread the galley bringing consistency to these pages.

About the Authors

CHRIS CHOUTEAU lives and writes in Sausalito, California. He has a master's degree in fisheries and wildlife biology which led to a career in energy and environmental research management, and regional and national energy policy. He has served on several energy efficiency and environmental advocacy boards. He lived and worked at Esalen Institute from 2003-2006 and continued to lead workshops there until 2012. He has been privileged to share in the fellowship of twelve step programs for over 30 years. He currently writes about his life growing up in the San Francisco Bay Area, leads workshops on recovery and walks in the hills of Marin daily.

RICHARD M. BALABAN is a clinical psychologist in private practice in Bloomington, Indiana. He has taught in the psychology departments of State University of New York at Buffalo and Indiana University. He is currently writing about his relationship with, and the life of, his father, who had Alzheimer's at the end of his life.

JULE D. BOWDEN, M.S. is a retired Marriage and Family Therapist in Santa Barbara, California. A founding Board Member of the National Association for Children of Alcoholics, she was its first treasurer. She led workshops at Esalen Institute for 25 years, conducted recovery retreats, individual and group psychotherapy, and educational seminars for adult children of alcoholics as well as other adult children of trauma and the professionals who serve them. She also co-authored with Dr. Herb Gravitz the classic *Recovery: A Guide for Adult Children of Alcoholics.*